CLASSIC HANDGUNS
of the 20th Century

David W. Arnold

Published by

 **krause publications**

An F+W Publications Company

700 East State Street • Iola, WI 54990-0001
715-445-2214 • 888-457-2873
www.krause.com

Our toll-free number to place an order or obtain
a free catalog is (800) 258-0929.

Library of Congress Catalog Number: 2004100739
ISBN: 0-87349-576-4

Designed by Brian Brogaard
Edited by Joel Marvin

Printed in the United States of America

ACKNOWLEDGMENTS

The idea for compiling this book originated several years ago when I was editor of *G&A HANDGUNS*, a Primedia magazine. It was decided to run a short series called *"CLASSIC HANDGUNS OF THE 20TH CENTURY"* that would examine some of the more notable handguns of that period.

After compiling the first few articles of the series, I quickly realized I was just scratching the surface and that the only way to do full justice to the subject was to write a book. I am grateful for being allowed to use some of the material previously used in the original HANDGUNS magazine series.

A number of people have helped in the compilation of this book. First is my lovely wife, Patricia, who has devoted many long hours creating the color renditions of all the handguns covered in this study.

I am grateful to Frank James for his assistance in compiling the chapter on the Glock pistol. Glen Barnes gave valuable assistance in researching the Walther P38.

Providing photographs to illustrate the various chapters proved to be quite a challenge and would not have been possible without the kind assistance of the following people.

Garry James was kind enough to allow me to photograph a number of handguns from his personal collection. Glen Barnes also helped by providing photographs from his extensive handgun collection.

Others who loaned me guns to photograph were Jeff John, Marty Kovacs, Jan Libourel, Jerry Lee, Lou Page, George Pedersen and Jerry Usher.

I am also indebted to my good friend Jan Libourel, editor of *Gun World* magazine, who kindly reviewed the text for accuracy. He offered a number of useful corrections and suggestions.

Finally, I must thank Don Gulbrandsen of Krause publications for his assistance and encouragement. To all the abovementioned and anyone I may have omitted, I tender my heartfelt thanks.

David W. Arnold
Canyon Country, California

CONTENTS

INTRODUCTION

A LOOK AT HANDGUN DESIGN DURING THE LAST TWO CENTURIES

Compared to the 20th century, the previous 100 years saw the greatest advances in handgun, and for that matter, firearms design. During the 20th century, handgun design had pretty much culminated by the 1930s. The remaining 70 years really saw just the refinement of the already established design principles.

High points of 19th century firearms development started with the invention of the percussion cap ignition system. This enabled Samuel Colt to perfect the revolving pistol or revolver, the first practical repeating firearm.

Shortly afterwards, self-contained ammunition was invented, which led first to the cartridge revolver and later, when combined with the advent of smokeless powder, to the first self-loading firearms.

Thus, by the start of the 20th century, the revolver design was fully developed and the semi-automatic pistol was well established as a viable weapon. By the 1930s, both handgun types had been developed to a point of maturity.

By the mid-1930s, most of the major handgun developments had occurred, including the introduction of the high-capacity FN High Power auto pistol. Revolver development of the same period saw the introduction of the first magnum cartridge and revolver in the form of the 357 S&W Magnum.

For the remainder of the century, handgun advances were directed mainly towards new and improved materials such as stainless steel, titanium and scandium aluminum alloy. Probably the most significant material advancement is in the use of plastics and carbon fibers. The Austrian Glock pistol broke new ground in this respect. All these materials have enabled handguns to become lighter and more compact.

HANDGUN AMMUNITION DEVELOPMENT

While no new significant handgun designs occurred after the end of World War II, there have been significant ammunition advances. Today's handgun ammunition is more reliable and effective than ever before.

In terms of reliability, improvements began during the 1970s and into the 1980s. This improvement in reliability was also accompanied by improvement in the stopping effectiveness of ammunition. Much of the latter was prompted by law enforcement concerns about the ability of 38 Special cartridges in neutralizing determined attackers.

While more effective cartridges already existed in the large caliber rounds and the magnums, their heavy recoil made them difficult to shoot quickly and accurately. A fairly effective solution was found by producing high-velocity 38 cartridges with hollow-point bullets. The latter were designed to expand on impact, creating a wounding effect comparable to that made by a larger caliber bullet.

Initially the hollow-point bullets did not work reliably

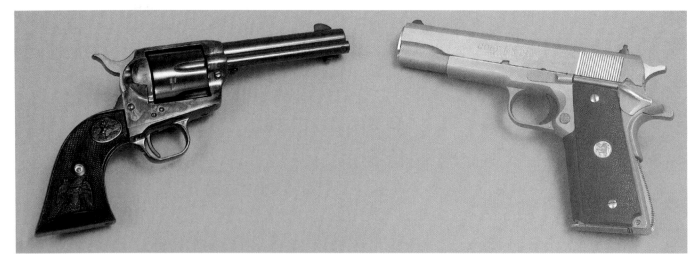

The previous century has produced a number of handguns that have become classics like the 1911 45 pistol (right). Some guns like the Colt Single-Action Army revolver (left) were actually made in the 19th Century.

in semi-automatic handguns. In time, these problems were overcome by both ammunition and handgun manufacturers.

SMART GUN TECHNOLOGY

Smart gun technology involves designing a handgun that can only be used by its lawful owner. From a police perspective, this provides protection for police officers who have had their sidearm taken by a criminal. A disturbingly high number of officers killed in the line of duty are shot with their own guns. In such instances, a smart gun becomes inoperable.

An early type of smart gun has been around for some time in the form of a magnetic-operated lock that prevents the gun's trigger mechanism from being operated. The key to unlock the mechanism is a magnetized ring worn on a finger of the shooting hand of a gun owner or police officer. When the gun is gripped in a normal manner, the trigger is unlocked. The ring is the key to the system, so for weak-hand operation of the gun, rings have to be worn on both hands. One disadvantage is that the ring or rings must be worn at all times. Another detraction is that the rings can adversely affect the magnetized strips on credit cards.

During the 1990s, Colt Manufacturing Company announced they were exploring the feasibility of developing a practical smart gun. No doubt, the company hoped that, if successful, they would capture a large share of the police handgun market. In addition, they hoped to score some good public relations by developing a handgun that could safeguard against accidental shootings involving children.

The new technology is based on the same concept of an internal method of locking the gun's firing mechanism in a manner similar to that of the magnetized ring. The main difference is the magnetic lock has been replaced by a microprocessor. The key is a microchip contained in a wrist bracelet.

Many firearms companies and Second Amendment proponents were concerned the gun control advocates would use the smart gun concept as a weapon to further their cause. Unfortunately, such warnings proved to be true as gun control supporters pushed for and sometimes succeeded in getting legislation requiring gun manufacturers to have smart guns in production by a fixed future date. When the due date arrived, only smart guns would be deemed as being legal.

All this coincided with a spate of lawsuits sponsored by city governments and gun control groups trying to make gunmakers liable for the wrongful and criminal misuse of their products.

The final blow came when the Clinton administration succeeded in pressing Smith & Wesson into an agreement where they accepted some responsibility for the sale and distribution of their firearms. Smith & Wesson also agreed to continue to explore the smart gun concept. In return, the company was offered favorable terms in limiting lawsuits against them by cities and the sale of their handguns to police departments. While Smith & Wesson was obviously motivated by the hope of reducing their legal costs in fighting the numerous lawsuits made against them, they were the only gun company to enter into this agreement. And this action has hurt them. There have been calls of "Sell out" by pro-gun supporters, who have penalized Smith & Wesson by boycotting their guns in the marketplace.

This has had the effect of dampening smart gun development. Colt, in serious financial difficulties, announced they were discontinuing their involvement in the project. A number of other companies, however, are offering built-in manual trigger and hammerlocks on their handguns.

The problem with the smart gun concept is the danger of a system failure that results in a gun that cannot be unlocked. The ideal goal is a system that unlocks when it identifies an authorized user by some personal characteristics such as fingerprint or even DNA. Smart gun technology is, at best, a concept that may be viable at some future undetermined date.

Except for a few pistols like the Glock 17 and the HKP7 (bottom) there have been few radical developments in handgun design during the post-World War II period. Instead, there have been some significant advances in handgun ammunition.

THE COLT SINGLE-ACTION ARMY REVOLVER

Born in the 19th Century and Still Going Strong

Although the Colt Model P "Peacemaker" revolver was introduced in 1873, the fact that it remains in production today is reason enough for it to qualify as a classic handgun. Production of the Single-Action Army (SAA) ceased twice, but popular demand brought it back on both occasions. It is probably safe to say that more SAAs have been sold during the last century than during the one prior. In addition, along with the Colt 1911 45 auto, the SAA is among the most cloned and copied handguns of all time.

HISTORY AND DEVELOPMENT

In 1855 a patent was granted to Rollin White, a Colt employee, for a revolver design with cylinder chambers bored all the way through. White offered his idea to Colt, who inexplicably failed to appreciate its significance and rejected it. Smith & Wesson later purchased the rights to White's patent and developed the first cartridge revolver.

Colt and other handgun manufacturers were thus prohibited from making cartridge revolvers of their own until the patent expired around 1869. Several novel conversions of cap-and-ball Colts were devised, which allowed for faster, more efficient ways of loading. When Colt was able to make cartridge revolvers, the company lost no time in coming out with a line of small house and pocket models.

The Single-Action Army began life in 1873 as a cartridge revolver that was really a development of previous percussion single actions like the Colt New Navy of 1862. It used the same trigger mechanism. The most significant difference was a solid frame that incorporated a topstrap, a loading gate and an ejector rod unloading system positioned on the left side of the barrel.

The first large cartridge revolver was the 44 rimfire. This revolver, the ancestor of the Single-Action Army, had an open top frame and a round, unfluted cylinder, giving it an appearance that closely resembled the earlier percussion conversion models.

The SAA was a considerable improvement with a topstrap added to the frame, a fluted cylinder and an ejector rod attached to left side of the barrel. The overall result was a very strong, impressive looking revolver. The company submitted samples to the Army for testing.

The revolver was awarded a U.S. military contract and the first models appeared with 7 1/2-inch barrels chambered for the 45 Colt cartridge. In the years leading up to the turn of the century, the revolver was made in other calibers that included Winchester 44/40, 38/40, 32/20 and 22 rimfire. By 1891, calibers ranged in size from 22 RF to 476 Eley.

The official designation of Colt's new revolver was the Model P Single-Action Army. Over the years, however, it has been given other unofficial names. Some of the best-known names are "Peacemaker", "Frontier Model" and "Colt Frontier Six-shooter" to name just a few.

DESIGN CHARACTERISTICS AND FEATURES

The Peacemaker was a solid-frame centerfire revolver with a single-action lock that closely resembled the single-action lock of the earlier Colt percussion revolvers.

For the purposes of loading and unloading, there was a gate in the rear left side of the frame and an ejector rod assembly on the left side of the barrel. As with the earlier percussion models, the hammer had a generous spur to facilitate fast thumb cocking.

The revolver was of iron and steel construction and consisted of seven major components: barrel, frame, cylinder, backstrap, trigger guard, ejector housing and ejector rod and spring; all of which were secured with machine screws. These could create some minor problems by being shaken loose by recoil during firing.

The Single-Action Army is a solid-frame large caliber revolver that differs from the earlier Colts by the addition of a topstrap to the frame. Even though this revolver is a third-generation model of 1980 vintage, it has changed little from the original made in the 19th century.

MODIFICATIONS AND UPGRADES

The revolver underwent remarkably few changes before 1900, the most significant being the replacement of the single screw center pin lock with a transverse bolt in 1894. This change is often used as a quick-and-easy method of identifying single actions made to handle smokeless powder ammunition when the fact is it was only in 1900 that Colt warranted the single action for modern cartridges. A more accurate method is to look at the serial number. If it is 192,000 or above, it is safe for smokeless powder ammunition provided it is in otherwise good mechanical condition.

TARGET MODELS

A special Flattop Target model was introduced in 1888 followed in 1894 by another target model called the "Bisley".

Some of the long-barreled revolvers had an adjustable tangent sight that flipped down into a recess in a flattop frame. In addition, such revolvers usually came with a detachable shoulder stock.

BARREL LENGTHS, GRIPS AND FINISHES

Single-Action Armys were made in three main barrel lengths of 4-3/4, 5-1/2 and 7-1/2 inches. Shorter and longer barrel versions were available on special order.

Of particular note were the 3-inch Storekeepers model and the 12-inch Buntline Special. Both the Storekeeper and Buntline were revived as second-generation models. While the Buntline Special was the most famous of the long-barreled models, even longer barreled revolvers were made, 16 inches being the most common.

Grips were generally of the one-piece type used on the percussion revolvers. After the turn of the century, two-piece grips of black hard rubber became standard. Special grips of ivory, mother-of-pearl, ebony and stag horn were available on special order. The standard finish was blued metal parts except for the frame, which was color case-hardened. Flattop Target models including Flattop Bisleys had an all-blue finish. Nickel-plating for all variations was offered as an option. The SAA has been a favorite canvas for engravers and Colt-grade A, B or C factory engraving could be had as a special order. Today the art of engraving continues through Colt's Custom Shop.

The Peacemaker has been a popular revolver for commemorative and special-issue models, as has the Single-Action Scout. The models usually had the reason for their issue roll stamped on the left side or were appropriately engraved.

CALIBERS

As previously mentioned, the Single-Action Army has been chambered for most popular revolver cartridges. The revolver began life chambered for the 45 Colt cartridge, which remains a popular chambering.

Other early popular calibers were the 44/40 and 38/40 because they were dual-purpose cartridges that could also be fired in the Winchester lever-action rifles of the day. This simplified the quandary of what ammunition to carry.

Other popular calibers of the 20th century included the 44 Special, 38 Special and 357 Magnum. A limited number of SAAs were chambered for the 45 ACP cartridge. The Single-Action Armys and Cowboys of today are available in 45 Colt.

FIRST-GENERATION SINGLE ACTIONS

This classification encompasses all black and smokeless powder revolvers made from 1873 to 1940. During the period of 1900 to 1940, the Single Action underwent relatively few changes apart from the cessation of the Bisley and Flattop Target models. Barrel lengths and most caliber options remained the same. The one-piece grips were changed to two pieces of hard rubber.

SECOND-GENERATION SINGLE ACTIONS

After World War II, Colt announced that a number of models in their revolver line were to be discontinued. The Single-Action Army was among these. The announcement created an immediate demand for the SAA, which was ironical in view of the fact that a lack of sales appeared to be the reason why the gun was dropped from production. Colt did make a few more post-war Single Actions, assembled from components in the spare parts inventory.

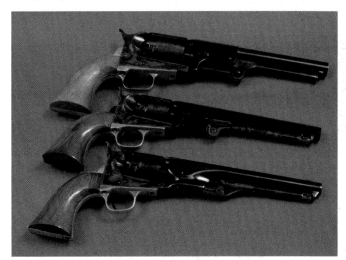

The Single-Action Army was a logical development of Colt's percussion revolvers such as the 3rd Model Dragoon 44 of 1851 (top), 36 Navy Model of 1851 (middle) and 36 New Model Navy of 1861 (bottom).

The Peacemaker has a single-action lock where the hammer must be cocked for every shot.

The renewed demand prompted Colt to bring the Single Action back into production in 1956. Referred to as "second-generation" models, these single actions—offered in the same standard barrel length and centerfire calibers as the original—differed little from the first-generation guns.

Also made were 12- and 3-inch barrel versions called "Buntline Specials" and "Sheriff's Models" respectively. These are included in the second-generation series, which remained in production until 1976. Second-generation models can be identified by the letters "SA" as a suffix to the serial number that began with 00001SA and ended with 74000SA.

THIRD-GENERATION SINGLE ACTIONS

Production of second-generation revolvers ended in 1976. Colt then made a few minor changes to the design mainly to simplify production. The most significant of these were the elimination of the separate cylinder bushing and a different method of securing the barrel to the frame. Apart from these, no other major changes were made to the original design. The series included the Buntline Specials and the Sheriff's Models.

This generation series remained in production until 1984. Some years thereafter, the Single-Action Army became a special order item made by the Colt Custom Shop.

Third-generation models start with serial number 80000SA and run to 99999SA before the "SA" becomes a prefix at SA00001 until SA99999. To confuse matters further, numbering began again in 1993 with S00001A. All revolvers within these number ranges are classified as third-generation models.

THE 22 SCOUT SERIES

In 1957, a year after the revival of the Single-Action Army, Colt introduced a seven-eighth-sized 22 version called the Frontier Scout. The revolver employed a frame and grip made of alloy metal. Duotone (silver frame/grips and blue barrel/cylinder) and all-blue finishes were offered.

Later, blue all-steel models as well as guns with color case-hardened frames were made. The latter revolver was called the Peacemaker Scout. In addition, flattop frame versions with adjustable sights, called the New Frontier Scout, as well as long-barrel (9 inches) revolvers called Buntline Scouts, were also made. Production of the Scouts ended in 1981.

THE NEW FRONTIER MODELS

In 1961 Colt introduced a flattop frame single action with adjustable sights called the New Frontier. The models were made in the same standard barrel lengths and calibers as the

regular Single Action line. The New Frontiers underwent the same production changes as the regular single action and are classified as second generation (1961-1975, with the letters "NF" a suffix to the serial number) and third generation (1978-1983, with the letters "NF" a prefix to the serial number).

THE COLT COWBOY

In 1999 Colt introduced a new single action with a modern action that included a transfer bar safety. Called the Colt Cowboy, this revolver was made to offer a more moderately priced revolver to the Cowboy Action Shooting market. It retained the traditional looks and feel of the original but had the added safety of the transfer bar action.

The first Cowboy was chambered for 45 Colt and was available in the traditional barrel lengths of 4-3/4, 5-1/2 and 7-1/2 inches. Finish was the usual color case-hardened frame and blue barrel, cylinder and grip frame. Grips were two-piece wood or checkered black plastic. Along with the regular Single-Action Army revolver, the Cowboy continues to be made at the time of this writing.

SINGLE-ACTION CLONES

Together with the 1911 45 auto, the Colt Single Action is one of the most copied handguns of all time, especially after it was first dropped from production after World War II. The first copies were made by Great Western, followed by Sturm Ruger. The latter company introduced a line of modern single actions that, while based on the original design, incorporated a new, stronger lockwork and improved sights.

In the years that followed, other companies have offered virtual clones of the original New Frontier model. These filled the niche as the Colt models escalated in price and were eventually dropped from regular production. The growing popularity of Cowboy Action Shooting has helped in keeping the demand for reasonably priced single-action revolvers. The following are some of the more popular brand of SAA models currently available: American Western Arms, Cimarron Arms, EAA, EMF, Navy Arms, Sturm Ruger & Company, U.S. Firearms and Dixie Gun Works, Inc.

THE COLT SINGLE ACTION IN THE 21ST CENTURY

The revolver continues to be made as a Colt Custom Shop item and as the Cowboy. Its long-term future really depends upon what happens to the Colt

Loading and unloading is accomplished by means of a loading gate in the frame and an ejector rod system.

Early Single-Action Armys had the cylinder pin secured with a single screw in the front of the frame.

Company. If the company survives, as hopefully it will, so will the old single action. While this remarkably graceful handgun may not enjoy the popularity it had in the 1950s, it still has a great deal of appeal to shooters worldwide.

LOADING AND UNLOADING THE SINGLE-ACTION ARMY

To unload the Peacemaker, always ensure the barrel is pointing in a safe direction. Place the revolver in the left hand, open the loading gate and carefully draw the hammer back to the second cock position. Then elevate the barrel and rotate the cylinder so that each chamber is aligned with the ejector rod, which is used to eject the cartridges or spent cases.

To load, hold the revolver in the same way. Point the barrel towards the ground. With the loading gate open, cock the hammer to the half-cock notch, rotate the cylinder and insert a fresh cartridge in each chamber.

To ensure an empty chamber is under the hammer, load only five cartridges. After loading the first chamber, leave the next one empty and then load the rest. When all cartridges

have been loaded, fully cock the hammer before gently lowering it completely so that it rests on the empty chamber.

SHOOTING AND HANDLING THE SINGLE-ACTION ARMY

In addition to its classic appearance, the Peacemaker has excellent handling and shooting characteristics, the attributes most responsible for the revolver's continuing popularity over the years.

Much of the revolver's fame is related to the role it played on the American frontier. While other revolvers were used, there is no doubt the SAA was the favored sidearm of most of the famous names on both sides of the law in the American West. Lawmen such as Wyatt and Virgil Earp, Bat Masterson, Pat Garret, Bill Tilghman, Heck Thomas and many others carried Peacemakers of one type or another.

The revolver began its life with the U.S. Army, especially as a cavalry sidearm. It remained in service until the Colt 38 double-action revolver of 1892 replaced it. It was rushed back into service several years later during the Philippine Insurrection because of the ineffectiveness of the 38 cartridge. It was finally retired when the Colt 45 ACP Government Model pistol was adopted by the military in 1911.

After solid-frame, swing-out cylinder, double-action revolvers by Colt and Smith & Wesson became the choice of most major police departments, many Western lawmen, especially the Texas Rangers, refused to part with their single actions.

Much of the revolver's success is due to its many strengths.

The Colt New Frontier featured adjustable sights and a flattop frame.

While it's internal mechanism is actually quite fragile and subject to breakages, its generally rugged construction enables it to remain functioning. Its strong solid frame enabled lawmen like Wyatt Earp to use it as a "Billy club" to "buffalo"(subdue) drunken cowboys by hitting them over the head with the revolver's barrel. Such treatment was not good for the revolvers and often resulted in the ejector housing and rod being broken away from the side of the barrel.

While the Peacemaker is generally very well made, there were other revolvers with a superior fit and finish. In spite of this, the SAA would continue to function when subjected to the dirt and dust that would jam its finer-made competitors.

When it comes to shooting, the revolver has many endearing features. Its simple plow-handle grips tend to be one size that fits all. In addition, the revolver has excellent balance regardless of barrel length. Both these attributes help in cushioning the recoil of heavy loads. The grips allow the revolver to slide up in the hand to place the hammer in an ideal position for cocking it back for a fast follow-up shot.

In terms of accuracy, the revolver can hold its own against most others. I witnessed an old blackpowder model in 44/40 being fired at a man-size silhouette target at a distance of 200 yards. A total of 10 shots were fired; seven hit the target. The three misses were all misfires, no doubt due to the age of the ammunition. I should add this revolver was well used and had a worn and pitted barrel.

In spite of its great accuracy potential, the revolver is not a target arm. Its fixed sights are rudimentary and rarely shoot to point of aim. Most of the SAAs I have shot required some sight adjustments. Even when adjusted, the sights present a small sight picture that is not conducive to pinpoint accuracy.

The revolver is not without its faults; it is slow to load and unload and has to be cocked for every shot. The latter is somewhat mitigated by its relatively light single-action trigger pull. With practice, the revolver can be fired quite quickly thanks to its generous hammer spur.

Even more speed can be achieved by using a two-handed

In 1894, the single screw securing the cylinder pin was replaced with an easier-to-operate transverse bolt. This feature is often mistakenly used to identify revolvers made for use with smokeless powder.

As pistol target shooting grew in popularity, Colt introduced two target versions of the Single-Action Army, the Flattop Target model (top) and the Bisley Model (bottom).

hold, using the thumb of the supporting hand to cock the hammer. Slip shooting, where the hammer is slipped off the thumb while the trigger is held or tied back, is another way of shooting the Single Action quickly.

Fanning the hammer, a method popularized by Hollywood, is an overrated method of quickly discharging a single-action revolver. It can be effective after much practice, but was little used on the frontier. Fanning can also cause serious damage to a Peacemaker by breaking the hammer notches, making the revolver dangerous to load and unload. Fanning is not the only way notches can be damaged or broken, however. A heavy blow on the hammer, or losing control of the hammer during cocking, so that it falls before engaging the trigger can break or

An early alloy frame Scout (bottom) and a late model with color case steel frame (top).

damage the lower notches or do the same to the trigger.

Shooting a Peacemaker fast requires a considerable amount of dexterity. The danger is the hammer slipping off the thumb before the hammer is fully cocked. Not only is this likely to break the half and safety notches, but the revolver may discharge. Many accidents have occurred by a shooter attempting to practice a fast draw from the holster. For this reason, both fast shooting and holster work must be approached with caution.

While broken hammer notches may not prevent a single action from being fired, safety is severely compromised. The first or safety notch is intended to keep the firing pin from contacting the cartridge primer. Its not being strong enough to resist fracturing from a heavy blow can result in an accidental firing of the revolver. For this reason, traditional Peacemakers must always be carried with an empty chamber under the hammer.

Both the functions of loading and unloading require placing the hammer in the half-cock notch so the cylinder is free to rotate. If the notch is broken, the hammer can slip off and fire a cartridge during the loading process.

The tendency of the screws to be jarred loose during firing is more an irritation than a serious fault. Giving the threads a thin coating of nail varnish or rubber cement is a simple way to lock the screws in place.

Another warning for Peacemaker owners is never to shoot modern smokeless ammunition in blackpowder models. Even though these revolvers will chamber modern ammunition, blackpowder single actions are just not stressed for the higher pressures generated by modern ammunition and are in danger of blowing up.

This 38/40 Single-Action Army of 1907 vintage is warranted for smokeless powder. It has the transverse bolt.

COLLECTOR INTEREST

Colt Single Actions are highly collectable and demand high prices completely out of proportion to their scarcity or vintage. Except for new revolvers, there is the question "Should a Single-Action revolver be fired at all?"

There are several factors to consider when answering this question, the first of which has already been discussed – is it a blackpowder or smokeless model? The other question is one of value. Single actions, even of fairly recent vintage, are demanding amazingly high values. As a general rule of thumb,

shooting should be confined to third-generation models of late vintage. I rarely shoot even my third-generation models and never my three first-generation revolvers. All my single-action shooting is done with one of the many fine replicas currently available.

Nevertheless, these revolvers are shot quite a bit by handgun hunters, single-action enthusiasts and Cowboy Action Shooters. Genuine Colt SAAs are in great demand by the latter. There are a number of gun shops that offer restoration services catering to the needs of such competitors. Ultimately, the decision to shoot must be left to the reader.

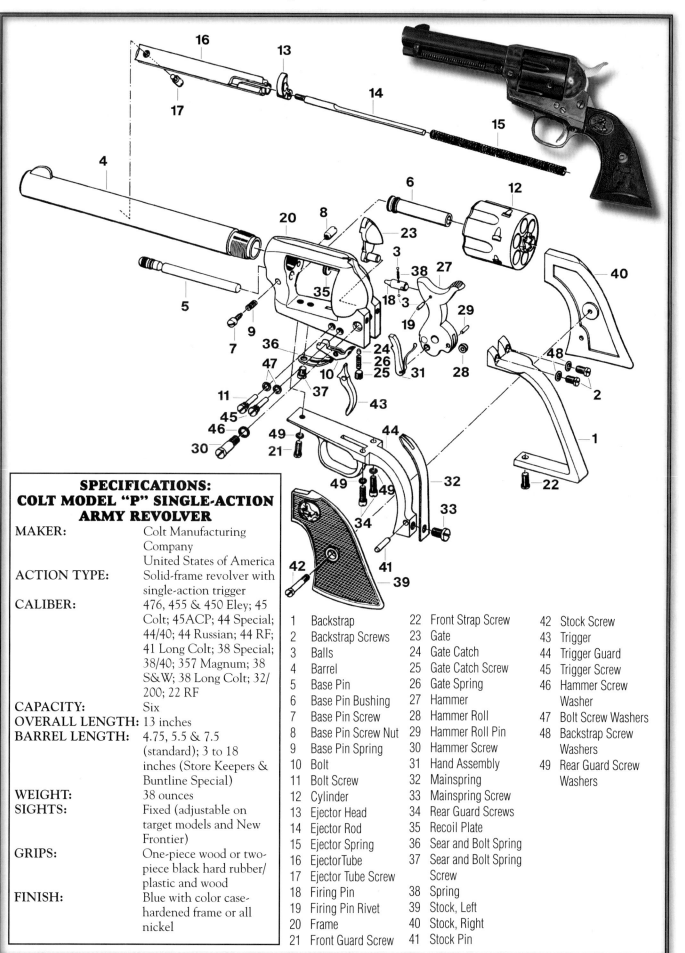

SPECIFICATIONS:
COLT MODEL "P" SINGLE-ACTION
ARMY REVOLVER

MAKER:	Colt Manufacturing Company United States of America
ACTION TYPE:	Solid-frame revolver with single-action trigger
CALIBER:	476, 455 & 450 Eley; 45 Colt; 45ACP; 44 Special; 44/40; 44 Russian; 44 RF; 41 Long Colt; 38 Special; 38/40; 357 Magnum; 38 S&W; 38 Long Colt; 32/200; 22 RF
CAPACITY:	Six
OVERALL LENGTH:	13 inches
BARREL LENGTH:	4.75, 5.5 & 7.5 (standard); 3 to 18 inches (Store Keepers & Buntline Special)
WEIGHT:	38 ounces
SIGHTS:	Fixed (adjustable on target models and New Frontier)
GRIPS:	One-piece wood or two-piece black hard rubber/plastic and wood
FINISH:	Blue with color case-hardened frame or all nickel

1	Backstrap	22	Front Strap Screw	42	Stock Screw
2	Backstrap Screws	23	Gate	43	Trigger
3	Balls	24	Gate Catch	44	Trigger Guard
4	Barrel	25	Gate Catch Screw	45	Trigger Screw
5	Base Pin	26	Gate Spring	46	Hammer Screw Washer
6	Base Pin Bushing	27	Hammer		
7	Base Pin Screw	28	Hammer Roll	47	Bolt Screw Washers
8	Base Pin Screw Nut	29	Hammer Roll Pin	48	Backstrap Screw Washers
9	Base Pin Spring	30	Hammer Screw		
10	Bolt	31	Hand Assembly	49	Rear Guard Screw Washers
11	Bolt Screw	32	Mainspring		
12	Cylinder	33	Mainspring Screw		
13	Ejector Head	34	Rear Guard Screws		
14	Ejector Rod	35	Recoil Plate		
15	Ejector Spring	36	Sear and Bolt Spring		
16	EjectorTube	37	Sear and Bolt Spring Screw		
17	Ejector Tube Screw	38	Spring		
18	Firing Pin	39	Stock, Left		
19	Firing Pin Rivet	40	Stock, Right		
20	Frame	41	Stock Pin		
21	Front Guard Screw				

William Mason

Who designed the Single-Action Army? The answer is that no single person was responsible for the revolver's creation. As is the case with many large and well-established companies, the revolver was the product of the combined efforts of a number of talented individuals.

When the Model P is laid alongside the main percussion Colts that preceded it, its pedigree is obvious, and it is clear it evolved from these by way of improvements and various upgrades. In fact, its basic action is little changed from Sam Colt's very first revolver design.

Nevertheless, when the single action was being created, the company no longer had the creative talents of its founder or Elisha Root, both of whom were deceased. William Mason was the man who was key in pulling together the various elements that resulted in the creation of Colt's very successful solid-frame cartridge revolver.

Mason, who was born in Massachusetts in 1837, had run the Mason Machine Works during the Civil War. Before coming to Colt, Mason had assigned two of his revolver patents to Remington. During his life, Mason registered over 100 patents for inventions that included mechanical devices, firearms, machinery and bridges.

When Mason arrived at Colt in 1869, his technical expertise and innovation was especially important. He was responsible for the design of the side-mounted ejector rod system of the Single-Action Army while Charles B. Richards designed the loading gate. It seems these two men had much to do with the design and development of the revolver.

Later, Mason would play a major role in the design of the company's first double-action revolvers. William Mason died in 1913.

THE
GERMAN P08 LUGER
The Auto Pistol with the Most Sex Appeal

In many ways, the Luger is to semi-automatic pistols what the Colt Single-Action Army is to revolvers. Its classic flowing lines make it one of the most appealing auto pistols of all time. It is also the pistol that introduced the 9mm Parabellum cartridge, which became one of the most popular pistol and submachine gun cartridges ever made. As a military sidearm, it saw service in both world wars and was widely used by the armies of a number of European and other nations. Not surprisingly, Lugers are keenly sought by collectors and some models are extremely valuable.

HISTORY AND DEVELOPMENT

The Luger owes much of its design, especially its toggle action, from the Borchardt pistol. Although initially chambered for a bottlenecked 7.65mm cartridge, it was later chambered for the new more powerful 9mm cartridge that remained its main caliber for most of its long production life.

Apart from being offered with a variety of barrel lengths, its basic mechanism remained unchanged until production finally ceased in World War II. Lugers have always been admired for the high quality of workmanship they display. As with many military arms, this was the main reason for its eventual demise because it was very expensive to manufacture.

As a result, it has been replaced with the more modern designs that, while undoubtedly efficient, lack the appeal of old-time craftsmanship and eye appeal that is fast becoming only a memory.

DESIGN CHARACTERISTICS AND FEATURES

The Luger is a magazine-fed, semi-automatic pistol that uses a toggle action developed for the earlier Borchardt pistol to lock the breech momentarily during firing. The toggle action is a locking mechanism that moves rear-wards for a short distance together with the barrel and then pivots upwards once chamber pressures have reached a safe level. The action is then unlocked as the toggle continues its upward/rearward motion at the same time it is ejecting the spent case and cocking the firing mechanism. On its forward movement, the lock pivots down to close the action, stripping a fresh round from the magazine and feeding it into the chamber. If the magazine is empty, the toggle will be locked open.

The pistol's controls consisted of a takedown latch located in the front of the frame, a button-type magazine catch positioned behind the trigger and a safety catch set at the top rear left side of the frame. Early models often had a safety in the rear of the grip although this was eliminated in later pistols.

Characteristics of the Luger were its clean flowing lines that included a tapered barrel of various lengths and a grip that housed the magazine, which was angled acutely to the barrel centerline. The sharply angled grip contributed to the pistol's natural pointing characteristics and its pleasant mild recoil.

While most standard Lugers had fixed sights, most of the long-barrel models had an adjustable tangent sight position forward of the breech.

During its long period of service, the pistol underwent relatively few major modifications, evidence of the soundness of its basic design.

MILITARY LUGERS IN FOREIGN SERVICE

Although Deutsche Waffen & Munitionsfabriken's (DWM) ultimate goal was to obtain a German military contract for the Luger, this occurred only after a number of foreign nations had adopted the pistol for their armies. In 1900, the armies of Bulgaria and Switzerland were the first to express an interest in the Luger. In both cases, the pistols were chambered for a 7.65mm bottlenecked cartridge (known in the US as the 30 Luger).

Both pistols had 4 3/4-inch, slim, tapered barrels and were made by DWM, which is roll-stamped on the rear of

Lugers employ the unique toggle breech locking system that first appeared in the earlier Borchardt pistol.

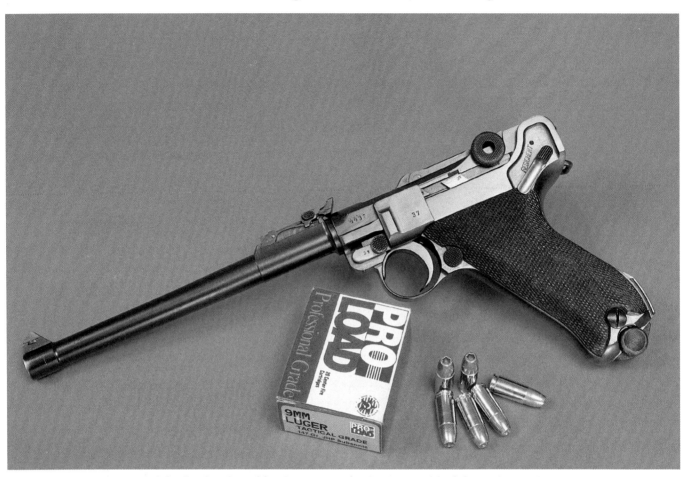

Although the Luger was originally chambered for the 7.65mm (30 Luger cartridge), its main cartridge was the 9mm Luger specially created for it. Shown here is an artillery model with a 7 1/2-inch barrel.

the toggle. Swiss military models are marked with the Swiss cross in a sunburst stamp on top of the chamber while the Bulgarian models have the Bulgarian royal family crest stamped in the same location. Commercial versions were also sold in both countries. Other foreign users of the pistol were Brazil, Chile, China, Holland, Iran, Luxemburg, Mexico, Norway, Portugal, Rumania, Russia and Turkey.

LUGERS IN THE UNITED STATES

In 1900, similar 30 Lugers were submitted to the US military for trials. It performed well enough for an order for 1000 pistols to be placed. These continued to be tested until 1908. The main complaint was over the small caliber of the cartridge. Around the same time, a number of similar pistols were made for commercial sales in the US.

Due to the complaints about the striking power of the

7.65mm, Luger developed a new cartridge for the pistol in 1902, a 9 x 19mm round that became universally known as the 9mm "Parabellum." The term Parabellum came from the Latin phrase "Si Vis Pacem Para Bellum" (If you want peace, prepare for war). The Parabellum subsequently became the most widely used pistol and submachine gun cartridge in the world.

The new 9mm version of the Luger was not well received in the US, however, where DWM hoped it would enjoy good sales. The testing conducted by the Cavalry Board and the Field Artillery Board, while admiring the Luger's accuracy, was disappointed with its continual jamming during the testing. The jamming and the need to constantly use two hands when firing or clearing jams rendered it "practically useless" according to the Cavalry Board report. The Colt revolver would remain the mainstay of the US military until the arrival of the Colt 1911.

In 1907, a few Lugers were made for the 45 ACP cartridge to compete in the US military trial then taking place, but the pistol eventually lost out to the Colt Government model. All American Lugers were made by DWM and carry the American Eagle crest over the chamber.

While the Luger failed to interest the US military, it did quite well as a civilian arm. Among the main US importers and distributors were Abercrombie & Fitch and Stoeger. The latter company even copyrighted the name Luger.

The Luger's controls are all on the left side and consist of a takedown lever, magazine catch and a thumb safety.

The Luger's safety is applied by depressing it so that the marking "Gescihert" (safe) is exposed.

GERMAN MILITARY LUGERS

The Luger's lackluster reception in the US would not be duplicated on its home turf. DWM had previously tried, unsuccessfully, to market the Luger to the German military. The army had tested variations of the Luger for several years and found it wanting. The navy, as usual, thought differently than its sister branch. In December of 1904, the Reichsmarineamt (German Naval Office) made the 9 x 19mm Pistole, Marine Model 1904, System Borchardt Luger its official sidearm. The 1904 Marine model was equipped with a 6-inch barrel, a unique two-position rear sight (graduated for 100 and 200 meters) and a combined extractor-loaded chamber indicator. The early Marine model featured the flat-faced knurled toggle grips with the older anti-bounce lock mechanism.

In 1906, an improved version of the Marine model was introduced. It had a coil spring instead of the flat mainspring and the anti-bounce lock was discontinued. The 1906 model remained the mainstay until the arrival of the world-famous Pistole '08. Not much had changed from the 1906 model when the P08 first made its appearance, the most apparent alteration being that the grip safety was discarded. As a result, the P08 safety catch had to be pulled downward to make the pistol safe. The P08 was accepted by the German Army as its official sidearm in 1908.

The P08 models were made with a 4-inch barrel and were in 9mm. Originally, the P08 had no device to keep the action open for cleaning or inspection as the old type of toggle link lock had been abandoned. This was later fixed by fitting a spring-loaded lever that, when pushed upward by the magazine platform button, engaged a slot cut into the bottom of the bolt.

The German Navy had its version of the P08, the Navy Parabellum, which lacked the grip safety, but kept the two-position rear sight and the 6-inch barrel. The German military version came with a special holster that had space for a spare magazine and a small pocket underneath the flap for a combination tool.

In 1914, the Navy Parabellum was produced with an 8-inch barrel and was known as the Model 08/14 or Model 14. The Model 14 was identical to the '08 except for the longer barrel and a special elevating rear sight mounted on the rear of the barrel. A special holster was issued with the Model 14 that doubled as a shoulder stock and came with a 32-round drum magazine. The drum magazine was later abandoned due to its bulky weight and tendency to jam.

After World War I, the P08 remained in service with German military forces right up to the early years of the Second World War. Production ceased in 1942 with adoption of the P38 pistol.

In the 1930s and 1940s, Mauser manufactured pistols identical in design to the original Luger. Most collectors view these more as replicas rather than as genuine Lugers.

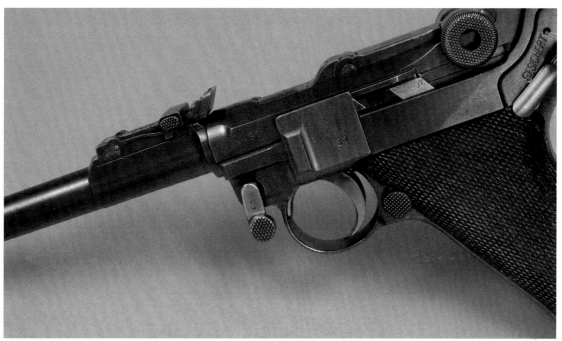

Depressing the takedown latch allows the barrel and action to be removed from the frame.

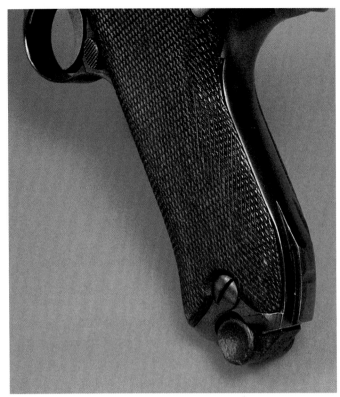

Many of the military Lugers, especially the long-barreled models, have the bottom of the grip frame machined to accept a shoulder stock.

LUGER MANUFACTURERS

While DWM was the main manufacturer of Luger pistols, eventually other companies were brought in to cope with the wartime demand. These included the following companies, whose names are usually stamped on the top of the rear toggle:

DWM - Deutsche Waffen & Munitionsfabriken, Karlsrube, Germany

Erfurt - Royal Arsenal of Erfert, Germany

Spandau - Spandau, Germany

Simpson & Company - Suhl, Germany

Mauser - Obendorf, Germany

Krieghoff - H. Krieghoff Waffenfabrick, Suhl, Germany

In addition, several foreign companies were licensed to make Lugers, such as:

Vickers Ltd - Vickers-Armstrong Ltd, England

Waffenfabrick Bern - Bern, Switzerland.

CALIBERS

The most common Luger calibers are 9mm and 7.65 (30 Luger). Other chamberings include 32 ACP, 380 ACP and 45 ACP, all of which are very rare. Also scarce are 22 LR, 4mm and 6mm conversion units.

BARREL LENGTHS

Lugers were made in a variety of barrel lengths. The most common lengths of 3-3/4, 4 and 4-3/4 inches are found on the military and commercial models. Naval and presentation models include 6-inch barrels while artillery models and some commercial models had 8-inch barrels.

Luger carbines had 11 3/4-inch barrels, detachable wooden stocks and fore-ends. The 1920 commercial models had barrel lengths between 12 and 20 inches. The shortest Luger barrel is 3-1/4 inches, of which only one was made. This was the personal pistol of Georg Luger himself and it is stamped with his personal monogram.

SIGHTS, STOCKS AND FINISHES

Luger pistols with standard barrels of 6 inches or less had fixed sights. The artillery, long-barrel and carbine models had adjustable tangent sights on the barrel just in front of the chamber.

Most but not all Lugers had the bottom rear of the grip frame machined to accept a detachable stock. This resulted in a number of Luger carbine models being made.

All Lugers exhibit a high degree of fit and finish. Metal parts are either rust or salt blued while a few presentation guns are engraved. Grip panels are generally a finely checked wood although some late-production World War II models have checkered plastic grips.

FIELD STRIPPING THE LUGER

First remove the magazine and check that the chamber is empty. Press the muzzle against a flat piece of wood to relieve spring tension. In this position, the takedown lever can be rotated down allowing the trigger plate to be removed from the side of the pistol.

The barrel and toggle assembly can now be slid forward off the frame. Buckle the toggle slightly to remove the axle pin so the toggle assembly can be removed from the rear of the barrel group. This is as far as the pistol needs to be taken down for normal cleaning and maintenance.

The pistol is assembled in reverse order.

SHOOTING AND HANDLING THE P08 LUGER

In terms of shooting and handling, the P08 is similar in many respects to the Colt Single-Action Army revolver.

Most regular Lugers have fixed sights, but long-barrel versions like this artillery model have an adjustable tangent sight mounted on the barrel forward of the breech. Manufacturer marking are stamped on top of the toggle. These indicate a Luger made by DWM.

Not only is it an attractive looking pistol but also one that has many endearing shooting qualities.

The Luger's long service with the German forces and the armies of other nations is proof enough of its worth as a military sidearm. Probably because of its flowing lines and high-grade workmanship, Lugers were prized trophies among allied servicemen during both world wars. Their new owners pressed a number into service.

There is an unsubstantiated claim that the American World War I hero Sgt. Alvin York, used a liberated Luger in his final shootout with a German squad of soldiers instead of a 1911 45 pistol.

The pistol has very pleasant shooting characteristics, thanks to its sharply angled grip that makes it point naturally at the target. It also gives good access to the trigger and controls with the exception of the safety, which has to be pushed up to be disengaged. This can be a little difficult to perform without having to change one's grip on the pistol. Recoil is relatively mild enabling fast recovery of the sights.

While the trigger has a relatively short throw, the pull is a little on the heavy side. The fixed sights are rudimentary, consisting of a barleycorn front blade and a small rear notch. The tangent sights on the long-barrel models are an improvement.

Even though the Luger is not a target arm, I have shot a number that have produced impressive accuracy. This is especially so of the long-barrel versions.

Probably the greatest complaint against the Luger is questionable reliability. Even though it appears to have served the German troops well enough in the dirt and mud of the trenches, it has a reputation for poor feeding with some types of ammunition.

In my experience, Lugers perform reliably enough if fed the correct ammunition. They seem to perform best with 124-grain military ball ammunition loaded to velocities around 1250 fps. Failures generally occur with underpowered ammunition that lacks the energy to drive the toggle action back far enough to eject the spent case or pick up a fresh round from the magazine. With this in mind, it is worth remembering that European military 9mm is loaded to higher velocities than American commercial ammunition.

COLLECTOR INTEREST

As with the Colt Peacemaker, Lugers have high collector interest and can demand high prices. There is also the familiar question of whether they should be fired at all. This stresses the need to identify what type of Luger one has and its potential worth. Lugers of recent vintage and issue don't command the very high values of the long-barrel and the older, more exotic models and are candidates for shooting provided they are mechanically sound. On the other hand, I would be hesitant to shoot one that is in pristine condition for fear of marring its finish and reducing its potential future value.

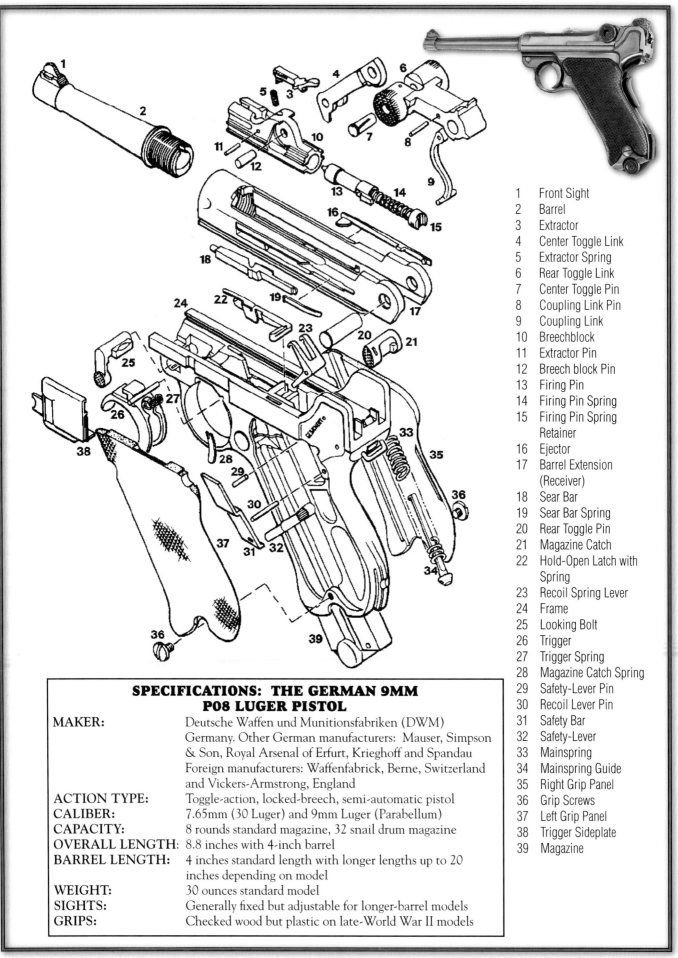

1 Front Sight
2 Barrel
3 Extractor
4 Center Toggle Link
5 Extractor Spring
6 Rear Toggle Link
7 Center Toggle Pin
8 Coupling Link Pin
9 Coupling Link
10 Breechblock
11 Extractor Pin
12 Breech block Pin
13 Firing Pin
14 Firing Pin Spring
15 Firing Pin Spring
   Retainer
16 Ejector
17 Barrel Extension
   (Receiver)
18 Sear Bar
19 Sear Bar Spring
20 Rear Toggle Pin
21 Magazine Catch
22 Hold-Open Latch with
   Spring
23 Recoil Spring Lever
24 Frame
25 Looking Bolt
26 Trigger
27 Trigger Spring
28 Magazine Catch Spring
29 Safety-Lever Pin
30 Recoil Lever Pin
31 Safety Bar
32 Safety-Lever
33 Mainspring
34 Mainspring Guide
35 Right Grip Panel
36 Grip Screws
37 Left Grip Panel
38 Trigger Sideplate
39 Magazine

SPECIFICATIONS: THE GERMAN 9MM P08 LUGER PISTOL

MAKER:	Deutsche Waffen und Munitionsfabriken (DWM) Germany. Other German manufacturers: Mauser, Simpson & Son, Royal Arsenal of Erfurt, Krieghoff and Spandau Foreign manufacturers: Waffenfabrick, Berne, Switzerland and Vickers-Armstrong, England
ACTION TYPE:	Toggle-action, locked-breech, semi-automatic pistol
CALIBER:	7.65mm (30 Luger) and 9mm Luger (Parabellum)
CAPACITY:	8 rounds standard magazine, 32 snail drum magazine
OVERALL LENGTH:	8.8 inches with 4-inch barrel
BARREL LENGTH:	4 inches standard length with longer lengths up to 20 inches depending on model
WEIGHT:	30 ounces standard model
SIGHTS:	Generally fixed but adjustable for longer-barrel models
GRIPS:	Checked wood but plastic on late-World War II models

Georg Luger
and
Hugo Borchardt

The two men responsible for creation of the Luger, Georg Luger and Hugo Borchardt, both worked at the company that was closely associated with the manufacture of the pistol, the Deutsche Waffen und Munitionsfabriken (DWM).

DWM was the result of the business activities of two brothers, Ludwig and Isidor Lowe. Their company, Ludwig Lowe und Companie, originally specialized in the manufacture of machine tools and sewing machines. After gaining a government contract in 1870 during the Franco-Prussian War, the company began to manufacture rifle sight assemblies. Lowe und Companie's skill and precision at this venture soon led to further government contracts, both domestic and foreign. It was not long before sewing machines were traded for weapons as the successful company began making firearms full time.

In 1886 Ludwig died, and Isidor began a joint venture with Waffenfabrik Mauser, AG to produce rifles for Turkey. As time passed, the activities of these two companies intertwined together around the successful manufacture of firearms. Lowe acquired controlling interest in Waffenfabrik Mauser as well as Deutsche Metallpatronenfabrik Lorenz, a German ammunition factory. The resulting company purchases and corporate shuffling led to the creation of the Deutsche Waffen und Munitionsfabriken (DWM).

Georg Luger and Hugo Borchardt worked together at the Lowe firm and both had a serious interest in and no small measure of success with self-loading firearm designs and patents as well as ammunition loads.

Borchardt, a German-born, naturalized US citizen, worked at several small companies before working for the Winchester Repeating Arms Company of New Haven, Connecticut. His first patent for a machine to cut lubrication grooves into bullets was given while he was with Winchester. In 1890, after employment at various companies in the US and Europe, Borchardt joined the Lowe firm and later designed the large toggle-action semi-automatic pistol that bears his name.

Georg Luger, an Austrian, became involved with firearms as a result of his involvement with Ferdinand von Mannlicher. Luger experimented with rifle designs for bolt actions and self-loaders for twenty years before joining Lowe in 1891.

Luger used Borchardt's pistol as a basis for his now famous pistol. His final design was a pistol that was smaller and lighter than the big cumbersome Borchardt. As a result, the new Luger pistol had much more potential as a military sidearm than the Borchardt.

THE COLT 45 GOVERNMENT MODEL OF 1911

Possibly the Best Combat Handgun of All Time

The Colt 45 Government Model of 1911 is arguably the most popular handgun ever made. The number of imitations of the 1911 is countless and continues to increase. No other handgun has the dedicated following of the venerable Colt.

Based on John Browning's patent, the 1911 established a reputation for being an extremely rugged, reliable and hard-hitting auto pistol. The US Army, Navy and Marine Corps used it for close to a century. It has also been the first choice of many civilians and law officers.

HISTORY AND DEVELOPMENT

The 1911 was developed from Browning's first semi-automatic pistol, the Colt 38 pistol of 1900. Colt and Browning had entered into an agreement for the company to distribute his handguns in America as well as using his patents in pistols that Colt decided to manufacture in the future.

In 1898, the US army was considering replacing the Colt 38 revolver with a self-loading pistol. A board of officers had began trials for a new handgun and was testing a number of auto pistols including the 1896 Mauser and the blow-forward Mannlicher as well as the Colt Browning Model of 1900.

Some 6000 rounds were fired through the Colt with only minor breakages occurring. In fact, the only thing that stopped the test was the running out of ammunition.

The pistol was submitted to field-testing by army units. After complaints from some officers about the pistol's balance and handling procedures, Colt began fine-tuning the pistol. The pistol's muzzle heaviness was reduced and the grip elongated, allowing space for a larger cartridge to be accommodated in the magazine.

THE CALIBER QUESTION

The real problem was deciding on a caliber for an updated Model 1900, which was only a 38 caliber at the time. Complaints about the lack of stopping power of Colt New Model Army and Navy revolvers in the Philippines had brought the realization that a larger caliber was required as well as a new sidearm.

These days there is a popular myth that the 38 revolver and its cartridge proved to be complete failures in the Philippine campaign. In fact, during the early stages, it performed quite adequately, even holding its own against other weapons.

This situation changed dramatically when operations moved to the southern island. It was against the tough, fanatical Moro warriors who inhabited the island that the 38 proved to be inconsistent in its fight-stopping abilities. The myth of its ineffectiveness against a fanatical enemy was born. More stopping power was required.

Thompson and LeGarde, two officers in the US Army, conducted experiments with a variety of projectiles of different weight, diameter and velocity. The tests were conducted using human cadavers, steers and horses.

Stopping power and wounds were compared and judged. For the military, the best performing round was judged to be one that entered the body and then stopped and delivered all

In its final configuration, the Colt pistol was chambered for the newly developed 45 ACP cartridge. It was officially designated as the Colt Government Model 45 pistol of 1911. Photo courtesy of Garry James.

its inherent energy. The 45 caliber (11.43mm) was the bullet judged best to fit the bill.

Colt developed a new 45-caliber automatic pistol in 1905 from the Model 1900. Called the Colt 45 Automatic Pistol, it had a 5-inch barrel chambered for the new 45 ACP cartridge and had a seven-shot magazine.

The pistol and cartridge went through several stages of metamorphosis before it reached this point. The initial cartridge was too heavy to achieve the hoped-for performance so Colt and Winchester combined their efforts to produce an effective cartridge for the new pistol. The case was shortened and bullet weight reduced. The resulting cartridge reached the desired level of 853 fps and retained accuracy up to 147 feet.

The pistol underwent exhaustive trials during the period of 1907 to 1911. The trials included other arms and continued until the field had been narrowed down to two competitors, the 45 Colt and a pistol in the same caliber from Savage.

Both were found to have the desirable features required by the army, but with several flaws inherent in each, which would need correction before a final decision could be made. Both guns were cited as having insufficient safety mechanisms and each needed some fine-tuning, including wood grips for the Savage and a better trigger for the Colt.

In 1907, Colt received the list of improvements necessary for the next incarnation of its design—an almost-vertical ejection port, a loaded-chamber indicator and an automatic safety. In 1909, the pistol was overhauled into what was nearly the end result of the 1911. The two-link locking system was replaced by a one-link system. The grip safety, a fairly late

addition, was worked on and made easier to manipulate. The magazine release catch and ejector were both enhanced.

In 1910, the Cavalry Board, still nervous about the safety of an autoloader, requested more work done on the safety mechanism of the gun. After attempts with several designs, Colt came up with a safety that allowed the pistol to be "cocked and locked" safely. But after a test that resulted in a cracked barrel and a damaged slide on the Colt, the Army determined that neither it nor the Savage was ready in their present forms and that strengthening of the guns was necessary, as was work on the reliability of the actions of both pistols.

Both companies resumed work in correcting these defects. In March of 1911, the board of officers met to test the two updated pistols for the last time. The Savage had 31 malfunctions and a number of parts breakages. The Colt performed without a hitch. In March of 1911, the secretary of war announced a new sidearm for the US Army – the Colt Government Model 45 pistol.

The 1911 is often referred to as the Colt/Browning 45 pistol, implying that Browning was its sole designer. While his contribution was considerable, engineers from both Colt and the Army Ordnance Department were equally involved in creating improvements and refinements. In addition, the patents of other inventors were incorporated into the pistol.

DESIGN CHARACTERISTICS AND FEATURES

The 1911 was a locked-breech semi-automatic pistol chambered for the 45 ACP cartridge. It used Browning's single swinging-link system to lock the action during firing. It had a single-action trigger that required the hammer to be cocked for every shot. Its controls consisted of multiple safeties, a slide stop and a magazine catch. One of the safeties was a manual thumb catch located with the two other controls on the left side of the frame. The other safeties included a disconnector that prevented firing until the action was fully closed, a half-cock hammer notch to prevent the pistol from going full auto and grip safety positioned in the top rear of the frame. The latter permitted firing only when the pistol was correctly gripped in the hand. The slide stop was positioned above the safety and a button-style magazine catch was located behind the trigger. The pistol had a seven-shot single-column magazine.

DESIGN CHANGES

During its long service with the US armed forces, the 1911 has undergone relatively few changes.

In the early 1920s, important changes were made that included a longer grip safety tang, an arched mainspring housing and a shorter trigger. Pistols with these changes became standard military issue and are designated as the Colt Government Model 1911A1.

No further changes were made to military Government models until the last GI models were made at the end of World War II.

In the post-war years, Colt continued making the 1911 for the civilian market and continued to update and improve the design when appropriate. Virtually all of these changes were minor in nature.

One of the first noticeable changes was a slightly larger

The 1911 employed John Browning's swinging-link system to lock the breech momentarily during firing. Photo courtesy of Garry James.

The Colt Series 80 Mark IV stainless steel model.

thumb safety that was easier to manipulate. During the 1970s, the Mark IV Series 70 model was introduced. This model replaced the old-style barrel bushing with a new collet finger-style design intended to improve accuracy.

During the decade that followed, the Series 80 was introduced. This pistol reverted to the old-style plain barrel bushing but had an internal passive firing pin lock to prevent firing should the pistol be dropped on its muzzle. The Series 80 also introduced much-improved fixed sights.

The final changes of significance occurred several years later with the so-called "Enhanced Series." These pistols had features that had become popular in competition and customized versions of the Government model. These include a ribbed slide, improved fixed sights, speed safety, modified beavertail grip safety and a round spur hammer.

OTHER 1911 MANUFACTURERS

During World Wars I and II, there was an urgent need for firearms, and Colt could not produce enough pistols for the expanding army. As a result, other companies were licensed to produce the pistols. These included:

Remington Arms Co of Ilion, New York
North American Arms Co Ltd, Canada
Remington Rand Co, Syracuse, New York
Ithaca Gun Co. Ithaca, New York
Union Switch & Signal Co, Swissdale, Pennsylvania
Singer Sewing Machine Co, New York, New York

The Springfield armory ordnance factory made a number of pistols. In addition, some countries like Norway and Argentina were also licensed to make the 1911 for their military and police forces.

The pistol's controls are all on the left side and consist of a slide stop, magazine catch and thumb safety. Photo courtesy of Garry James.

PISTOLS BASED ON THE 1911

During its long life, the 1911 has spawned a number of other Colt pistols based on its design. Although intended as a military service pistol, gunsmiths in the years between the wars discovered that the pistol could be fine-tuned to deliver enough accuracy for target shooting. This was enough to prompt Colt to produce a target 1911 especially for competition. Eventually called the National Match, it was first introduced in 1933. It was tuned for accuracy, given a match trigger and target sights. A 38 Special National Match was made in 1960.

The National Match underwent further refinements to its sights and action, eventually becoming the Gold Cup in 1957. Since its introduction, Colt has always billed the Gold Cup as its premier 1911 model.

In 1949 Colt introduced a special, lightweight, more-compact 1911 called the Commander. It had an alloy frame, a shortened barrel and slide, and was chambered for 45 ACP, 9mm Luger and 38 Super. In 1971, a steel frame version called the Combat Commander was introduced.

The year 1985 saw the introduction of the even more compact Officers ACP series. These pistols were shortened both in length and height and were later offered with light alloy frames and in stainless steel.

CALIBERS

While the 1911's main caliber has always been the 45 ACP, over the years models in other calibers have been made. These include 455, 7.65 Luger, 9mm Luger, 9mm Largo and 38 Super. In recent years, the pistol has been made in modern calibers such as 10mm and 40 S&W as well as a 9x23mm cartridge made by Winchester.

In 1931, the Ace appeared, which was a 1911 chambered for the 22 Long Rifle cartridge. This pistol has a lightened slide and a special floating chamber.

Later, Colt offered 1911 owners a 22 conversion unit consisting of a barrel, slide, bushing recoil spring ejector and magazine.

FINISHES AND MATERIALS

The first 1911s had Colt's brightly polished fire-blue finish but later military pistols had a matte non-glare Parkerized finish. Civilian models with bright blue finishes continued to be made.

Grips began with checkered-wood side panels. Military models later had panels made of a brown plastic material. For a time, Colt used a special synthetic material with a wood-like appearance called "Coltwood" for most of their handgun grips, including the 1911.

While carbon steel has been the material used for most 1911s, an aluminum alloy called "Coltaloy" was substituted for lightweight versions like the Commander and Officers ACP. During the 1980s, Colt offered a stainless steel Government model and this material is now used throughout the 1911 line.

THE COLT 1911 TODAY

As already mentioned, the 1911 continues to be made by Colt in several versions. Even though Colt's future is uncertain, the 1911 continues to thrive in the form of a variety of clones and copies made by other companies.

FIELD STRIPPING PROCEDURES

The following is the field strip procedure for the standard Government model. Customized pistols and those with full-length guide rods have a slightly different procedure.

First remove the magazine and check that the chamber is empty. Then rotate the barrel bushing clockwise so the recoil spring and plug can be removed. Next, rotate the barrel bushing counter-clockwise so it can be removed from the slide.

With the recoil spring removed, pull back the slide until the smaller detent on the left side is aligned with the rear of the slide stop. When in this position, the slide stop can be removed from the frame.

The slide and barrel assembly can then be pulled forward off the frame. The final step is to remove the barrel from the front of the slide. The pistol is assembled in reverse order. With Series 80 models that have the firing pin lock, the levers operating the same need to be pushed back in the frame when refitting the slide.

SHOOTING AND HANDLING THE GOVERNMENT MODEL 1911

In spite of its continuing popularity, not everyone has praised the pistol as a shooting arm. Many a GI has cussed it for its lack of accuracy and heavy recoil. This is in sharp contrast to those who extol it as one of the best combat handguns ever made. The simple fact is the pistol would never have survived as long as it has if it did not have many virtues and few faults.

Its strength, reliability and great hitting power are at the top of its many attributes. In spite of the pistol's great strength, prolonged shooting of high-performance ammunition can result in accelerated wear and even frame and slide cracking. Regular maintenance and recoil spring replacement can go a long way towards preventing this.

The pistol's large components and generous tolerances enable it to continue functioning in the most arduous of circumstances. Nevertheless, like other pistols of the period, it is designed for

In addition to the thumb safety, the Model 1911 had a grip safety positioned in the back of the grip. It incorporated a relatively short tang and a flat mainspring housing. Photo courtesy of Garry James.

One of the pistol's first major changes occurred after World War I in the revised 1911A1 model. The changes consisted of a revised grip safety with a longer tang and an arched mainspring housing. The new thumb safety shown here was only made after World War II.

shooting full metal case ammunition. Problems therefore may be experienced with modern hollowpoint ammunition, although some 1911s handle them as well as hardball.

In my experience, malfunctions often occur with pistols that have been tricked up, accurized or otherwise customized for high performance. To avoid this, use only the services of a gunsmith who is well acquainted with the 1911. Such gunsmiths can also improve the reliability of 1911s with functioning problems.

In terms of shooting performance, the Government model has many excellent qualities. Its controls are all well placed for easy operation with the thumb of the shooting hand. The thumb and other safeties enable a well-trained shooter to carry it "cocked and locked" (chamber loaded, hammer cocked and safety applied).

The pistol's grip provides a very comfortable hold. Recoil is surprisingly mild, especially when a two-handed grip is used. The only problem that can occur, depending on how the pistol is gripped, is failure to completely push in the grip safety. This may happen if a very high thumb position is taken.

Taking a high thumb position with a Model 1911 also may result in hammer bite (the fleshy part of the web of the hand being pinched between the hammer and the grip safety spur). This is less likely to occur with a 1911A1 because of its longer grip safety tang. The problem can be resolved either by taking a different hold or having a custom Beavertail grip safety fitted.

Except for 1911s of later than 1990 vintage, the fixed sights tend to be on the small side and trigger pulls on the heavy side. The former can be vastly improved by fitting a set of one of the many excellent aftermarket sights while the services of a good gunsmith can provide a trigger equal to that of any target pistol.

Most Government Models have accuracy that is adequate for service and defense purposes, although it is possible to get a pistol that has superior accuracy. My first Government Model, a 1911 of fairly early vintage delivered excellent accuracy. The fact is the 1911 and the 45 ACP have great accuracy potential.

There are gunsmiths specializing in 1911 custom work who can create a match-grade target arm out of a military GI 45. Accuracy can be improved by simply fitting tighter barrel bushings and longer barrel links. A device called a Group-Gripper that is relatively simple to install can produce remarkable improvements in accuracy.

No other handgun has been subjected to such extensive gunsmithing. Such pistols dominate the target and action shooting ranges. The things that can be done to improve the pistol's performance are one of its most endearing qualities.

COLLECTOR INTEREST

Model 1911s of early vintage have high collector value as do some of the later models. Customizing can destroy their value and there is also the question of whether to shoot such a pistol. It is, therefore, important to know exactly what type of 1911 you have.

In the 1930s, Colt offered a slide 22 barrel and magazine conversion unit to allow the 1911 to shoot 22 LR cartridges.

A trigger-activated lever in the rear of the frame disengages the firing pin lock in the slide.

The Series 80 also introduced new fixed sights that were a vast improvement over those of the earlier models.

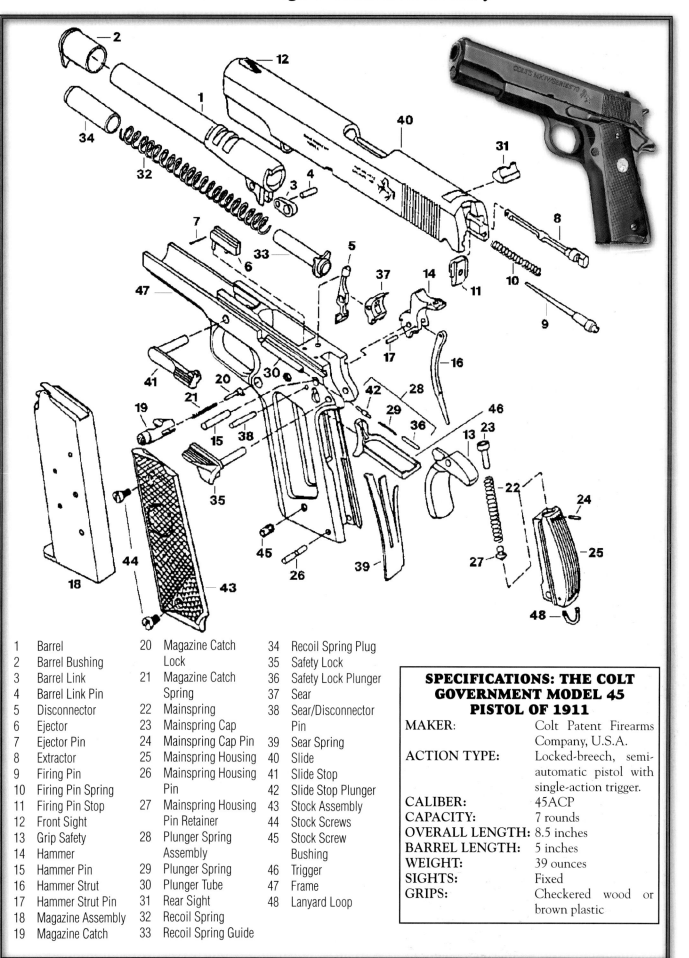

1	Barrel	20	Magazine Catch	34	Recoil Spring Plug
2	Barrel Bushing		Lock	35	Safety Lock
3	Barrel Link	21	Magazine Catch	36	Safety Lock Plunger
4	Barrel Link Pin		Spring	37	Sear
5	Disconnector	22	Mainspring	38	Sear/Disconnector
6	Ejector	23	Mainspring Cap		Pin
7	Ejector Pin	24	Mainspring Cap Pin	39	Sear Spring
8	Extractor	25	Mainspring Housing	40	Slide
9	Firing Pin	26	Mainspring Housing	41	Slide Stop
10	Firing Pin Spring		Pin	42	Slide Stop Plunger
11	Firing Pin Stop	27	Mainspring Housing	43	Stock Assembly
12	Front Sight		Pin Retainer	44	Stock Screws
13	Grip Safety	28	Plunger Spring	45	Stock Screw
14	Hammer		Assembly		Bushing
15	Hammer Pin	29	Plunger Spring	46	Trigger
16	Hammer Strut	30	Plunger Tube	47	Frame
17	Hammer Strut Pin	31	Rear Sight	48	Lanyard Loop
18	Magazine Assembly	32	Recoil Spring		
19	Magazine Catch	33	Recoil Spring Guide		

SPECIFICATIONS: THE COLT GOVERNMENT MODEL 45 PISTOL OF 1911

MAKER:	Colt Patent Firearms Company, U.S.A.
ACTION TYPE:	Locked-breech, semi-automatic pistol with single-action trigger.
CALIBER:	45ACP
CAPACITY:	7 rounds
OVERALL LENGTH:	8.5 inches
BARREL LENGTH:	5 inches
WEIGHT:	39 ounces
SIGHTS:	Fixed
GRIPS:	Checkered wood or brown plastic

John Moses Browning

John Browning is generally recognized as one of the greatest firearms designers. His designs extend not just to handguns, but encompass rifles, shotguns and machineguns. He is best known for his many contributions to the design of self-loading firearms.

Browning was born in 1855 in Utah. His father was a gunsmith by trade and his son showed an aptitude for firearms as a young boy and worked in his father's shop. At the age of 14, he made his first rifle from scrap he found in the shop.

In 1878, he received his first patent. By the time he was married and a father, he was a full-time gun maker. His career as a firearms designer was ensured when T.G. Bennett, vice president of Winchester, purchased one of Browning's single-shot rifles. This spawned a partnership with the company that lasted for some 19 years. During that time, the company purchased Browning's Models 1886, 1894 and 1895 lever-action rifles as well as his 1887 lever-action and 1897 slide-action shotguns.

After returning from his compulsory two-year service as a Mormon missionary, Browning continued with his work as a gun designer. He began experimenting with self-loading firearms in 1889. Browning's first successful machinegun design was the Model 1895, a gas-operated weapon that was ultimately made and sold by Colt.

His first self-loading pistol was also a gas-operated design. Shortly afterwards, Browning and Colt entered an agreement where that company would make and sell his pistols in the United States.

Browning intended to sell his pistols in Europe and that led to another partnership with Fabrique Nationale (FN) in Belgium. It was in this adopted country that Browning worked on his final pistol design, the P35 High Power. He died in Belgium before the pistol was completed. At his funeral, he was lauded by countless of his co-workers.

THE SMITH & WESSON MILITARY & POLICE MODEL 10 REVOLVER

Mainstay of America's Police Force for Almost 100 Years

Smith & Wesson's Military and Police (M&P) revolver, or Model 10, is one of that company's most successful designs. In addition to its long service life, it has also been the platform from which many of the company's other popular revolvers have been developed.

Much of this revolver's success and that of the other models that have been developed from it can be attributed to its size, especially its grip. It uses a frame designated as the "K" size, which is a major factor why the M&P is considered a classic handgun.

HISTORY AND DEVELOPMENT

The Military and Police revolver traces its ancestry back to Smith & Wesson's swing-out cylinder revolvers. Prior to 1895, all Smith & Wesson revolvers were either tip-up or break-top designs. The company never copied Colt by developing a solid frame revolver like the Single Action Army.

Nevertheless, Smith & Wesson was interested in Colt's new swing-out cylinder 38 revolver of 1892. The company came out with their own such design called the "hand ejector models." According S&W historian Roy Jinks, the first prototype was made by modifying a Colt Model 1892 revolver.

The first production model was a 32-caliber six-shot cylinder revolver called the Hand Ejector. The cylinder was locked in place in the frame by means of its ejector rod. Pulling the rod forward released the cylinder from the frame for loading and unloading.

In the years that followed, Smith & Wesson improved the design until they arrived at a swing-out cylinder revolver much like the models in production today.

Calibers were expanded from 22 and 32 to include larger cartridges like 38, 44 and 45. The first 38 was the Hand Ejector Model of 1899 introduced in that same year. It was later called the 38 Military and Police model. This revolver is significant in that it introduced the now famous K-frame and the 38 Special cartridge.

DESIGN CHARACTERISTICS AND FEATURES

The M&P Model of 1905 is a six-shot solid-frame swing-out cylinder double-action revolver chambered for the 38 Special cartridge. It is built on the medium-size K-frame and employs

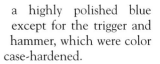

a highly polished blue except for the trigger and hammer, which were color case-hardened.

the cylinder locking and trigger system of the Hand Ejector models.

The cylinder was locked in the frame at both ends by a spring-loaded plunger rod that was released by a sliding latch on the left side of the frame behind the recoil shield. When released, a crane with the cylinder swung out of the left side of the frame.

To clear the cylinder chambers of cartridges and spent cases, the ejector rod in front of the frame was pushed to the rear. When the cylinder was swung back into the frame, it automatically locked in place. Up until 1959 all revolvers had tapered barrels.

Sights were fixed and grips were of checkered wood containing brass S&W medallions. The revolver was of all-steel construction. All major metal components were finished with

THE 38 SPECIAL CARTRIDGE

Smith & Wesson hoped the U.S. military would show interest in the new revolver. The first models were chambered for the 38 Colt cartridge, but because this round had developed a poor reputation for putting down determined attackers in the Philippine insurrection, better ammunition was needed.

A new, more powerful 38 cartridge was designed by lengthening the case and changing the bore size so that the powder charge could be increased from 150 to 215 grains and the bullet size increased from 150 to 158 grains. The result was a round that has become a favorite for both defense and competition.

MILITARY USE

Military interest in the M&P was adversely affected by the fact they were already committed to the semi-automatic pistol. Nevertheless, the navy and army purchased some of the early 38 models. In later years, more revolvers were purchased, but it was never universally adopted by the military, even though it saw considerable use during World War II. During the Korean and Vietnam conflicts, the M&P was issued to navy and marine pilots.

A considerable number of M&Ps saw service with British and Commonwealth forces during World War II. After the evacuation of its army at Dunkirk, the British were desperately

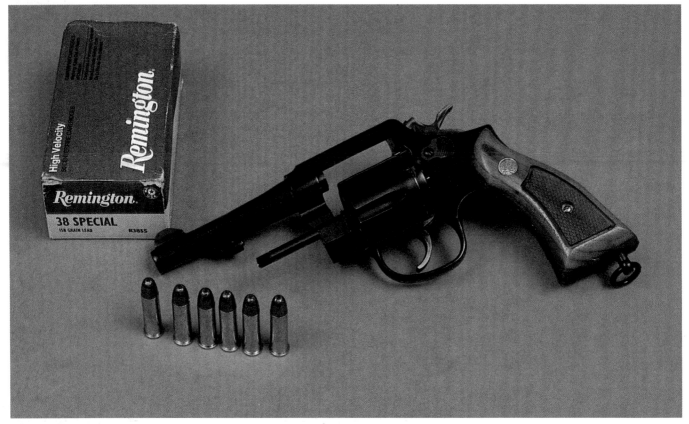

The Military & Police (Model 10) revolver was a solid-frame, swing-out cylinder revolver chambered for the popular 38 S&W cartridge, which was actually made for the M&P when it first appeared in 1905.

The Victory Model M&P was made for both the British and U.S. militaries. The British revolvers were chambered for the shorter 38/200 and the U.S. version, the 38 Special cartridge. Victory Models have a plain, rough, parkerized finish. Photo courtesy of Garry James.

short of firearms of any type. As a result, various U.S. arms companies were contracted to manufacture arms for the British including Smith & Wesson, which was given a $1,000,000 down payment to develop a 9mm carbine.

The project was never completed because the British were not satisfied with the gun the company delivered. Instead, they agreed to accept a large quantity of 38 revolvers in full settlement of the down payment.

Smith & Wesson used the M&P model for the revolver, chambering it for the British 38/200 cartridge, and the revolvers were so marked. Sometime after the revolvers went into production, the prefix "V" was added to their serial numbers. These are known as the "Victory" model M&Ps. Instead of the highly polished blue finish of the civilian M&Ps, the Victory models have a sandblasted parkerized finish.

After America entered the war, the Victory model production was expanded to include revolvers chambered for the 38 Special cartridge. These have the same sandblasted parkerized finish and were used largely by navy and marine aviators as well as other military personnel. A total of 568,204 Victory models were made for the British and several hundred thousand more were used by the U.S. After the war's end, many Victory models saw service with the military and police of countries such as Australia, New Zealand, South Africa and Rhodesia. In addition, many were sold to defense plants, postal services and other such organizations.

CIVILIAN AND POLICE

The M&P and the 38 Special cartridge have proven to be extremely popular with police and civilians. The 38 Special is an extremely versatile round that is powerful enough for defense, especially in the modern +P loadings, as well as being extremely accurate. The latter characteristic has made it a longtime favorite with serious target shooters.

As far as the revolver is concerned, its frame and grip size are such that it generally suits most hands, which helped increase its popularity with both civilians and police. Since being introduced in 1905, it has seen service with many police departments including the NYPD, the RCMP, the Royal Hong Kong Police and the London Metropolitan police to name but a few.

POST-WAR PRODUCTION

After the war ended, Smith & Wesson resumed civilian production of the M&P about September 1945. In 1957 Smith & Wesson began a number system to classify their handguns and the M&P was designated as the Model 10. It is a tribute to the soundness of the revolver's original design that the post-war models have changed very little from the

M&Ps were made for many foreign police forces. This 4-inch barrel model carries the marking of the British Colonial Royal Hong Kong Police.

After 1959, Smith & Wesson introduced a Model 10 with a plain non-tapered bull barrel with a top rib.

originals. In addition, the Model 10 and many of its variants are still in production today with only minor changes.

M&P VARIANTS

The first M&P Model of 1905 introduced a square butt frame that was used on many subsequent M&P models. Towards the end of the last century, Smith & Wesson made all their swing-out cylinder revolvers with round butt grip frames using a Hogue-style rubber grip available in either a round or square butt configuration.

All revolvers were equipped with tapered barrels up until 1959 when a heavy barrel version was introduced. This consisted of a four-inch-long parallel bull-type barrel.

M&Ps and Model 10s are mostly constructed of blued carbon steel although an optional nickel finish was offered.

Lightweight models with aluminum alloy frames called the 38 Military & Police Airweight were introduced from 1952 to 1986. Prior to this, lightweight models with both alloy frames and cylinders were made for the U.S. military. The latter are known as the Aircrewman Models. Apparently, the first civilian Airweights also had aluminum cylinders, but in the later models, this was changed to steel.

An all-stainless steel version of the Model 10—the Model 64—was introduced in 1970.

British Victory models were made with barrels of 4, 5 and 6 inches while the American versions had 2-, 4-, 5- or 6-inch barrels.

Airweights had 2-, 4-, 5- and 6-inch barrels while Model 13s had 3- or 4-inch barrels.

RELATED REVOLVERS

The introduction of the K-frame by the M&P has spawned a number of other popular centerfire revolvers such as the Model 19/66 and Model 15/67 as well as target models like the K-38 Masterpiece or Model 14. With its unbroken record of service from 1905 to the present, the M&P is truly one of the classic handguns of all time.

As with all Smith & Wesson revolvers, the M&P has undergone the usual design alterations such as the elimination of pinned barrels, reduction of frame screws from five to three and various grip design changes.

THE MODEL 13 357 MAGNUM

In 1974, a 357 Magnum version called the Model 13 was introduced. A few years later a stainless steel model called the Model 65 appeared. Both the 13 and 65 have heavy barrels and are virtually identical to the Models 10 and 13 except for caliber.

BARRELS LENGTHS

All of the above-mentioned models have been made in a variety of barrel lengths. While the most popular length for all models is 4 inches, other lengths for the M&P 1905 include 4, 5, 6 and 6-1/2 inches.

After 1970, stainless steel and 357 Magnum versions of the Model 10 were introduced. The latter was designated the Model 13. This Model 65 is the stainless version of the Model 13.

Even though the Model 10 has grips that fit most hand sizes, it can be improved by adding either custom stocks or a grip adapter, which fills in the annoying gap at the back of the trigger guard.

LOADING AND UNLOADING PROCEDURES

To unload a M&P, place it in the left hand, press the cylinder catch forward and push the cylinder out of the left side of the frame using the fingers of the hand holding the revolver.

With the cylinder swung open, elevate the barrel and strike the top of the ejector rod smartly with the palm of the right hand to clear the chambers of spent cases.

To load, hold the revolver in the same hand with the barrel pointing to the ground and insert fresh cartridges in the chambers. When the cylinder is loaded, push it firmly back into the frame.

SHOOTING AND HANDLING CHARACTERISTICS

The M&P is truly a handgun with few defects. It has a grip and frame size that really does fit all hand sizes. The 38 Special cartridge for which it is chambered delivers excellent accuracy that is more than adequate for self-defense purposes. In fact, I have seen a 6-inch-barreled M&P custom fitted with an adjustable target rear sight that proved to be a very fine target revolver.

Being a solid-frame swing-out revolver design, it is simple to load and unload.

It is of rugged construction, and if properly cared for and maintained, it should outlive its owner without difficulty.

Except for the very early models, the revolver has very good fixed sights that are easy to acquire when brought quickly up into the aim. Admittedly, they don't always shoot to points of aim, but I have found that most M&Ps of post-war vintage have sights well regulated for standard velocity 38 Special 158-grain ammunition.

Most M&Ps I have shot have had very good single- and double-action trigger actions. The latter is a good example of the relatively light, smooth, even pull for which Smith & Wesson is famous and is enhanced by a grip that permits proper engagement of the double-action trigger.

All of these attributes make for a revolver that is easy and pleasant to shoot. Recoil is mild, allowing for fast recovery between shots. This is especially so with the modern heavy-barrel versions, which probably have the best feel and balance thanks to the additional weight in the front.

Can the revolver stand some improvement? Even though its grip is quite suitable as is, I have found that fitting a set of well-designed custom grips will improve the revolver's overall shooting performance. As with many similar revolvers, the M&P has the annoying gap behind the trigger guard that can cause it to move in the hand during firing. When this is filled with either a grip adapter or custom grips, a firmer hold is provided, which helps considerably in improving both speed and accuracy.

COLLECTOR INTEREST

The only M&Ps that have much collector value are Victory models that are stamped on the side plate and top strap with N.Y.M.I., U.S.G.C and U.S.M.C. Except for these and the rare aluminum alloy Aircrewman, most other M&P values rarely exceed $300, so they can be shot.

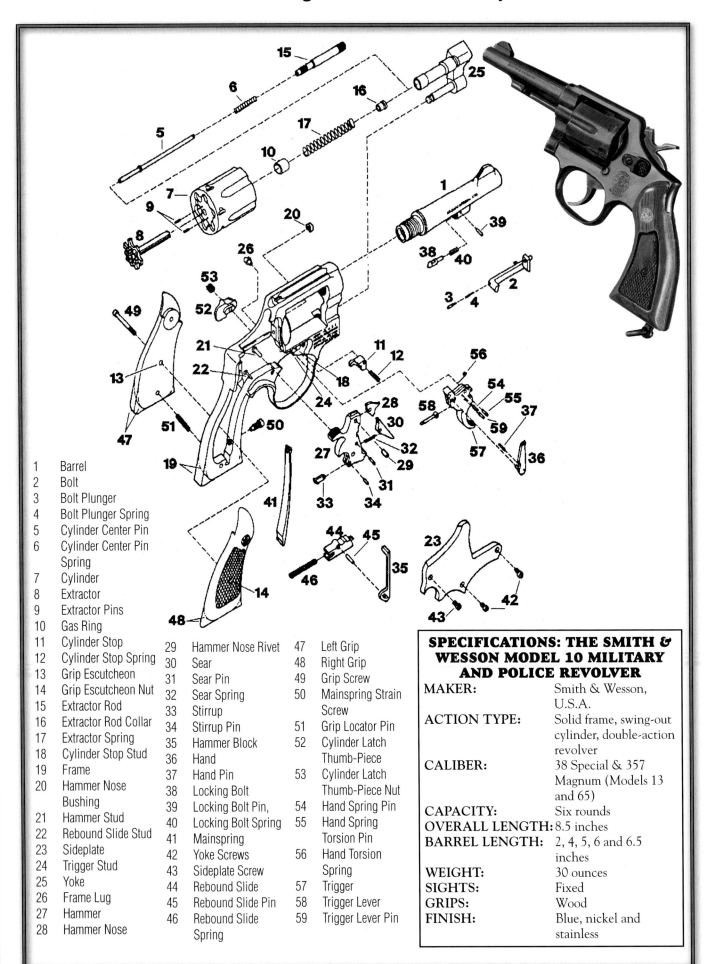

1	Barrel	29	Hammer Nose Rivet	47 Left Grip
2	Bolt	30	Sear	48 Right Grip
3	Bolt Plunger	31	Sear Pin	49 Grip Screw
4	Bolt Plunger Spring	32	Sear Spring	50 Mainspring Strain
5	Cylinder Center Pin	33	Stirrup	Screw
6	Cylinder Center Pin	34	Stirrup Pin	51 Grip Locator Pin
	Spring	35	Hammer Block	52 Cylinder Latch
7	Cylinder	36	Hand	Thumb-Piece
8	Extractor	37	Hand Pin	53 Cylinder Latch
9	Extractor Pins	38	Locking Bolt	Thumb-Piece Nut
10	Gas Ring	39	Locking Bolt Pin,	54 Hand Spring Pin
11	Cylinder Stop	40	Locking Bolt Spring	55 Hand Spring
12	Cylinder Stop Spring	41	Mainspring	Torsion Pin
13	Grip Escutcheon	42	Yoke Screws	56 Hand Torsion
14	Grip Escutcheon Nut	43	Sideplate Screw	Spring
15	Extractor Rod	44	Rebound Slide	57 Trigger
16	Extractor Rod Collar	45	Rebound Slide Pin	58 Trigger Lever
17	Extractor Spring	46	Rebound Slide	59 Trigger Lever Pin
18	Cylinder Stop Stud		Spring	
19	Frame			
20	Hammer Nose			
	Bushing			
21	Hammer Stud			
22	Rebound Slide Stud			
23	Sideplate			
24	Trigger Stud			
25	Yoke			
26	Frame Lug			
27	Hammer			
28	Hammer Nose			

SPECIFICATIONS: THE SMITH & WESSON MODEL 10 MILITARY AND POLICE REVOLVER

MAKER:	Smith & Wesson, U.S.A.
ACTION TYPE:	Solid frame, swing-out cylinder, double-action revolver
CALIBER:	38 Special & 357 Magnum (Models 13 and 65)
CAPACITY:	Six rounds
OVERALL LENGTH:	8.5 inches
BARREL LENGTH:	2, 4, 5, 6 and 6.5 inches
WEIGHT:	30 ounces
SIGHTS:	Fixed
GRIPS:	Wood
FINISH:	Blue, nickel and stainless

Ed McGivern
World Speed Record Holder

Ed McGivern and the Smith & Wesson double-action revolver, especially the 38 Military & Police Model, are forever linked because of the amazing speed records he shot with the gun.

Ed McGivern was a native of the state of Montana who, between the wars, did a considerable amount of experimentation with speed shooting with handguns. Somewhat short and stocky in stature, McGivern performed most of his feats when he was in his fifties and sixties. In fact, his experimentation was interrupted by a severe attack of arthritis.

McGivern's shooting exploits included the speed shooting of multiple rounds, shooting at long ranges out to 600 yards, shooting at single and multiple aerial targets and fast draws from the holster as well as speed shooting with frontier single-action revolvers.

Initially, he started out his speed shooting with Colt 1911 45 semi-automatic pistols, but soon switched to double-action revolvers because he found them to be better for speed work.

After honing his double-action shooting techniques through a considerable expenditure of ammunition, Ed McGivern began demonstrating his remarkable skills by performing at fairs and shows. On November 30, 1919, in Denver, Colorado, he set a world record by shooting six shots in three-fifths of a second at a distance of 15 feet, placing all six shots in a group that could be covered with the palm of a hand.

To perform this remarkable feat, the revolver he used was a Colt Officers target model 38 Special revolver. As with all of his records, the shooting was performed in the presence of witnesses and the time recorded by a specially made timing mechanism attached to the revolver. McGivern repeated this record several times with the same revolver.

Although McGivern used a Colt for this record, he seems to have preferred the Smith & Wesson Military & Police for most of his subsequent feats. Using such a revolver, he shot five shots in two-fifths of a second on September 13, 1932. He repeated this feat several times with the same M&P revolver.

It is worth pointing out the Ed McGivern did all of his shooting using the then traditional one-handed shooting stance. None of the modern two-handed shooting techniques for him! In addition, an examination of the revolvers he used to set his records indicates that all were pretty much standard in respect to their triggers. It seems he never resorted to having the double-action pulls lightened. About the only modifications his revolvers had were better sights.

In addition to his speed work, McGivern found time to help law enforcement in honing their revolver skills. A full account of his shooting efforts can be found in his book *Fast and Fancy Revolver Shooting*, which is long out of print although reprinted editions do appear from time to time.

THE COLT DETECTIVE SPECIAL REVOLVER

The First "Snubby" 2-inch Barrel Revolver

Colt's Detective Special revolver's claim to fame is that it is the first of the short 2-inch "bellygun" 38 revolvers. The name "bellygun" originates from an early misguided belief that the only way to hit an opponent with a very short-barreled handgun was to stick the gun against his abdomen and fire. The fact is these little revolvers are surprisingly accurate, although they can be difficult to control.

HISTORY AND DEVELOPMENT

The first Detective Special was introduced in 1926 and was really nothing more than a Police Positive Special with a 2-inch long barrel. The Police Positive Special revolver had evolved from the New Police revolver of 1896. These were small swing-out-cylinder revolvers developed in 1895 and chambered for the 32 New Police cartridge. Serial number 1 was presented to Theodore Roosevelt, who was then head of the New York Police Department.

In 1905, the revolver had Colt's positive safety lock installed. This is a sliding steel bar between the hammer and the frame that prevents the firing pin from reaching the cartridge primer if the revolver is accidentally dropped or struck a heavy blow. It is connected to the trigger by means of small levers. Properly cycling the trigger pulls the bar away from the hammer. The new revolver's name was then changed to the Police Positive.

In 1907, the Police Positive was followed by the Police Positive Special. The latter revolver was really just a Police Positive chambered for the 38 Special and the 32-20. Its cylinder was lengthened by a quarter inch to accept the longer cases of these cartridges. After the Police Positive was taken out of production, the Police Positive Special was also chambered for 38 S&W, 32 S&W, 32 S&W Long and the 32 Colt New Police.

Barrel lengths were 4, 5 and 6 inches until 1926 when the first 2-inch model was introduced. Initially, the name remained the same and the new revolver retained the square-shaped butt of the Police Positive Special. In 1934, however, the bottom edges of the grip were given a round profile. Not long after its introduction, the name was changed to "Detective Special."

DESIGN CHARACTERISTICS AND FEATURES

The Detective Special was a solid-frame, swing-out, double-action revolver. It was built on a small-size frame that Colt designated as their D-frame series. It had a six-shot cylinder that was chambered for the 38 Special cartridge.

The revolver had the internal positive safety lock and the usual Colt double-action lockwork of the period. The latter employed a "V"-type leaf spring that operated both the hammer and the rebound lever. The latter reset the trigger and controlled the cylinder stop.

This cylinder capacity was a feature that Colt always emphasized because the capacity of many competitors' revolvers

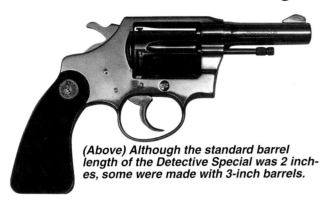

(Above) Although the standard barrel length of the Detective Special was 2 inches, some were made with 3-inch barrels.

(Right) The first revolvers had "Police Positive Special" roll-stamped on the 2-inch barrels. Not long afterwards, this was changed to " Detective Special." Photo courtesy of Glen Barnes.

the barrel. This provided a more positive ejection of spent cases.

Most subsequent changes were also frame related. The first was a shortening of the grip frame to match that of the very similar Agent model. This was obviously done to simplify the manufacture of both revolvers. By making wood grips that have filler at the bottom, the actual size and profile of the Detective Special remained unchanged.

The most radical change occurred in 1972 when the revolver was given a new streamlined appearance. This involved a new barrel with an under lug that incorporated a protective shroud to protect the ejector rod. The barrel also had a small rib that incorporated a ramped front sight blade. The revolver was also given new wood combat-style grips that filled the gap behind the trigger.

In 1986, Colt announced they were ceasing production of the Detective Special and all D-frame guns. The reason appeared to be they were too expensive to manufacture. Just prior to this, the revolver appeared with rubber combat grips.

of a similar size is one round less. The Detective Special's usual barrel length was 2 inches.

The revolver's grip was a generous size that permitted a full hold, a useful feature in controlling recoil and the long heavy double-action trigger pull. The sights were fixed with the front post having a round profile on the first models and the rear sight having a large wide notch machined into the topstrap.

DESIGN CHANGES AND MODIFICATIONS

The Detective Special has had relatively few major changes during its long lifetime. As previously mentioned, early changes were to the name and grips. After World War II, the frames of both the Police Positive and the Detective Special underwent some slight changes.

After the war, an accessory called the "Hammer Shroud" was offered for Detective Specials and Colt's other 2-inch revolvers. This was an attachment that covered the hammer spur to prevent snagging in clothing. It still, however, permitted the hammer to be cocked for single-action shooting.

The original frame design had a narrow gap behind the trigger guard. To improve one's hold of the revolver, this gap was widened slightly in post-war models. In addition, the ejector rod was lengthened so that it was almost in line with the front of

Prior to 1972, the notable features of the Detective Special were its 2-inch barrel with exposed ejector rod and its rounded grip frame. Photo courtesy of Glen Barnes.

THE DETECTIVE SPECIAL AND SUBSEQUENT MODELS

Two years after ceasing production, Colt brought the Detective Special back in the same form it had been when production stopped. It retained the same lockwork, shrouded barrel, rubber grips and bright blue finish.

In 1995, the name was changed to "Colt 38 SF-VI." While the new revolver looked the same externally, internally it had a new mechanism that incorporated the transfer bar system of the King Cobra and Anaconda.

In 1996, a 38 SF-VI Special Lady model was introduced with bright finish and a bobbed hammer. This was followed a year later by a stainless version. With this was a return to the original name with the revolver being called the Detective Special II.

RELATED SHORT-BARREL REVOLVERS

Colt has made a number of other 2-inch-barrel revolvers, some of which are derived from the Detective Special and use the same D-frame. The "Banker's Special" was a 2-inch six-shot revolver chambered for 38 S&W and New Police as well as 22LR cartridges.

The post-war Detective Special underwent another change when the grip frame was shortened to conform to that of the Agent.

The first Detective Specials had a square butt grip. Not long afterwards, this was changed to a round butt configuration.

The ultimate version of the Detective Special was the 357 Magnum Carry introduced in 1999. Only in production for a brief time, it was strengthened for the 357 Magnum cartridge. This one of the author's has had the original rubber grips replaced with a set of custom Hogue stocks.

While similar to the Detective Special, it used the Police Positive frame, which gave it a shorter cylinder. It remained in production until 1943.

In 1950, Colt came out with a lightweight version of the Detective Special with an aluminum alloy frame called the "Cobra". Five years later, the "Agent" appeared, which is the same revolver but with a shorter grip frame. Both these revolvers underwent basically the same changes as the Detective Special. When production ceased in the mid-1980s, both had shrouded ejector rods and wrap-around wood grips.

The Magnum Carry is the last of the D-frame shorties and is simply a Detective Special II strengthened to handle the 357 Magnum cartridge. The revolver was introduced in 1999 and remained in production until the following year when Colt reduced the handgun line for economic reasons.

CALIBERS, BARREL LENGTHS, GRIPS AND FINISHES

When first introduced, the Detective Special was chambered for the 38 Special cartridge. In later years, it was offered in calibers that included 38 New Police, 38 S&W as well as 32 Colt and 32 S&W. By 1973, the Detective Special and all the other models were chambered only for the 38 Special cartridge. As mentioned earlier, 357 Magnum models became available in 1999.

While 2 inches has always been the Detective Special's standard barrel length, a few 3-inch revolvers have been made throughout its production. In addition, a 4-inch-barreled Cobra was offered with a square butt.

For a time, Colt fitted simulated wood grips made of a synthetic plastic material called Coltwood to all of the short-barrel models. In addition to the combat rubber grips, the Magnum Carry had a one-piece rubber design made by Hogue.

For most of its life, the Detective Special has been offered with an all blue or a plated nickel finish. In an attempt to reduce manufacturing cost, the "Commando Special" was introduced in 1984 with matte unfinished exterior metal surfaces and a matte parkerized finish.

After 1972, the Detective Special was completely revamped with a new barrel that had the ejector rod protected by a shroud and a small rib. New larger wood grips were also provided to encase the front strap. Late models were fitted with similar grips made of rubber.

UNCERTAIN FUTURE

It seems odd that what was once Colt's best-selling revolver has now been dropped from the line. In spite of its popularity, the Detective Special has become a victim of the company's financial problems. It seems Magnum Carry sales did not provide enough of a profit margin over its manufacturing costs. Nevertheless, there is a remote chance that the Magnum Carry may appear again if Colt's financial problems are resolved.

UNLOADING AND LOADING PROCEDURES

The Detective Special is unloaded and loaded in exactly the same manner as all swing-out cylinder revolvers. The revolver is held in the left hand and the cylinder swung open. The only thing to remember with a Colt is that the cylinder latch is pulled back, not pushed forward, to release the cylinder.

SHOOTING AND HANDLING THE DETECTIVE SPECIAL

The Detective Special was labeled a "bellygun" because of its short barrel. This is a complete misconception, however, because the Detective Special is capable of surprisingly good accuracy at respectable distances. This is also true of other makes of snubby revolvers.

The first Detective Special I shot delivered tight five-shot groups at 20 yards that matched what my 6-inch target revolver could shoot. Having said that, I am the first to admit that small 2-inch revolvers are not the easiest to shoot well. Most short-barrel revolvers have a lot of recoil as well as muzzle blast, and their small grips make them difficult to hold and shoot quickly without discomfort.

Partly because of its larger grips, the Detective Special is one of the biggest of the small revolvers, which does compromise its ability to be concealed.

I contend the larger grips are its biggest strength, however, because they help in making the revolver more controllable. The grips fit my hand very well and make the revolver quite pleasant to shoot even with the higher velocity +P ammunition. This is especially so with the combat wood and rubber grips fitted to late vintage revolvers. The rubber grips are especially good for shooting high-velocity ammunition.

The revolver's fixed sights provide a good sight picture, but like all short-barreled revolvers, they are not always perfectly regulated. This may require some off aim to hit a desired target at longer distances.

Detective Specials have good single-action trigger pulls. The double action is typical Colt with the hitch or stacking near the end of the stroke. Some complain this adversely affects fast double-action shooting.

Although not as smooth as the Smith & Wesson, I find this is offset by the better grips, and I have no problem in shooting my Detective Specials. It may not be the most concealable of the snubbies, but for me it is the most comfortable to shoot.

COLLECTOR INTEREST

On the question of collector value, Colt handguns no longer in production tend to command higher resale prices. With this revolver, the first-issue models made before World War II are currently listed at around $900. Later models are priced at around $300 - $400. Post-World War II Detective Specials can generally be considered shooters provided they are in sound mechanical condition.

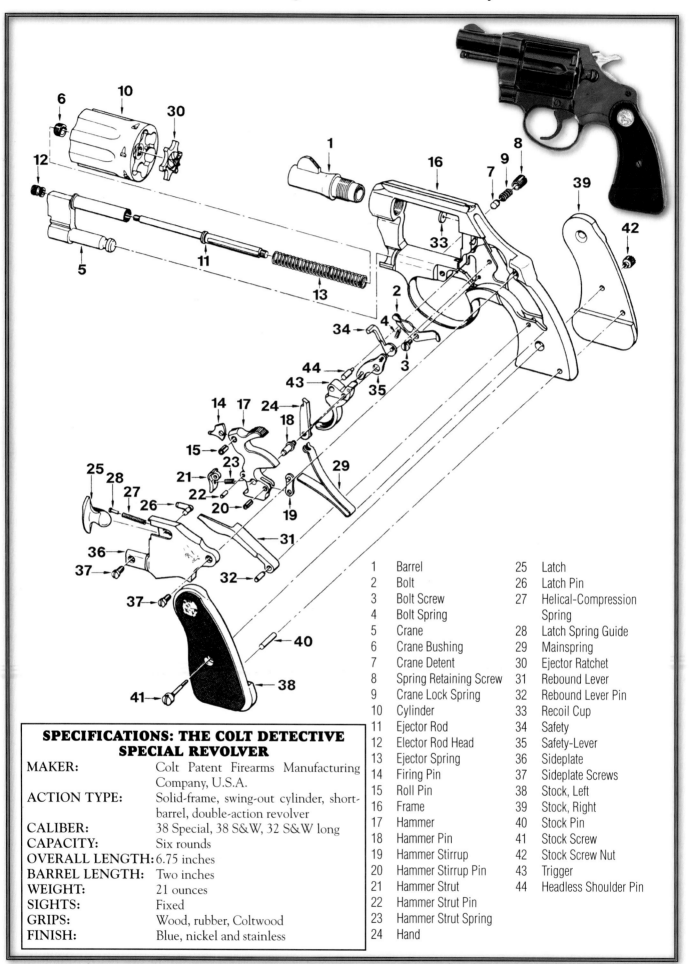

#		#	
1	Barrel	25	Latch
2	Bolt	26	Latch Pin
3	Bolt Screw	27	Helical-Compression
4	Bolt Spring		Spring
5	Crane	28	Latch Spring Guide
6	Crane Bushing	29	Mainspring
7	Crane Detent	30	Ejector Ratchet
8	Spring Retaining Screw	31	Rebound Lever
9	Crane Lock Spring	32	Rebound Lever Pin
10	Cylinder	33	Recoil Cup
11	Ejector Rod	34	Safety
12	Elector Rod Head	35	Safety-Lever
13	Ejector Spring	36	Sideplate
14	Firing Pin	37	Sideplate Screws
15	Roll Pin	38	Stock, Left
16	Frame	39	Stock, Right
17	Hammer	40	Stock Pin
18	Hammer Pin	41	Stock Screw
19	Hammer Stirrup	42	Stock Screw Nut
20	Hammer Stirrup Pin	43	Trigger
21	Hammer Strut	44	Headless Shoulder Pin
22	Hammer Strut Pin		
23	Hammer Strut Spring		
24	Hand		

SPECIFICATIONS: THE COLT DETECTIVE SPECIAL REVOLVER

MAKER:	Colt Patent Firearms Manufacturing Company, U.S.A.
ACTION TYPE:	Solid-frame, swing-out cylinder, short-barrel, double-action revolver
CALIBER:	38 Special, 38 S&W, 32 S&W long
CAPACITY:	Six rounds
OVERALL LENGTH:	6.75 inches
BARREL LENGTH:	Two inches
WEIGHT:	21 ounces
SIGHTS:	Fixed
GRIPS:	Wood, rubber, Coltwood
FINISH:	Blue, nickel and stainless

The Development of Modern Solid-Frame Double-Action Revolvers

The Detective Special was a small revolver based on the design of the Colt 38 double-action revolver of 1889. This was the first American-made revolver to use a solid-frame, swing-out-cylinder reloading system. As originally conceived, it was intended that spent cases would be automatically ejected on opening the cylinder from the frame. This was abandoned in the final design because of concerns that its complexity might compromise reliability. The Model 1889 was the work of William Mason and used improvements developed by Horace Lord, another Colt employee. While the 1889 is the first American revolver to use a swing-out cylinder, it was not the first to use the concept.

The first swing-out-cylinder solid-frame revolver actually appeared in Europe some 20 years earlier. In 1869 a British patent was granted to a Captain A. Albini for a solid-frame side-opening revolver. An examination of reproductions of the drawings that accompanied the patent applications reveals a number of similarities. Albini's shows a typical English revolver of the period with a cylinder that opens out to the right on a crane.

The Colt drawing shows a modified Double Action Frontier revolver with a left-opening cylinder that uses a similar crane device. Albini's design also has an ejector rod positioned in the crane to remove spent cases. The Colt design has a similar system. I am not aware if the Colt designers were influenced by Albini's system or if they came up with the idea on their own. It would not be the first time that similar ideas were developed independently of each other.

While Smith & Wesson replaced their break-top revolvers with a similar swing-out-cylinder design, they improved on it by providing a locking system in the front of the ejector rod. This made for a far stronger locking system.

Colt retained their original crane system using it on all of their subsequent double-action revolvers. The rear-locking latch has been retained up to the present time. This leaves the ejector rod exposed and unprotected, which some critics claim to be a weakness because it can be damaged or bent through rough usage.

Beginning with the Python, Colt did provide some protection by providing a protective shroud incorporated as part of the barrel under lug. Later, Detective Specials models were fitted with barrels that had a similar protective shroud.

Virtually all modern double-action revolvers use some form of Colt's or Smith & Wesson's swing-out-cylinder system. The fact that it continues to be used after 100 years is evidence of the soundness of the original design.

THE WALTHER PP, PPK AND PPK/S DOUBLE-ACTION AUTO POCKET PISTOLS

The First Commercially Successful Double-Action Self-Loading Pistols

When the words "double-action (DA) auto pistol" are mentioned, the name Walther immediately comes to mind, even though the company cannot really lay claim to the invention of a trigger-cocking semi-automatic pistol.

Walther did, however, develop the world's first pistol with a trigger-cocking and single-action system. The PPK, a small blowback-operated vest-pocket-size 6.35mm, was introduced in 1929 and was the first commercially successful double-action pistol. A number of similar models in this caliber and 7.65mm were made in the years that followed. During World War I, a number of Walther Model 4 pistols were used by police and military officers. The company's first full-caliber handgun was the Model 6, virtually an enlarged Model 4 chambered for the 9mm parabellum cartridge. It used a straight blowback design rather than employing a breech-locking system and was never made available for commercial sales, as there were concerns that it was stressed to the limits of safe operation with the more powerful cartridge.

DESIGN CHARACTERISTIC AND FEATURES OF THE MODEL

Although the concept of a semi-automatic pistol employing a trigger-cocking firing system had appeared in several earlier pistols before 1900, Walther was among the first to produce a practical, commercially successful design in the form of the Model PP, which was introduced in 1928. The PP was an immediate success and was adopted by a number of German and European police forces.

The pistol employs a blowback action that permits the barrel to be fixed to the frame. The barrel, which is contained within the recoil spring, acts as the spring's guide. The pistol has a firing pin that is activated by an exposed hammer. The pivoting trigger cocks the hammer for the first shot. All subsequent shots are fired single action with the hammer being cocked automatically by the rearward movement of the slide.

The controls include a button-style magazine catch position on the left side of the frame behind the trigger. There is a slide-mounted safety catch on the same side.

When the safety is depressed, it disengages the trigger and safely lowers the hammer. When pushed up, it puts the pistol in the double-action firing mode. The exposed hammer has a round, serrated spur that permits manual cocking for single-action firing.

The pistol has a loaded-chamber indicator consisting of a rod that protrudes out of the rear of the slide when there is a cartridge or case in the chamber.

DESIGN CHARACTERISTICS AND FEATURES OF THE MODEL PPK

The popularity of the Model PP prompted Walther to develop a smaller, more compact version. Known as the PPK (Police Pistole Kriminal), the pistol proved to be equally as popular, especially with plain-clothes personnel, detectives and civilians.

The PPK had the same firing mechanism and action as the PP. It differed in that it had a smaller, more compact frame with a shortened grip. The bottom of the grip frame is rounded while the magazine floor plate incorporates an extension to accommodate the little finger of one's hand. Its plastic grips also incorporate the pistol's backstrap.

MILITARY AND FOREIGN SERVICE

As already mentioned, both the PP and PPK were an immediate hit with law enforcement and were adopted by a number of European police agencies. During World War II, the pistols were pressed into military service (mainly by the Luftwaffe) as Germany became increasingly short of handguns.

A number were carried by high-ranking Nazi officials, including Adolph Hitler, who used one to end his life in the Berlin Bunker in 1945. As for civilian sales, the pistols were popular in countries outside of Germany, including the United States.

After the war, the PPK acquired somewhat of a cult following when author Ian Fleming armed his fictional agent, 007 James Bond, with a PPK. Actually, for a time, British Metropolitan Special Branch Officers assigned to the personal protection of the Royal Family and other dignitaries were issued PPKs. South African Police detectives were issued post-war PPK models.

Turkey made a copy of the Model PP called the "Krikkale" in 7.62mm. Hungary made a similar pistol based on the PP in 380 called the "Model 48 Walam."

POST-WAR PRODUCTION

After World War II ended, production of Walther firearms ceased because the factory was in the Russian occupied zone of Germany. As the company's patents were still valid, Walther licensed the manufacture of the Models PP and PPK to Manurhin of France.

This arrangement enabled Walther to recover financially and to resume production of most of its pistols including the PP and PPK in the mid-1960s.

THE MODEL PPK/S

In the United States, the PPK was popular with plain-clothes and undercover police officers because of its compact size and good handling qualities. For the same reason it was also popular with civilian shooters.

The passing of the Gun Control Act of 1968 prohibited the importation of the PPK because it failed to meet the size requirements of this law. After a 2-year hiatus, the pistol returned to American shooters in the form of the Model PPK/S.

By marrying a PPK slide to a re-configured PP frame, Walther was able to meet the requirements of the new legislation. The new pistol, now designated as the PPK/S ("S" for special), was made under license in the United States by Interarms of Virginia. Later, Interarms also made the PPK. Blue and stainless steel versions of both pistols were made.

RELATED MODELS

The PP series was the basis for two other similar pistols—the TPH and the Model PP Super. The former was chambered for the 22 LR cartridge, while the latter fired a longer case version of the 380.

CALIBERS AND FINISHES

The first PP and PPK pistols were chambered for the 7.65mm cartridge. In the years that followed, this was expanded to include 22 LR, 6.35mm and 9mm Short. Post-war chambering of both pistols was restricted to 7.65mm, 22LR and 9mm Short.

Both the PP and PPK are renown for the high quality of their fit and finish. A highly polished blue finish was applied to all the exterior metal surfaces, while the grip panels were a checkered black or brown plastic material. Pistols made during the war dispensed with the high polishing of the metal surfaces, and a matte blue with evidence of machine marks is common.

Post-war production guns have the highly polished blue finish. The stainless steel PPK/S models have a matte brushed finish. The factory did make a limited number of profusely engraved presentation models that were usually given to dignitaries.

THE SMITH & WESSON CONNECTION

Right at the end of the 20th century, Walther and this famous American company entered into an agreement whereby the latter would produce a version of the newly introduced P99

Both the PP and PPK and the subsequent models all employed blow-back actions. Their barrels were fixed and the recoil spring was mounted around the barrel. To comply with requirements of the U.S. Gun Control Act of 1968, Walther developed the PPK/S that used the frame of the Model PP and the shortened slide of the PPK. Photo courtesy of Garry James.

service pistol. Smith & Wesson also agreed to market Walther products (except for the company's target pistols) in the United States.

Prior to this, Walther's U.S. distributor had been Interarms of Virginia, which had also been responsible for the manufacture of the PPK/S. With Interarms out of the picture, Smith & Wesson stepped in, not only as Walther's U.S. distributor, but also as the new manufacturer of the PPK/S. This new pistol is significant in that in addition to the Walther trade name being roll-stamped on the slide, it also carries the name of Smith & Wesson.

Apart from this distinction, the PPK has been used as the basis for a number of similar pocket pistol designs, proving that imitation is the greatest form of flattery.

FIELD STRIPPING PROCEDURE

As with all small semi-automatic pistols, take care to keep the muzzle pointing in a safe direction and ensure your fingers are kept clear of the trigger. Then remove the magazine and check that the chamber is empty. Pull the front of the guard out of the frame and push it to the side so that it rests against the frame and remains out.

Pull the slide back as far as it will go and lift it up to release it from the frame rails. This permits the barrel and slide to be eased off the frame. Remove the recoil spring off the barrel to complete the procedure. The pistol is assembled in reverse order.

SHOOTING AND HANDLING THE PPK/S

The PP, PPK and PPK/S are all well designed pistols with a number of features that have stood the test of time and have been copied by a number of imitations. All three are compact and easy to conceal.

In spite of their small size, they are easy to handle and shoot. The controls are well positioned for operation by the thumb of the shooting hand. The grip provides a good firm hold and permits proper engagement of the double-action trigger. Even the shorter grip of the PPK is not adversely affected, thanks to the finger rest that is incorporated into the magazine floor plate.

The grips also contribute to the pistol's remarkably mild recoil. The sights are surprisingly good for such a small pistol and provide a nice clear sight picture that is easy to acquire when the pistol is brought quickly into the aim.

All three pistols are capable of very good accuracy for their size, which is why the PP was used as a service pistol by

During World War II, many PPs and PPKs were pressed into service with the German military forces. Photo courtesy of Garry James.

a number of European police forces. Even the pistol's minor detractions can actually be considered strengths.

On the debit side, the pistol's safety is rather stiff to manipulate. It also has to be pushed up to be disengaged, which is contrary to what American shooters prefer. Both the single- and double-action trigger pulls are on the heavy side.

A safety that is easy to engage or disengage and a light, double-action trigger are likely to severely compromise safety. This is especially so in the case of small pistols intended for easy concealment or pocket carry. The last thing one wants is a safety that can be disengaged by the pistol jostling around in one's pocket. In the same way, trying to draw the pistol in a hurry could cause the trigger to be inadvertently engaged and a light pull could have tragic consequences. Therefore, the stiff safety and heavy trigger on this pistol are actually positive attributes.

COLLECTOR INTEREST

PPs and PPKs with German military markings are quite collectable although catalog prices don't usually exceed $1000. Finely engraved pistols are worth a lot more. Both pistols, in sound mechanical condition, are suitable for personal defense.

(Left) The PP series all have the same controls of a magazine catch and thumb safety. When the latter is in the horizontal position, the pistols are in the firing mode.

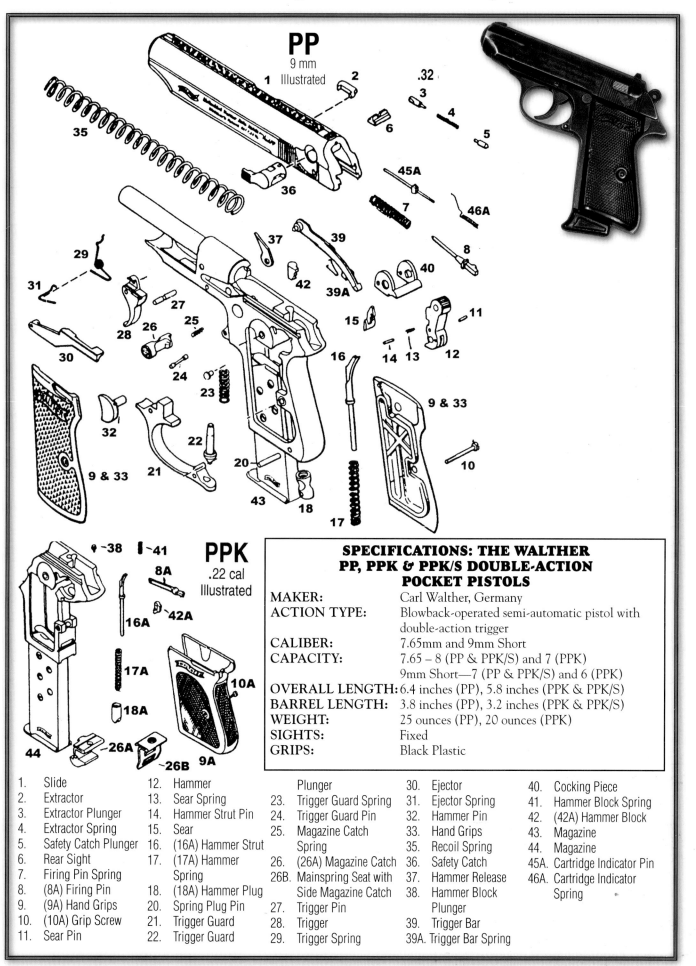

PP
9 mm
Illustrated

.32

PPK
.22 cal
Illustrated

SPECIFICATIONS: THE WALTHER PP, PPK & PPK/S DOUBLE-ACTION POCKET PISTOLS

MAKER:	Carl Walther, Germany
ACTION TYPE:	Blowback-operated semi-automatic pistol with double-action trigger
CALIBER:	7.65mm and 9mm Short
CAPACITY:	7.65 – 8 (PP & PPK/S) and 7 (PPK) 9mm Short—7 (PP & PPK/S) and 6 (PPK)
OVERALL LENGTH:	6.4 inches (PP), 5.8 inches (PPK & PPK/S)
BARREL LENGTH:	3.8 inches (PP), 3.2 inches (PPK & PPK/S)
WEIGHT:	25 ounces (PP), 20 ounces (PPK)
SIGHTS:	Fixed
GRIPS:	Black Plastic

1. Slide
2. Extractor
3. Extractor Plunger
4. Extractor Spring
5. Safety Catch Plunger
6. Rear Sight
7. Firing Pin Spring
8. (8A) Firing Pin
9. (9A) Hand Grips
10. (10A) Grip Screw
11. Sear Pin
12. Hammer
13. Sear Spring
14. Hammer Strut Pin
15. Sear
16. (16A) Hammer Strut
17. (17A) Hammer Spring
18. (18A) Hammer Plug
20. Spring Plug Pin
21. Trigger Guard
22. Trigger Guard
    Plunger
23. Trigger Guard Spring
24. Trigger Guard Pin
25. Magazine Catch Spring
26. (26A) Magazine Catch
26B. Mainspring Seat with Side Magazine Catch
27. Trigger Pin
28. Trigger
29. Trigger Spring
30. Ejector
31. Ejector Spring
32. Hammer Pin
33. Hand Grips
35. Recoil Spring
36. Safety Catch
37. Hammer Release
38. Hammer Block Plunger
39. Trigger Bar
39A. Trigger Bar Spring
40. Cocking Piece
41. Hammer Block Spring
42. (42A) Hammer Block
43. Magazine
44. Magazine
45A. Cartridge Indicator Pin
46A. Cartridge Indicator Spring

The Carl Walther Company

This company was founded by Carl Walther in 1886 and by the turn of the century had established itself as a manufacturer of sporting firearms. The company's first handgun was introduced in 1908.

Until the introduction of Models PP and PPK, the company's pistol line consisted of a number of small pocketsize auto loaders. With the introduction of these two pistols and the celebrated P38, the company was fully committed to wartime production throughout World War II.

The company survived the war and in 1928 introduced its first double-action design. Called the Model PP (for Polizei Pistol), it was an immediate success and was the platform for other successful models like the PPK and P38.

Walther survived World War II, but because its factory in Zela Mehlis was taken by the Soviets as war reparations, the company had to license the manufacture of many of its pistols to Manhurin in France. Walther was re-established in the early 1960s in West Germany and resumed manufacturing most of its pistol line, including the P38.

Today, Walther is still in business producing fine target and sporting pistols as well as a line of service models that have been developed from the P38. Walther's latest pistol, the P99, is a brand new design that incorporates the latest in new materials such as polymer.

Today, Walther and Smith & Wesson have joined forces. The latter company is marketing the P99 in America as the S&W 99. The pistol is in effect a slightly modified P99 with the frame being made in Germany by Walther and the slide, barrel and upper assembly made by Smith & Wesson.

As previously mentioned, Smith & Wesson is also currently making the PPK/S in a new company-owned facility.

THE WALTHER P38 DOUBLE-ACTION AUTO PISTOL

The First Military Double-Action Auto Pistol

The P38's main claim to fame is that it established the concept of a trigger-cocking auto pistol as a viable handgun mechanism for a service pistol.

Although the concept of a semi-automatic pistol employing a trigger-cocking firing system had appeared in several earlier pistols before 1900, Walther was among the first to produce a practical, commercially successful design in the form of the Model PP. The pistol employed a blowback action linked to a trigger-cocking hammer for the first shot. All subsequent shots were fired single action with the hammer being cocked automatically by the rearward movement of the slide. Other novel features included a hammer-lowering safety and a loaded-chamber indicator. The PP was an immediate success and was adopted by a number of German and European police forces.

Not long afterward, a smaller, more compact version known as the PPK (Police Pistole Kriminal) was introduced. It proved to be equally as popular, especially with plain-clothes personnel, detectives and civilians. These pistols are described in detail in a previous chapter.

DEVELOPMENT OF THE P38

Not long after Adolph Hitler become Chancellor of Germany, the German military began looking for a replacement for the P08 Luger. While the Luger had served Germany well, it was a complex design that was expensive to make.

Walther was among a number of arms companies that included Mauser and Sauer & Sohn to submit a pistol design for the new German military sidearm. Walther's first submission was the "Militarisches Pistole" (MP). This was followed by an improved design known as the "Armee Pistole"(AP). This version was similar to the final P38 in both appearance and design. A major difference was that its hammer was contained within the slide. The AP also had a double-action trigger system similar to that of the smaller PP and PPK models.

The new pistol had a number of unique design features for which Walther was awarded patents including the breechblock, extractor, firing pin, loaded-chamber indicator and breech-locking system.

While the Armee was judged to be the best of the pistols submitted for testing, the military wanted an exposed hammer. Walther responded with several additional prototypes with the required changes, calling these the "Heeres Pistole," which translates to "Army Pistol." This satisfied military personnel who adopted the pistol in 1938, giving it the official designation of P38.

Anticipating a good civilian market, the pistol was offered commercially, but sales were not as good as expected. In any event, with the coming of World War II, Walther was hard pressed to meet the demands of the military.

DESIGN CHACTERISTICS AND FEATURES

The P38 is a locked-breech semi-automatic pistol with a trigger action that cocks and drops the hammer for the first shot. Thereafter, the hammer is cocked by the cycling of the slide. The breech-locking system is commonly referred to as the "propped-up block" type, which employed a pivoting locking block underneath the barrel. It unlocked the barrel and slide without the former having to tilt or rotate. The top of the slide was open, providing for more positive ejection of spent cases.

The pistol's controls were all on the left side and consisted of a take-down latch, slide stop and safety catch.

The double-action trigger was similar to that on the Models

PP and PPK, as was the safety. The safety lever was positioned on the left and rear of the slide. When the lever was depressed, it locked the firing pin and safely lowered the hammer. This differed from the AP, where the firing pin was retracted into the slide. While a very safe system, it was expensive to manufacture, which is why it was changed. In addition, the first APs had a rectangular-shaped firing pin, instead of the rounded type of the P38.

The barrel was secured to the frame by a disassembly catch positioned at the front and left side of the frame. Rotating this down released the barrel and slide, enabling both to be removed from the front of the frame.

The magazine catch is of the heel-clip type and is positioned at the bottom rear of the grip.

The P38 replaced the P08 Luger as Germany's military service pistol in 1938. It was chambered for the same 9mm cartridge, had a locked breech and a double-action trigger. Photo courtesy of Garry James.

P38 USERS AND MANUFACTURERS

German military forces were the main users of the P38, but Sweden apparently purchased a large quantity of HP models. These are very rare and can be identified by the letter "H" that appears before the serial number. The pistol will also have the Crown N proof mark. Switzerland also showed an interest in the pistol and managed to acquire a number for its armed forces.

While Walther produced the greatest number of P38s during the war, output fell short of what the military required, especially as World War II intensified. In an attempt to meet the demand, the factories of Mauser and Spreewerke were pressed into service. As Germany's control of Europe expanded during the early years of the war, a number of foreign arms companies became involved in P38 production. Usually this was confined to the manufacture of components like frames and barrels. Companies involved included CZ in Prague and FN in Belgium.

P38s manufactured by Walther, Mauser and Spreewerke have the left side of the slide stamped with the factory codes of "ac", "byf" and "cyq" respectively. Late in the war, the Mauser code was changed to "SVA."

As mentioned in the previous chapter, the Walther factory fell into Soviet hands at the war's end and all production ceased. The French army did, however, continue production of the P38 at the Mauser factory, which was in their zone of occupation. The pistols were issued to the French occupation forces.

POST-WAR P38s

Walther handgun production ceased after the war when their factory fell into Soviet hands. Walther was allowed to make handguns again after the German Federal Republic was constituted in the 1950s and production of the P38 resumed. The new model, known as the P1, differed from the originals only in that the steel frame has been replaced with one made of a lightweight metal alloy.

P1s were issued to the German military and some police departments. After several years use, the P1s were found to be susceptible to cracked slides due to locking-block wear to the alloy frame. This was corrected by first strengthening the steel slide with thicker sides. Later, a steel block was inserted into the alloy frame where it engaged the locking block.

One of the final versions of the P38 line is the P4, which has all these improvements in addition to a slightly shorter barrel and a decocking lever in place of the safety. It was used by a number of German police departments.

In addition to its use by the German military and police, P38s were used by the police and military of other nations. Pistols were also made for civilian sales and a number were imported into this country up until around 1983.

CALIBERS, BARRELS, GRIPS AND FINISHES

While the main caliber of the P38 is the 9mm Parabellum, early Walther catalogs mention it would be made in other calibers such as 45 ACP, 38 Super and 30 Luger. There are,

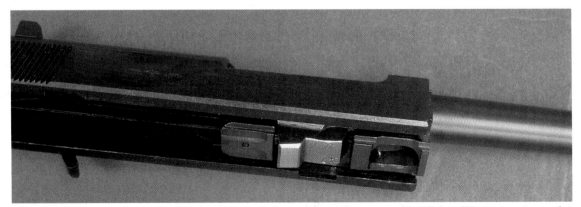

The pistol uses a unique pivoting block to lock the action at the moment of firing. Photo courtesy of Garry James.

One of the P38's notable features was the open top slide that exposed most of the barrel. Photo courtesy of Garry James.

supposedly, a few 45 ACP and 38 Super pistols in circulation. These are such rarities that they command very high prices from collectors. Post-war P38s and P1s were made in calibers of 9mm Luger, 7.65mm Luger and 22 LR.

The standard barrel length of the military P38s is 5 inches. Before the war, there were a few long barrel (up to 8 inches) versions made. Some of these had a detachable shoulder stock that was also a holster/carrying case. Of the post-war models,

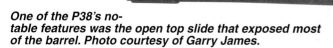

there was a short barrel (2.8 inches) version made called the P38 K.

The early P38 models exhibited a very high quality of fit and finish with highly polished slides and checkered wood grips. Wartime P38 finishes deteriorated as the demand for more pistols increased. The highly polished blue finish was soon replaced with a black or gray matte finish. In addition, the grips were soon replaced with one made of black or red/brown synthetic Bakelite material.

While the quality of the internal mechanism was the last to deteriorate, a number of pistols were apparently deliberately sabotaged by slave labor used in some of the factories. Inmates from the infamous Buchenwald death camp were known to have worked in the Walther factory. Defective guns can fire when the safety is applied. A competent gunsmith should, therefore, check late-war Model P38s before they are fired.

Fit and finish improved with the post-war P38s, especially after Walther resumed complete control of production. The only glitch was the slide cracking caused by wear to the alloy frame. As already mentioned, this was corrected in the final models by beefing up the slide in the critical areas and the use of a steel insert in the frame.

INFLUENCE ON OTHER PISTOL DESIGNS

Although no longer in production, the P38 was used as a design platform for subsequent Walther service pistols like the P5 series. Many of the P38's design features are used in many other double-action auto pistols like the S&W Models 39 and 59 series as well as the Beretta Model 92.

In many ways, the P38 was instrumental in introducing some of the most significant advances in semi-automatic pistol development of the 20th century.

FIELD STRIPPING PROCEDURE

First place the safety catch on the safe position and remove the magazine. Then pull back the slide and lock it open by pushing up on the side stop. After making sure the chamber is empty, push the barrel catch down and forward to release the barrel. The slide and barrel can now be pulled off the front of the frame.

To complete the field strip, push in the plunger at the back of the locking block and push it up so that the barrel can be removed from the frame. The pistol is assembled in reverse order. Depending upon the model, some levers at the rear of the frame may pop up. To get the slide back on the frame, these may need to be pushed back in again.

The pistol's plastic grip panels encase the back of the grip frame. Photo courtesy of Garry James.

The magazine catch is of the heel clip type and is located at the bottom rear of the grip. Photo courtesy of Garry James.

SHOOTING AND HANDLING THE P38

I carried a P38 for many years as a police officer in the British South Africa Police, the national police force of the former British colony of Rhodesia. As a result, I am quite familiar with the pistol's strengths and weaknesses.

On the credit side, the P38 has an excellent grip and good fixed sights. The controls are easy to access and manipulate. Being a double action for the first shot, it can be carried fully loaded and brought into action immediately.

With the magazine catch being positioned in the bottom of the grip, reloading is not as quick as with pistols that have button-type magazine catches. On the plus side, it is a most secure method of keeping the magazine in the pistol and also works well for left-handed shooters.

The pistol's well-designed grip helps considerably in controlling recoil. It also provides good access to the double-action trigger. This is important because the trigger, in both double- and single-action modes, is not as good as the triggers of the double-action pistols currently available.

The single-action pull has a rather spongy hammer release while the double-action pull tends to stack just before the hammer is released. I found that with practice I could control the double-action trigger by quickly applying pressure until I felt the pull getting harder. At that point, I would hesitate momentarily, to ensure the sights were aligned, before completing the pull. In this manner, I was able to maintain accuracy at distances beyond 10 yards. While the spongy single-action pull was not good for target shooting, I found it was surprisingly satisfactory for fast follow-up shots.

None of the P38s I have shot have ever delivered stellar accuracy, but they were good enough for defensive purposes. To be fair, my issued P38's accuracy may have been affected by the slide developing fatigue cracks.

Taking everything into consideration, I found the P38 to be perfectly satisfactory as a service pistol.

COLLECTOR INTEREST

Walther pistols of any model and vintage have commanded high prices. Any of the development models like the MP and AP have values exceeding $1000. Post-war P38s in mint condition can command quite high values, especially steel-frame models of 1987. Check, therefore, what you have before you decide to shoot it.

Rotating the takedown latch enables the slide/barrel assembly to be removed off the front of the frame. Photo courtesy of Garry James.

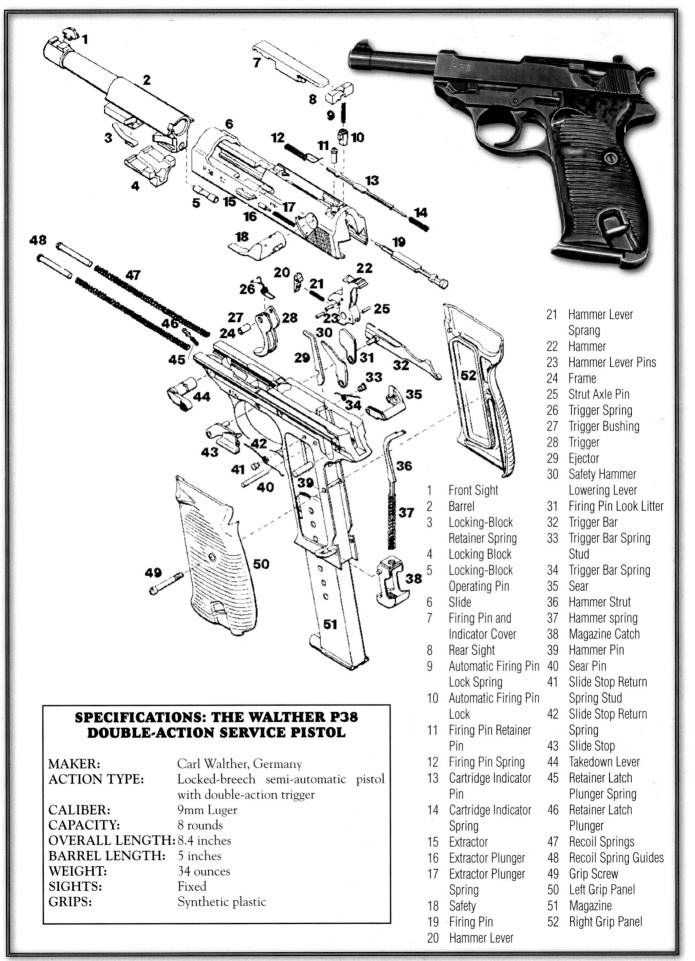

1. Front Sight
2. Barrel
3. Locking-Block Retainer Spring
4. Locking Block
5. Locking-Block Operating Pin
6. Slide
7. Firing Pin and Indicator Cover
8. Rear Sight
9. Automatic Firing Pin Lock Spring
10. Automatic Firing Pin Lock
11. Firing Pin Retainer Pin
12. Firing Pin Spring
13. Cartridge Indicator Pin
14. Cartridge Indicator Spring
15. Extractor
16. Extractor Plunger
17. Extractor Plunger Spring
18. Safety
19. Firing Pin
20. Hammer Lever
21. Hammer Lever Sprang
22. Hammer
23. Hammer Lever Pins
24. Frame
25. Strut Axle Pin
26. Trigger Spring
27. Trigger Bushing
28. Trigger
29. Ejector
30. Safety Hammer Lowering Lever
31. Firing Pin Look Litter
32. Trigger Bar
33. Trigger Bar Spring Stud
34. Trigger Bar Spring
35. Sear
36. Hammer Strut
37. Hammer spring
38. Magazine Catch
39. Hammer Pin
40. Sear Pin
41. Slide Stop Return Spring Stud
42. Slide Stop Return Spring
43. Slide Stop
44. Takedown Lever
45. Retainer Latch Plunger Spring
46. Retainer Latch Plunger
47. Recoil Springs
48. Recoil Spring Guides
49. Grip Screw
50. Left Grip Panel
51. Magazine
52. Right Grip Panel

SPECIFICATIONS: THE WALTHER P38 DOUBLE-ACTION SERVICE PISTOL

MAKER:	Carl Walther, Germany
ACTION TYPE:	Locked-breech semi-automatic pistol with double-action trigger
CALIBER:	9mm Luger
CAPACITY:	8 rounds
OVERALL LENGTH:	8.4 inches
BARREL LENGTH:	5 inches
WEIGHT:	34 ounces
SIGHTS:	Fixed
GRIPS:	Synthetic plastic

THE BROWNING P-35 HIGH POWER

John Browning's Last Pistol

The Browning P-35 High Power is a notable handgun of the last century for a number of reasons. It is John M. Browning's final pistol design. It introduced the concept of the high-ammunition-capacity double-column magazine. It is considered by many to be an improvement of the famous Colt Government Model of 1911. Finally, it is one of the most widely used military service pistols of all time. In fact, during World War II, the High Power saw service not only with a number of the allied forces but was also used by the German military as well. The fact that the P-35 remains in production today without major changes speaks volumes of the soundness of its basic design.

JOHN M. BROWNING AND FN

Although the P-35 is often called the "Browning High Power," after the American gun designer of the same name, its country of origin is in fact Belgium. It is a product of that country's huge arms company, Fabrique Nationale, or FN as it is often called.

FN was created in 1889 by a consortium of Belgian financiers to manufacture Mauser rifles under license for the military of that country. Ironically, Ludwig Lowe of Berlin helped them set up the machinery and factory. Lowe is known for his involvement in the development of the Luger pistol.

The manufacture of Mauser rifles did not provide the profit margin anticipated and the company began to look for other firearms to manufacture to increase their profits. FN began production of bicycles, sporting rifles and shotguns, but even these did not take full advantage of the company's production capacity.

During the late 1890s, FN came in contact with the American gun designer John M. Browning. At the time, Browning was working with Winchester but was dissatisfied with that company over the manufacture of one of his shotgun designs.

FN showed great interest in the shotgun and also a pocket pistol designed by Browning. The company began production of the latter, completing the first pistol in 1899. The pistol was a success and it began an association that was to last until Browning's death in 1926.

Belgium became Browning's second home and he and FN collaborated in developing a number of successful firearm designs. Some four years before he died, Browning was working on a project that proved to be his final pistol design.

The pistol in question was a 9mm semi-automatic pistol. Browning made several prototypes, but the design was incomplete before he died. The project was completed by his protégé, Dieudonne Saive. The final design became known as the Modele 1935 Pistolet Automatique Grand Puissance, or in English speaking countries, as the Model 1935 High Power Pistol.

DESIGN CHARACTERISTICS AND FEATURES

Many 1911 adherents view the High Power as Browning's ultimate design, one that simplified the Colt 45 Government Model and corrected what few faults it had. It is certainly true that the High Power does share many of the 1911's characteristics and has a similar appearance.

Like the 1911, the High Power was a locked-breech semi-automatic pistol that had a single-action trigger. Instead of the swinging-link barrel locking system, a simpler cam-operated action, also developed by Browning, was employed to unlock the action immediately after firing.

While the pistol had an exposed hammer and the same controls of slide stop, magazine catch and thumb safety, the grip safety was absent. Instead, the pistol had a magazine disconnect that disabled the action when the magazine was removed.

The stirrup-type trigger used in the 1911 was replaced by a connecting bar contained in the slide that released the hammer when activated by the trigger.

Perhaps the pistol's most innovative feature was its 13-round, double-column magazine. It was Browning's intention to retain a single-column magazine because he was concerned about the reliability of the double-column type. Saive, however, decided to use the double-column magazine. The amount the double-column magazine adds to the width of the grip is surprisingly small and does not detract from the pistol's handling characteristics.

The FN P-35 was John Browning's last pistol design and was chambered for the 9mm Luger cartridge with an ammunition capacity of 13 rounds. Photo courtesy of Garry James.

While the High Power is a simpler design than the 1911, its trigger cannot be custom tuned to the same extent. In addition, the thumb safety on the original models is small and stiff to operate. This has been improved on the current models.

MILITARY AND CIVILIAN USE

The Model 35 is one of the most widely used military pistols of all time. When it first appeared, it was immediately adopted by the Belgian military. Later, sales were made to Estonia, Lithuania, China, Peru and Rumania. The war interrupted further foreign sales.

The High Power is unique in that both sides used it during World War II. When the Germans invaded Belgium, FN management refused to work for them. The factory was confiscated and German

The pistol had a cam-operated tilting-barrel locking system in place of the Browning swinging-link design. Photo courtesy of Garry James.

management was installed to run it. Over 300,000 High Powers were made for the German military that designated it as the Pistole 640(b).

British, Canadian, and Chinese forces used High Powers made by the John Inglis Company of Ontario, Canada. High Powers were generally issued to Special Forces such as airborne and commando units.

After the war, FN resumed production of the Model 35. Post-war military pistols are designated as the Model 1946, while the civilian models are simply called the High Power. The British Army adopted the High Power as its official pistol to replace the Webley and Enfield 38 revolvers. Numerous other countries also adopted the pistol for their military forces including Argentina (where it was made under license), Denmark, Holland and Rhodesia.

The High Power has enjoyed good civilian sales worldwide thanks to its cartridge, reliability and high-capacity magazine. For many users, the latter feature is the reason the pistol ranked high as an effective combat arm. In the United States, the High Power and other FN arms were distributed by Browning in Utah.

MODIFICATIONS AND UPGRADES

The High Power of today remains little changed from the original pistols of 1935. Some of the first models had a tendency for the internal extractor to break. This was corrected by replacing it with a shorter, more rugged, external extractor.

The first High Powers were made with fixed and adjustable sights. The latter was a tangent-type rear assembly. Post-war civilian High Powers included a sports model that featured a small fully adjustable rear sight.

Early High Powers all have a round external hammer. This has since been replaced with a spur-type hammer. A number of military models were made to accept a detachable stock that also contained a flap holster.

During the war, the Inglis Company experimented with lightening the High Power by machining scallops to the slide, but it was never produced in quantity.

High Power finishes vary from profusely engraved presentation models to drab parkerized military-issue guns. Civilian models usually have a bright polish blue finish. Late German High Powers often have a very rough exterior gray parkerized finish with much evidence of machine marks. Allied wartime Model 35s usually have a matte parkerized finish although some may also have a black paint-like coating on the slide.

Post-war High Powers have checkered wood grip panels. Since the war, this has changed to grips made of black-checkered plastic.

The pistol's high ammunition capacity is due to the double-column magazine. Photo courtesy of Garry James.

THE HIGH POWER TODAY

FN continues to make the High Power much as it was in 1935. Changes include a spur hammer, larger ambidextrous thumb safety and form-fitting black plastic grips with a built-in thumb rest.

The High Power remains in service with a number of armies even to this day and has been used by FN as a platform for double-action, fast-action and compact versions.

FIELD STRIPPING PROCEDURE

First remove the magazine and check that the chamber is unloaded. The bottom edge of the left slide has two recess cuts. The rear one is for applying the safety. Pull back the slide and lock it with the safety catch using the front notch.

When the slide is locked in this position, the slide stop can be removed from the left side of the frame. Once the slide stop is out, release the safety from the notch and ease the slide and barrel forward off the frame.

With the slide off the frame, remove the recoil spring assembly from under the barrel. Removing the barrel out of the bottom of the slide completes the field strip. The pistol is assembled in reverse order.

SHOOTING AND HANDLING THE HIGH POWER

The high ammunition capacity of the High Power is one feature that makes it a great combat pistol. It has paved the way for the numerous high-ammunition pistols that have followed over the years. Providing 13 or 14 shots compared to a mere six or seven gives a soldier or police officer a tremendous tactical advantage. Even more important is the fact the pistol's grip size is not compromised in any way that might affect the shooter's ability to properly engage the trigger.

My experience with the High Power was in competing in what is now called Practical Pistol Shooting. The majority of the Rhodesian National Combat Pistol Team, of which I was a member in 1976, used it. In that year, we won the team event of the Second World Combat Pistol Championships held in Austria. The pistol was used the following year by the 1977 Rhodesian team to again win the world team title. The winner of the individual title, also a Rhodesian, used a High Power. The pistols used by the team were fitted with aftermarket adjustable sights.

I found the pistol's 14-shot capacity gave me a distinct advantage in not having to reload as often as with my 1911 (then considered the best pistol for this type of shooting).

Accuracy was more than adequate for this type of competition, and while the trigger pull was a little on the heavy side, it could be improved enough by a competent gunsmith.

The safety, which is on the small side, locks the sear when the hammer is cocked. Photo courtesy of Garry James.

The High Power has the usual controls of slide stop, magazine catch and safety, all positioned on the left side of the frame. Photo courtesy of Garry James.

The pistol did have a few faults. The fixed sights of the early models were rather small and the trigger pull was rather heavy. But, again, both can be improved by custom gunsmithing.

One thing I did not like was the pistol's short tang at the rear. This caused me to suffer hammer bite when the web of my hand was pinched between the hammer and the frame. The thumb safety is small and stiff to operate, making it difficult to disengage quickly. I also found that my thumb could inadvertently engage the button-style magazine catch. This occurred at a critical stage in the 1977 World Match that cost me a place among the winners.

As a combat pistol, I found the High Power more than adequate for defensive shooting. Most of its minor detractions can be resolved with sensible customizing.

COLLECTOR INTEREST

Current production High Powers are generally priced in the $500-$600 range.

Factory-engraved pistols have collector values in excess of $1000. Some pre-war models have collector values that range between $600 and $1500.

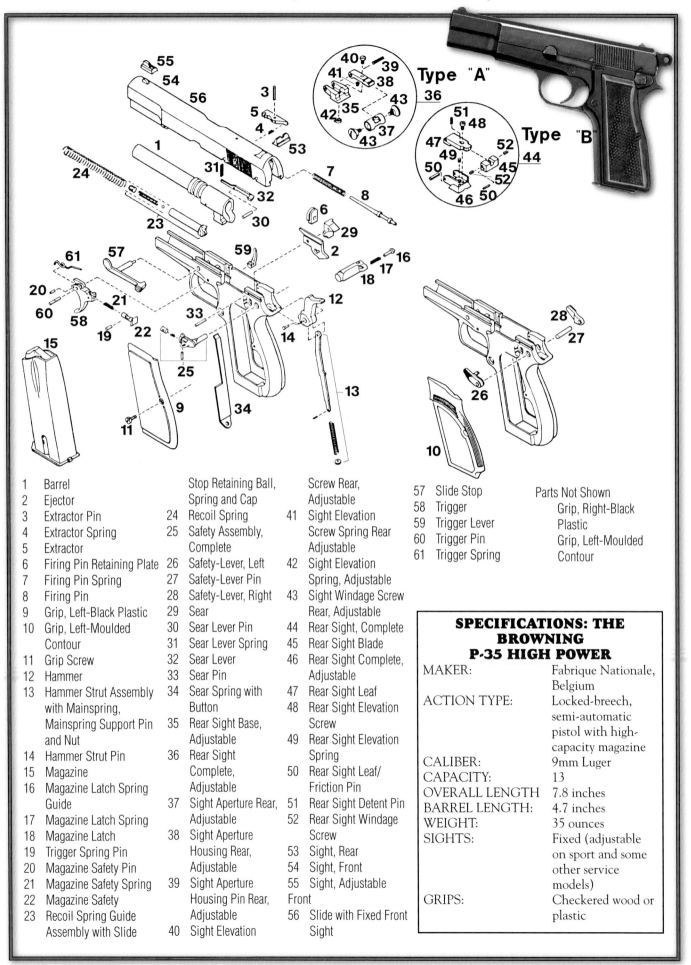

Type "A"

Type "B"

1	Barrel		Stop Retaining Ball, Spring and Cap
2	Ejector	24	Recoil Spring
3	Extractor Pin	25	Safety Assembly, Complete
4	Extractor Spring	26	Safety-Lever, Left
5	Extractor	27	Safety-Lever Pin
6	Firing Pin Retaining Plate	28	Safety-Lever, Right
7	Firing Pin Spring	29	Sear
8	Firing Pin	30	Sear Lever Pin
9	Grip, Left-Black Plastic	31	Sear Lever Spring
10	Grip, Left-Moulded Contour	32	Sear Lever
11	Grip Screw	33	Sear Pin
12	Hammer	34	Sear Spring with Button
13	Hammer Strut Assembly with Mainspring, Mainspring Support Pin and Nut	35	Rear Sight Base, Adjustable
14	Hammer Strut Pin	36	Rear Sight Complete, Adjustable
15	Magazine		
16	Magazine Latch Spring Guide	37	Sight Aperture Rear, Adjustable
17	Magazine Latch Spring	38	Sight Aperture Housing Rear, Adjustable
18	Magazine Latch		
19	Trigger Spring Pin	39	Sight Aperture Housing Pin Rear, Adjustable
20	Magazine Safety Pin		
21	Magazine Safety Spring	40	Sight Elevation
22	Magazine Safety		
23	Recoil Spring Guide Assembly with Slide		

	Screw Rear, Adjustable
41	Sight Elevation Screw Spring Rear Adjustable
42	Sight Elevation Spring, Adjustable
43	Sight Windage Screw Rear, Adjustable
44	Rear Sight, Complete
45	Rear Sight Blade
46	Rear Sight Complete, Adjustable
47	Rear Sight Leaf
48	Rear Sight Elevation Screw
49	Rear Sight Elevation Spring
50	Rear Sight Leaf/ Friction Pin
51	Rear Sight Detent Pin
52	Rear Sight Windage Screw
53	Sight, Rear
54	Sight, Front
55	Sight, Adjustable Front
56	Slide with Fixed Front Sight

57	Slide Stop
58	Trigger
59	Trigger Lever
60	Trigger Pin
61	Trigger Spring

Parts Not Shown

Grip, Right-Black Plastic

Grip, Left-Moulded Contour

SPECIFICATIONS: THE BROWNING P-35 HIGH POWER

MAKER:	Fabrique Nationale, Belgium
ACTION TYPE:	Locked-breech, semi-automatic pistol with high-capacity magazine
CALIBER:	9mm Luger
CAPACITY:	13
OVERALL LENGTH	7.8 inches
BARREL LENGTH:	4.7 inches
WEIGHT:	35 ounces
SIGHTS:	Fixed (adjustable on sport and some other service models)
GRIPS:	Checkered wood or plastic

Dieudonne Saive
Co-Designer of the High Power

As already mentioned, John Browning died before the development of his High Power pistol was completed. The task of completing it fell to a talented Belgium engineer, Dieudonne Saive.

Saive had worked closely with Browning but was a competent gun designer in his own right. Prior to World War II, Saive was the principle engineer working on a self-loading military rifle that eventually became the FN FAL, one of the most successful military rifles of the post-war period.

When Belgium was overrun by the German army, Saive escaped to England together with a number of FN engineers. There he worked on a number of firearm projects. The Belgians also brought with them complete drawings of the High Power, which were used to manufacture the pistol in Canada by the Inglis Company.

In completing the design of the High Power, Saive included a high-capacity double-column magazine that housed a total of 13 rounds of 9mm ammunition. This could be increased to 14 if the chamber was also loaded.

Browning was not in favor of high-capacity magazines because of concerns about increased size of the pistol's grip and the likelihood of functioning problems. To Saive's credit, the pistol's grip was kept to a reasonable size and the double-column magazine proved to be perfectly reliable. The fact is that the inclusion of a high-capacity magazine ensured the success of the High Power as a military service pistol more than any of its many other features.

The Smith & Wesson 357 Magnum (Model 27) Revolver

The First Magnum Revolver

When Smith & Wesson first introduced their 357 Magnum revolver in 1935, it was touted as the most powerful handgun in the world. Although the 357 Magnum has been superseded by even more powerful ammunition, it still is a formidable defense round.

For many years, Smith &Wesson's 357 Magnum revolver was one of the company's premier handguns. In addition to its connection with the cartridge, the revolver also introduced a number of features that were to become standard items in the company's handgun line. These included sights and grips as well as some internal modifications.

HISTORY AND DEVELOPMENT

During the late 1920s and on through the 1930s, American law enforcement began calling for ammunition with greater velocity and power than the 38 Special then in common use. The reason was to counter the increasing use by criminals of bulletproof vests and armored automobiles.

Smith & Wesson responded by offering their 38/44 Heavy Duty model. This was a 38-caliber revolver that employed a 44 Hand Ejector frame. The bigger and stronger frame enabled the revolver to handle 38 ammunition of much higher velocities. The ammunition companies began manufacturing ammunition especially for these revolvers that were designated as the 38/44 models.

Phil Sharpe, a well-known gun writer of the period, began experimenting with ammunition hand loaded to even higher velocities. He communicated the results of his work to Smith & Wesson, urging the factory to develop a suitable revolver to handle the ammunition.

The company was interested enough to ask the Winchester Repeating Arms Company to develop a special new cartridge. By 1934, Winchester produced a new cartridge to Smith & Wesson's specifications. Smith & Wesson then developed a revolver for the cartridge.

The cartridge used a 38 Special case lengthened by one-eighth inch to prevent it being loaded in standard 38 Special revolver cylinders. It was loaded with a 158-grain bullet and had a muzzle velocity of 1515 ft/sec.

The first revolver called the 357 Magnum rolled off the production lines in 1935 and was presented to J. Edgar Hoover, the FBI director. Initially, Smith & Wesson did not anticipate much commercial interest in the new revolver, and it was decided that civilian sales would be made on a special order basis.

The 357 Magnum was the most deluxe revolver the company had produced up to that date. Each revolver would be sighted in out to 200 yards for an ammunition load specified by the customer. The revolver cost $15 more than any other revolver made by the company at that time.

Contrary to Smith & Wesson's expectations, the demand for the new 357 Magnum soon exceeded what was being produced. The revolver became popular with law enforcement and hunters. The 357 Magnum gave the latter a cartridge and a handgun that was a viable hunting arm. Even though it is generally agreed that the 357 Magnum cartridge is too small for large, dangerous game animals, hunters have successfully hunted black bear and even grizzly with it.

Smith & Wesson kept the revolver in production until 1941 when its manufacture was suspended because of the war. The revolver was brought back into production in 1948 and Smith & Wesson continued to make it until 1994. The revolver was assigned the model number 27 in 1957.

DESIGN CHARACTERISTICS AND FEATURES

The Smith & Wesson 357 Magnum was a solid-frame, swing-out cylinder, double-action revolver that used the large N frame. Its internal lockwork followed that

The 357 Magnum used the frame and the basic mechanism of the earlier hand-ejector, large, N-frame revolver like this Model 1917 45 ACP. The frame, barrel and cylinder were all strengthened to handle the increased pressures of the new magnum cartridge.

employed in the company's other large-frame hand-ejector models like the 38/44 Heavy Duty and the 38/44 Outdoorsman. It had a six-shot cylinder and a round barrel that incorporated a top rib. On the underside of the barrel there was a shroud to protect the ejector rod.

The revolver had a fully adjustable rear sight while the topstrap and barrel rib were finely checkered. The wood grips were of the Magna type with the option of a grip adapter.

Customers could order the revolver in barrel length ranging from 3-1/2 to 8-3/4 inches with a choice of seven front sight blades and the new Magna-style grips with or without a grip adapter.

Each revolver was registered to its new owner and was accompanied by a certificate bearing the customer's name. In addition, the registration number on the certificate, which had the suffix "Reg," was stamped on the crane recess of the frame.

The revolvers had a bright blue finish in keeping with its fine fit and finish.

UPGRADES AND IMPROVEMENTS

During its production life, the revolver underwent relatively few major changes. Many of the changes were ones applied to the entire Smith & Wesson revolver line. The practice of

The 357 Magnum revolver was first made in two main barrel lengths—3-1/2 and 8-3/4 inches. The first revolver, presented to J. Edgar Hoover, had a 3 1/2-inch barrel. This 3 1/2-inch example has the large target stocks normally fitted to the longer barrel versions in place of the smaller Magna grips. Photo courtesy of Glen Barnes.

making the 357 Magnum a special order item was discontinued just before the start of the war as was the practice of issuing certificates and the stamping of the crane recess with registration number.

This resulted in the revolver becoming a normal production item, and barrel lengths were then standardized to 3-1/2, 5, 6 and 8-3/8 inches. Post-war models saw the introduction of the rebound-slide-operated hammer block and a hammer with a shortened fall. Along with other S&W revolvers, the five screws securing the side plate to the frame were reduced to four.

What is probably the most significant change was made in 1960 when the extractor rod screw twist was reversed to a left-hand thread. The purpose of this change was to prevent the ejector rod from being jarred loose by recoil and causing difficulty in opening the cylinder.

In 1975, the revolver was fitted with a target hammer and trigger as well as oversize Goncalo Alves grips and sold with a fitted mahogany presentation case.

RELATED REVOLVERS

The Model 27 is really just one of a number of large N-frame Smith & Wesson revolvers. Similar revolvers using this frame have been made for other large handgun cartridges such as 45 Colt, 45 ACP, 44 Magnum, 44 Special, 41 Magnum, 40 S&W and 10mm.

The only other N-frame revolver in 357 Magnum was the Model 28 Highway Patrolman. This revolver was introduced in 1954 at the request of the Texas Highway Patrol for a less expensive 357 Magnum revolver.

The Highway Patrolman is virtually identical to the Model 27 in terms of size and internal mechanism. It has a fully adjustable rear sight but lacks the superb highly polished blue finish, target hammer and trigger of the 357 Magnum. It was made with 4- and 6-inch barrels.

The Model 27 was one of the last Smith & Wesson revolvers to go stainless. The first stainless version, called the Model 627, appeared in 1989. The revolver is also known as "The Model of 1989" and has this roll-stamped on the barrel. The revolver has a 5 1/2-inch fully lugged barrel, a round grip frame and an un-fluted cylinder.

Manufacture of the Models 28, 27 and 627 ceased in 1986, 1987 and 1994, respectively.

BARREL LENGTHS, GRIPS AND FINISHES

The first 357 Magnums were made with 3 1/2-inch and 8 3/4-inch barrels and had the new Magna-style grips. Customers could also list other barrel lengths of their choice when ordering their registered revolvers.

When the barrel lengths were standardized after the war, the 8 3/4-inch length was changed to 8-3/8 inches to conform to NRA target requirements. The other lengths were 4 and 6 inches. After 1975, the grips were changed to the large target designs commonly fitted to most other S&W target-sighted revolvers.

The most popular finish applied to the revolver was a deep highly polished blue although nickel-plated 27s were offered. The Model 27 was one of the last all-blue large-frame revolvers to be made by the company. When in production, it was one of Smith & Wesson's most popular magnum revolvers.

LOADING AND UNLOADING THE 357 MAGNUM

Both these procedures are exactly the same as for the Model 10 Military & Police 38 revolver described in an earlier chapter.

SHOOTING AND HANDLING THE 357 MAGNUM

As Smith & Wesson's top-grade revolver, the 357 Magnum's performance matches its good looks. It is capable of excellent accuracy out to surprisingly long ranges, especially with 357 Magnum ammunition. It is also usually able to deliver above-average accuracy with the milder 38 Specials. Two good friends of mine used 6-inch-barreled Model 27s in serious target competition and were more than content with the revolvers' overall performances.

The revolver's target shooting capability should come as no surprise considering that it has excellent adjustable sights and a

The revolver's tapered barrel had a top rib and a protective shroud for the ejector rod.

single-action trigger. Its wide hammer spur facilitates fast and easy hammer cocking.

It handles the recoil of magnums extremely well thanks to its large frame. This is especially so with the longer barrel models. In comparison, shooting mild 38 Special target wadcutters is like shooting a 22 revolver in terms of recoil.

With the shorter barrels, the Model 27 is an excellent defensive handgun. Its double-action trigger has a smooth, even pull throughout its stroke. Small wonder that it was the first choice of many FBI agents in the gangster era of the 1930s.

If the revolver has any fault, it is its large size. This makes it difficult for small-handed shooters to reach the double-action trigger. This must be balanced against the revolver's mild recoil and great strength.

Unlike some of the smaller 357 revolvers, the Model 27 is more than able to handle a steady diet of hot 357s. One friend of mine put thousands of hot hand-loaded 357 Magnums through his Model 28 (the budget version of the 27) without affecting its accuracy or its action in any way.

COLLECTOR INTEREST

There is very limited interest in collecting these revolvers or, for that matter, most any other Smith & Wesson handguns. This is odd, considering the quality of fit and finish as well as the overall excellence of the design. Catalog values rarely exceed $1000, even for the registered 357 Magnums. Any Model 27 in good condition is still an excellent choice for defense or sport shooting.

For many years, the 357 Magnum was Smith & Wesson's most prestigious revolver. Its features included square checkering on the pistol's topstrap. Photo courtesy of Glen Barnes.

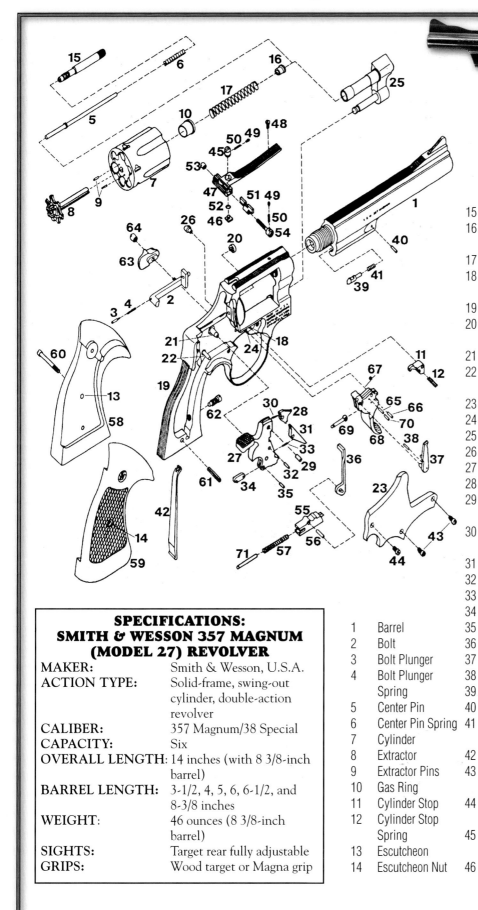

		15	Extractor Rod		Elevation Stud
		16	Extractor Rod	47	Rear Sight Leaf
			Collar	48	Rear Sight Leaf
		17	Extractor Spring		Screw
		18	Cylinder Stop	49	Rear Sight
			Stud		Plunger
		19	Frame	50	Rear Sight
		20	Hammer Nose		Plunger Spring
			Bushing	51	Rear Sight Slide
		21	Hammer Stud	52	Rear Sight
		22	Rebound Slide		Spring Clip
			Stud	53	Rear Sight
		23	Sideplate		Windage Nut
		24	Trigger Stud	54	Rear Sight
		25	Yoke		Windage Screw
		26	Frame Lug	55	Rebound Slide
		27	Hammer	56	Rebound Slide
		28	Hammer Nose		Pin
		29	Hammer Nose	57	Rebound Slide
			Rivet		Spring
		30	Hammer Nose	58	Stock, Left
			Spring	59	Stock, Right
		31	Sear	60	Stock Screw
		32	Sear Pin	61	Stock Pin
		33	Sear Spring	62	Strain Screw
		34	Stirrup	63	Thumb-Piece
1	Barrel	35	Stirrup Pin	64	Thumb-Piece
2	Bolt	36	Hammer Block		Nut
3	Bolt Plunger	37	Hand	65	Hand Spring
4	Bolt Plunger	38	Hand Pin		Pin
	Spring	39	Locking Bolt	66	Hand Spring
5	Center Pin	40	Locking Bolt Pin		Torsion Pin
6	Center Pin Spring	41	Locking Bolt	67	Hand Torsion
7	Cylinder		Spring		Spring
8	Extractor	42	Mainspring	68	Trigger
9	Extractor Pins	43	Plate Screws,	69	Trigger Lever
10	Gas Ring		Crowned	70	Trigger Lever
11	Cylinder Stop	44	Plate Screw, Flat		Pin
12	Cylinder Stop		Head	71	Trigger Stop
	Spring	45	Rear Sight		Rod
13	Escutcheon		Elevation Nut		Parts Not Shown
14	Escutcheon Nut	46	Rear Sight		Barrel Pin

SPECIFICATIONS:
SMITH & WESSON 357 MAGNUM
(MODEL 27) REVOLVER

MAKER:	Smith & Wesson, U.S.A.
ACTION TYPE:	Solid-frame, swing-out cylinder, double-action revolver
CALIBER:	357 Magnum/38 Special
CAPACITY:	Six
OVERALL LENGTH:	14 inches (with 8 3/8-inch barrel)
BARREL LENGTH:	3-1/2, 4, 5, 6, 6-1/2, and 8-3/8 inches
WEIGHT:	46 ounces (8 3/8-inch barrel)
SIGHTS:	Target rear fully adjustable
GRIPS:	Wood target or Magna grip

THE RUGER STANDARD 22 PISTOL

The Beginning for Sturm, Ruger & Company

This pistol is notable for, if no other reason, being the handgun that started the firearms company of Sturm Ruger. The pistol was the fledgling firearms company's first handgun. Its success enabled Ruger to expand and develop other handguns.

The pistol owed much of its success to its low cost, which was considerably below what most popular 22 autos were selling for at that time. Much of this was due to modern manufacturing methods used in its construction—a trend that Ruger has followed with most of its subsequent guns.

BASIC DESIGN AND FEATURES

The Ruger Standard Pistol was a blowback-operated semi-automatic pistol chambered for the 22 Long Rifle cartridge. While the pistol employed well-established auto pistol principles, its most notable feature was the manner in which it was constructed.

The design was simplicity itself and consisted of a barrel and a tubular receiver that contained the bolt and firing pin mechanism. The grip frame was made of two metal pressings, which were welded together to form a single unit.

The controls originally included a safety and a magazine catch. The introduction of the later Mark II pistols saw the addition of a slide. The magazine catch was of the heel clip type and was located at the bottom rear of the grip.

The first Standard models had a tapered 4 3/4-inch or 6-inch barrel and fixed sights. The 9-shot magazine was contained within the grip. The pistol was of all-steel construction except for the grip panels, which were made of black checkered plastic.

The first production models had grips with silver medallions containing the famous Ruger hawk logo in red. After 1951, this was changed to black to commemorate Alexander

The Ruger 22 was a very simple design that employed a number of notable manufacturing techniques such as a frame made of two metal pressings welded together to form a single unit. Shown here is a Mark II Target Model with a 5 1/4-inch barrel.

Sturm's passing. Red logo pistols are highly desirable as collectors' items.

Apart from its reasonable cost, the Ruger appeal was enhanced by it close resemblance to the shape of the famous Luger P08 9mm service pistol.

Field stripping the pistol could be a little tricky, in spite of its simple design.

STANDARD 22 PISTOL VARIATIONS

The popularity of the pistol prompted Ruger to offer models with other features, such as longer barrels and target sights. Although the pistol began life as a plinker or sport pistol, its impressive accuracy indicated its potential as a target pistol.

In 1951, the Mark I target model was introduced with a fully adjustable rear sight and a choice of a 5 1/2-inch heavy barrel or tapered 5 1/4- and 6 7/8-inch barrels. These versions, together with the fixed-sight versions, remained in production until replaced by the Mark II models in 1982.

THE MARK II 22 PISTOLS

In 1982, the Mark II model replaced the 22 Standard pistol line. These followed the same basic design but had enhancements that included a revised safety catch that permitted the bolt to be cycled when applied and an additional catch to hold the bolt open on an empty magazine. Finally, the rear of the receiver was scalloped so that a more positive grip could be taken on the protruding serrated ears of the bolt.

To celebrate the debut of the Mark II, a limited number of stainless steel models were made with Bill Ruger's signature roll-stamped on top of the receiver. The pistols also had the Ruger hawk emblem on the medallions outlined in red instead of black and were shipped in salt cod box cases just like the originals.

The Mark II was made in most of the configurations of the Standard model with both stainless and blue steel finishes being offered.

MILITARY SERVICE

During the 1960s, the military purchased a large number of Ruger 22 pistols for training purposes and a number were worked by the gunsmiths of the Army's Marksmanship Unit at Fort Benning for use by members of the unit in target competition. These military models are marked "U.S."

In 1987, Ruger introduced a commercial version of these pistols with a 6 7/8-inch barrel that was called the Government Target Model (MK678G). These pistols do not have the military markings. In 1993, a stainless steel version with a 6 7/8-inch bull barrel was introduced.

THE 22/45 PISTOL

This pistol, which has a synthetic polymer frame made of Zytel patterned after the shape of the Colt 1911, first appeared in the same year as the Government Target Model. It was made in both stainless and blue steel and at the time of writing is the last of the Ruger 22 auto pistols to be made.

The Ruger Mark II continues in production in most of its configurations, signifying the excellence of its concept and design.

The pistol's controls include a safety and a slide stop, which was added with the introduction of the Mark II series.

The magazine catch is of the heel clip design and is located in the bottom rear of the grip.

FIELDSTRIPPING THE RUGER 22

In spite of its simple design, the Ruger 22 has a quite complicated field takedown procedure. After removing the magazine and checking that the chamber is unloaded, pull the trigger to release the mainspring tension.

Next, direct your attention to the back of the grip where you will see three long narrow steel strips. Using a screwdriver or a firm piece of plastic, pry open the middle one, which is the mainspring housing latch.

When the latch has been pried open, the housing can be swung out of its recess in the frame and pulled down out of the back of the bolt. With the housing removed, the bolt can be pulled from the rear of the tubular receiver.

This completes the fieldstripping and permits access to the chamber and bore for cleaning. The pistol is assembled in reverse order. When replacing the mainspring, take care to ensure that the hammer fits into its recess in the top of the housing.

SHOOTING AND HANDLING THE RUGER 22 STANDARD PISTOL

The Ruger 22's simple design and low price belies its great potential as a competition target pistol. Even the fixed sight version out of the box is more than just a plinker.

The target versions are excellent entry-level pistols for anyone contemplating serious target shooting. They are accurate and their factory-installed adjustable target sights compare well to those found on more expensive target arms.

The single-action trigger pull, while not quite equal to those of the more expensive target pistols, is quite adequate for the novice to learn on. Probably the Ruger 22's greatest asset is how much it can be improved by a gunsmith who is familiar with the pistol.

By fitting a custom heavy barrel, adding an improved adjustable rear sight and honing the trigger so that it has a light crisp pull, the Ruger can be turned into a target pistol that can hold its own against most of the more expensive European-made target 22s.

The pistol's acutely angled Luger-style grips provide an excellent hold that aligns the sights with the target when brought up to shoulder level. While I can quite happily live with the grips as they are, I have fitted my personal custom Ruger 22 with a set of orthopedic target stocks made by K.N. Nill. These, together with an air gauge, heavy bull barrel, custom match trigger and a Bomar rear adjustable sight, have created a superb target pistol that delivers accuracy far beyond what I am capable of shooting.

If the pistol has one detraction, it is that it is somewhat tricky to field strip. Even this can be corrected, however, with a custom modification that greatly simplifies the procedure.

COLLECTOR INTEREST

Ruger handguns are beginning to attract interest by some collectors. In spite of this, very few command high prices. The most sought after of the Ruger 22s are the early models with the red-backed logos.

The Ruger 22 has great accuracy potential. This Mark II has been customized for the International Standard Pistol Match. It has Nill target grips, a match trigger, new adjustable sights and a match barrel.

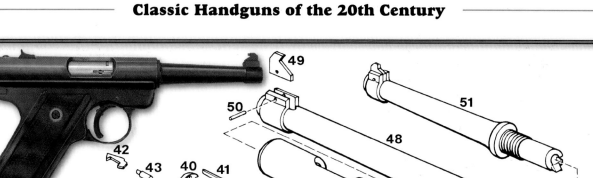

1	Frame	17	Mainspring	33	Hammer Pivot Pin
2	Disconnector		Housing	34	Recoil Spring Guide
3	Trigger	18	Bolt Stop	35	Recoil Spring
4	Trigger Pin	19	Bolt Stop Pivot	36	Bolt
5	Trigger Pin Lock		Pin	37	Firing Pin Stop
	Washer	20	Magazine Catch	38	Rebound Spring
6	Trigger Stop Screw		Spring	39	Rebound Spring Support
	(Mk. I)	21	Housing Latch	40	Recoil Spring Support
7	Trigger Spring		Pivot Pin	41	Firing Pin
	Plunger	22	Magazine Catch	42	Extractor
8	Trigger Spring	23	Housing Latch	43	Extractor Plunger
9	Sear	24	Mainspring	44	Extractor Spring
10	Sear Spring		Plunger	45	Receiver
11	Sear Pivot Yin	25	Mainspring	46	Rear Sight (Standard)
12	Sear Spring Stop	26	Detent Bail	47	Micro Rear Sight (Mk. I)
	Pin	27	Magazine	48	Barrel (Mk. I)
13	Magazine Catch		Assembly	49	Front Sight Blade (Mk. I)
	Stop Pin	28	Safety Catch	50	Front Sight Pin (Mk. I)
14	Magazine Catch	29	Hammer Bushing	51	Barrel Assembly
	Pivot Pin	30	Hammer		(Standard)
15	Grip	31	Hammer Strut		
16	Grip Screws	32	Hammer Strut Pin		

SPECIFICATIONS: THE RUGER 22 STANDARD PISTOL

MAKER:	Sturm Ruger & Company, U.S.A.
ACTION TYPE:	Blowback-operated semi-automatic pistol
CALIBER:	22 LR
CAPACITY:	Nine
OVERALL LENGTH:	11.1 inches (6.9-inch barrel)
BARREL LENGTH:	4.73 inches to 6.9 inches
WEIGHT:	46 ounces (6.9-inch barrel)
SIGHTS:	Fixed or adjustable (Target models)
GRIPS:	Black checkered plastic

William Batterman Ruger

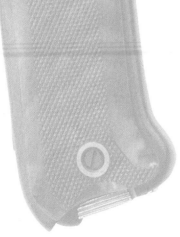

As a youth, Bill Ruger had an early interest in firearms and automobiles that was to last throughout his long career. In addition to participating as a member on his school's rifle team, he tinkered with firearms with a view to improving their performance.

Ruger and Alexander Sturm formed Sturm Ruger in 1949. The two men purchased a building in Southport and Bill Ruger set about designing the company's first firearm, a 22 auto pistol.

When the first production pistol was introduced, it received rave reviews and was an instant success. So much so that it enabled the company to expand into the manufacture of other handguns, which began with a single-action 22 revolver. By the end of the 1950s, the Ruger line included a 357 Magnum single-action revolver. Like the Ruger 22, this gun proved to be a great success.

Alexander Sturm died in 1951. In the years following his death, Sturm Ruger has grown into one of this country's most successful firearms companies. Bill Ruger died in 2002.

Much of the success of the Ruger company was due to Bill Ruger's knack for knowing just what the shooting public wanted and then filling this desire with well-made, reliable, accurate, and reasonably priced guns. All of these attributes are found in the Ruger 22 auto pistol.

THE SMITH & WESSON MODEL 39 DOUBLE-ACTION PISTOL

America's First Double-Action Service Pistol

The Model 39/59 series of pistols are significant in that they were the first American-made 9mm double-action service pistols. They were also the pistols on which many of the current line of Smith & Wesson double-actions pistols are based.

The man most responsible for developing the Model 39 was Carl Hellstrom (see sidebar), the company's head of production through the war years and company president during the post-war period.

HISTORY AND DEVELOPMENT

Shortly after the war ended, Hellstrom decided the company should design a new semi-automatic pistol, anticipating that the military would want to replace the Colt Government Model of 1911 with a 9mm pistol of modern design. It was decided that the pistol would have a double-action trigger mechanism.

Work on the project began in 1946 and by 1948 a prototype was ready for testing. While the pistol was not accepted by the military, the company decided that there might be a market for the pistol with law enforcement and civilians and the pistol went into production, making its debut in 1954.

DESIGN CHARACTERISTICS AND FEATURES

The pistol was a locked-breech, semi-automatic pistol that used the Browning cam-operated, tilting-barrel system to lock the action at the moment of firing. It was chambered for the 9mm Luger cartridge and had a magazine with an eight-shot capacity. Although the 39 was best known as a double-action pistol, a limited number (6) of single-action versions were made at the request of the military.

The double-action version used a trigger and safety mechanism similar to that of the Walther P38. It had a slide stop and button-style magazine catch, similar to that of the Colt 1911.

The pistol had a well-designed grip that featured a curved backstrap with raised checkering. Sights were fixed, although the rear assembly was screw adjustable for windage.

The first pistols submitted to the military had steel frames, but the first full-production guns had steel slides with alloy frames. The pistol underwent a few modifications and upgrades. Probably the most significant was the extractor, which was changed to one of a shorter, more robust design. This was because the longer original version had the propensity to break.

MILITARY AND LAW ENFORCEMENT USE

Initially, the pistol enjoyed modest civilian sales with little interest being shown by the law enforcement community. Then, in the 1960s, the pistol was adopted by the Illinois State Police, the first major agency in the country to adopt a self-loading pistol as its official sidearm.

While this did not result in a large-scale adoption of the pistol by other agencies, a number were interested enough to order some for test and evaluation. Civilian sales were strong enough to keep the pistol in production, enabling further development and improvements.

Smith & Wesson's Model 39 was the first 9mm double-action auto pistol to be made in the U.S.A. Its design served as the base for an extensive line of similar pistols made by the company.

The pistols had a double-action trigger similar to that on the Walther P38, but used the Browning titling-barrel, cam-operated, breech-locking system.

The pistol has the usual controls of slide stop, magazine catch and hammer-lowering safety, all positioned on the left side.

Even though the Model 39 was not adopted as the army's service pistol, it was used in limited quantities by some units, one of which was the Army's Marksmanship Unit (AMU), which was interested in the pistol's potential as a target arm. The unit requested Smith & Wesson to build some 39s for a 9mm cartridge with which they were experimenting. The cartridge was similar to a 38 Special wadcutter but with a rimless case. The pistols were designated as the AMU models and were further developed into the Model 52 (38 Master) competition pistol.

In 1964, Smith & Wesson began developing a 14-shot version of the 39. In 1968, the navy wanted the company to make a small quantity of high-ammunition-capacity pistols and the 14-shot models were forwarded to the navy for evaluation. The navy then requested that the pistols be made of stainless steel. Even though the factory did not have the necessary machinery to manufacture the pistol, they successfully filled the order by making the pistols in the experimental department. It was from these pistols the Model 59 was developed.

THE MODEL 52 (38 MASTER) TARGET PISTOL

This well-known target pistol was developed from the AMU pistol previously mentioned. The pistol was based on the Model 39 and had a steel frame and an adjustable target-style rear sight. The internal lockwork was the same except for a set-screw that locked the trigger so that it could only function as a single action. Later models were designed with single-action triggers. The pistol also came with a removable muzzle weight.

The pistol was eventually made for commercial sales and chambered for the 38 Special wadcutter target cartridge. It was given the official name of "Model 52 38 Master" pistol.

The pistol was well received by the target shooting community and it won a number of honors including winning a World International Center Fire Match.

The 38 Master enjoyed but a brief period of popularity in American centerfire matches because shooters found it offered little or no advantage over the target model 45-caliber pistols. The pistol remained in production until 1993. Recently, Smith & Wesson introduced a new version of the Model 52 made by the Performance Center and chambered for the 9mm Luger cartridge.

THE MODEL 59 WONDERNINE PISTOL

This pistol was developed from the high-capacity pistol built for the navy during the Vietnam War, but it differed in several respects. Like the 39, it used an alloy frame with a steel slide and barrel. The first models came with a blue finish. The pistol had a double-column magazine with a capacity of 14 9mm cartridges. Accommodating this large capacity magazine required the pistol's grip frame to be made thicker.

To keep the grip's width within reasonable proportions, the pistol had slim grip panels made of black checkered plastic instead of wood. In all other respects, the pistol was the same as the Model 39.

Unlike the Model 39, the new pistol received a modestly enthusiastic reception by law enforcement with a number of agencies adopting it in favor of the tried and tested revolver. To a large extent, this was due to the timing of the 59's introduction, which occurred as police were beginning to feel the need for increased firepower because of the rise in criminal gang and drug trafficking activity.

While the Model 59 performed reasonably well in police service, there were some complaints about reliability, which resulted in the pistol being called a "Jam-o-matic" by some of its users. In spite of this, the company persevered with the pistol, making the necessary changes and modifications to improve its performance.

THE JSSP MILITARY PISTOL TESTS

In the late 1970s, the military began a series of exhaustive tests to select a replacement for the 1911 45 service pistol. Various domestic and some foreign handgun companies were invited to submit test guns for evaluation. Smith & Wesson was among the companies involved and submitted a version of the Model 59 modified to meet the called-for specifications. By all accounts, the pistol performed very well in all aspects of the stringent test programs. In spite of this, the pistol lost out by a narrow margin to the Beretta Model 92 and the SIG-Sauer P226. The pistol's good performance justified the perseverance and effort that Smith & Wesson had devoted to both the Models 39 and 59.

THE WONDERNINE ERA

The acceptance by the military of a 9mm double-action high-capacity semi-automatic pistol had a dramatic effect on the American handgun market. Suddenly, such auto pistols became all the rage, especially among the law enforcement community.

By persevering with the original Models 39 and 59, Smith & Wesson had two handguns that could compete in the quickly expanding law enforcement market as departments began to switch from revolvers to auto pistols. Incorporating the various improvements developed for the military trials, the company produced new versions of both models.

These new versions are known as "second generation" models (prior-made pistols are classified as being "first generation") and were initially offered with steel and alloy frames. In addition, they had improved sights as well as improvements to the internal mechanism that improved reliability. Another important addition was an internal passive firing pin lock to prevent the pistol from discharging if accidentally dropped.

Not long afterwards, stainless steel models appeared. To identify these various new pistols, the model number was prefixed by another number. The numbers were "4" for alloy frame, "5" for all-blue carbon steel models and "6" for stainless steel. Thus a 459 signified an alloy-framed Model 59 while 539 indicated an all-steel 39.

The company also expanded the line to include a larger stainless steel pistol chambered for the 45 ACP cartridge called the Model 645. In addition, several single-action pistols—called the Model 745—were made for competition shooters by the newly created Performance Center in 1986.

THE MODEL 469 COMPACTS

The switch from revolver to auto pistol created a need for a more compact pistol to replace the small-framed, short-barreled revolvers used by detectives and other plain-clothes personnel.

The 39 has a well-designed grip with a curved backstrap with raised checkering for a firmer hold.

While the pistol had a low-mount fixed sight, the rear unit was adjustable for windage.

The long extractor of the first Model 39 was subject to numerous breakages and was soon replaced with a shorter, more robust one.

The Model 52 was a target version based on the Model 39. It had a steel frame, single-action trigger and an adjustable rear sight.

Some pistolsmiths were already offering customized, chopped versions of Smith & Wesson's double-action autos. One of the most celebrated was a pistol called the "Asp."

Smith & Wesson responded with a sub-compact, 12-shot, double-action pistol called the 469. Stainless steel and alloy frame models of the pistol were also offered.

THE THIRD GENERATION MODELS

The rapidly expanding police auto pistol market caused the company to develop a third generation of double-action service and compact pistols. While these drew heavily on the design of the original Model 39, they had a number of new features such as a single grip molding that encased the pistol's backstrap. The grip was made of a tough synthetic polymer called Delrin. This enabled the width to be reduced, providing a grip that suited most hand sizes. Initially, stainless and alloy frame models were offered as well as fixed and adjustable sight options and grips with either straight or curved backstrap grips.

The Model 59 (bottom) was based on the 39 (top) but had a large double-column, 14-shot magazine.

The 459 replaced the 59 and resolved most of the latter's reliability problems.

In the late 1980s and at the request of the FBI, the company produced a third generation pistol with a de-cocking lever instead of the usual safety. In addition to this de-cocking FBI model, Smith & Wesson also came out with pistols that had triggers that could only be fired double-action. These were adopted by a number of police departments that liked the additional safety and simplicity that these double-action-only pistols provided.

THE 40 S&W CARTRIDGE

The FBI specified that the de-cocking pistol they requested be chambered for a new shortened 10mm cartridge the bureau was testing. This coincided with a 40-caliber round that the company was developing. Although offered to the FBI, the agency rejected it and stuck with the 10 mm. The 40 S&W had the advantage of being able to be safely accommodated in a 9mm-size pistol. The Model 4006, introduced in 1990, was the first pistol made for the cartridge.

The 40 S&W cartridge was quickly adopted by a number of police agencies that believed it to be superior to the 9mm. As a result, other major handgun companies scrambled to come out with a pistol chambered for the new cartridge.

Smith & Wesson was able to offer most of its third generation pistols for the 40 S&W cartridge. The third generation models also were platforms for a number of other pistols in other calibers including the popular 45 ACP.

From a modest start, the Model 39 has developed into a very successful design that has sired a number of groundbreaking pistols and cartridges. It has also enabled Smith & Wesson to become a major manufacturer of semi-automatic pistols.

FIELD STRIPPING THE MODEL 39

The takedown procedures for the 39, 59 and all the subsequent models are very similar to that of the Browning High Power.

After removing the magazine and ensuring that the pistol is unloaded and safe, the slide is withdrawn until the front of the slide stop is aligned with the slide stop notch on the left of the slide.

When held in this position, the slide stop can be removed from the left side of the frame. Once this is done, all that remains is for the recoil spring assembly and the barrel to be removed from the bottom of the slide. This is as far as the pistol needs to be taken down for normal cleaning and maintenance.

The pistol is assembled in reverse order. In doing this with some of the later models, the levers that protrude up from the rear of the frame need to be pushed down when fitting the slide assembly.

SHOOTING AND HANDLING THE 39/59 PISTOL FAMILIES

My first introduction to the Model 39 was through shooting pistols owned by two close friends of mine. The time was in the early 1960s and it is important to remember that the only other double action of any consequence was the P38.

I found the shooting and handling characteristics of the 39 far superior to the P38. The grip seemed to suit my hand perfectly, allowing easy access to all the controls and the trigger.

The trigger was the pistol's strongest suit. It had an excellent single-action pull while the double action was surprisingly light with a nice smooth and even stroke. The sights were also good and the pistol delivered better accuracy than any of the P38s I had shot up to then.

On the debit side, the pistol did not have great reliability. Not long after one friend bought his 39, its extractor broke. My other friend's 39 was a later model with the improved extractor. It too had all the delightful shooting characteristics of the earlier model, but also like the first one, it had its own reliability problems. These problems included misfires due to light hammer strikes and the pistol failing to keep the hammer cocked. The problem, I was later told, was a worn drawbar.

Not long afterwards, I got to shoot a Model 59. While appreciating the increased magazine capacity, I found its larger grip inferior to that of the Model 39. In addition, I ran into the same worn drawbar problem, which resulted in the gun virtually becoming a double-action-only pistol.

In 1982, I got to fire the second generation versions of Models 39 and the 59. In terms of reliability, both pistols performed flawlessly. Once again, I much preferred the grip of the 39 to that of the 59. I did feel that the trigger pull was not quite as good as the original 39s I had fired in the past.

Some years later, I was exposed to third generation models. What really impressed me with these was how much the grip of the 59 version had been improved. I found the curved back grips were just as good as those on the 39. Reliability was flawless, and I eventually purchased a stainless Model 5906 that I later had polished and engraved. This pistol has always been completely reliable.

Since then, I have shot most of the subsequent models in 45, 40 S&W and 9mm. All have proved perfectly reliable and good shooters. I was especially impressed with the accuracy delivered by two early 4506 models that I shot. The groups both guns delivered were close to some of the best from my match custom 1911.

On the other hand, while all of the third generation 9mm

pistols I have shot have been accurate enough for defense, they were not as accurate as some other pistols I have shot.

Without question, the model that impressed me the most was the double-action-only Model 5946. I really appreciated the simplicity of its loading and unloading procedure and its double-action trigger is by far the best I have experienced in almost all such pistols that I have shot.

COLLECTOR INTEREST

Except for some of the very early Model 39s, especially those with single-action triggers and steel frames, this series of pistols does not command high prices on the used and collector market.

This Model 5906 of the author's has a bright, stainless steel finish and is profusely engraved. It sports custom-checkered wood stocks instead of the factory Delrin grips. The latter encased the backstrap and substantially reduced the grip's size.

SPECIFICATIONS: THE SMITH & WESSON MODEL 39 PISTOL

MAKER:	Smith & Wesson, U.S.A.
ACTION TYPE:	Locked-breech, semi-automatic pistol with double-action trigger
CALIBER:	9mm Luger
CAPACITY:	Eight
OVERALL LENGTH:	7.4 inches
BARREL LENGTH:	4 inches
WEIGHT:	27 ounces
SIGHTS:	Fixed (rear adjustable for windage only)
GRIPS:	Checkered wood

#	Part	#	Part	#	Part	#	Part
1	Barrel	23	Insert	45	Recoil Spring	67	Trigger Play Spring
2	Barrel Bushing	24	Insert Pin	46	Recoil Spring Guide Assembly	68	Trigger Play Spring Rivet
3	Disconnector	25	Magazine Buttplate	47	Sear		
4	Disconnector Pin	26	Magazine Buttplate Catch	48	Sear Spring		Parts Not Shown
5	Drawbar	27	Magazine Follower	49	Sear Spring Plunger		Recoil Spring Guide
6	Drawbar Plunger	28	Magazine Spring	50	Sear Spring Plunger Pin		Recoil Spring Guide
7	Drawbar Plunger Spring	29	Magazine Tube	51	Sear Pin		Bushing Recoil Spring
8	Ejector Depressor Plunger	30	Magazine Catch	52	Sear Release Lever		Guide Plunger Recoil
9	Ejector Depressor Plunger Spring	31	Magazine Catch Nut	53	Sideplate		Spring Guide Plunger
10	Ejector Magazine Depressor	32	Magazine Catch Plunger	54	Slide		Spring Hammer Pin
11	Ejector Spring	33	Magazine Catch Plunger Spring	55	Slide Stop		Sideplate Button
12	Extractor	34	Mainspring	56	Slide Stop Plunger		
13	Extractor Pin	35	Mainspring Plunger	57	Slide Stop Plunger Spring		
14	Extractor Spring	36	Manual Safety	58	Slide Stop Spiral Pin		
15	Firing Pin	37	Manual Safety Plunger	59	Stock, Left		
16	Firing Pin Spring	38	Manual Safety Plunger Spring	60	Stock, Right		
17	Frame	39	Rear Sight Body	61	Stock Screws		
18	Frame Stud	40	Rear Sight Plunger	62	Trigger		
19	Slide Stop Button	41	Rear Sight Plunger Spring	63	Trigger Plunger		
20	Hammer	42	Rear Sight Slide	64	Trigger Plunger Pin		
21	Stirrup	43	Rear Sight Windage Nut	65	Trigger Plunger Spring		
22	Stirrup Pin	44	Rear Sight Windage Screw	66	Trigger Pin		

Carl R. Hellstrom

Carl Hellstrom was an outstanding production engineer who joined Smith & Wesson at the beginning of World War II at the request of the company president, Harold Wesson.

At the time, the company was in serious financial difficulties after having contracted with the British government to develop a 9mm carbine and then delivering a gun with which the British were not satisfied. As a result, they demanded return of their $1,000,000 cash advance. Smith & Wesson could not comply as they had spent the money developing the carbine. At Hellstrom's suggestion, the company reached a settlement where it would supply the British with an agreed-upon number of M&P revolvers.

Hellstrom continued to manage the company's production through the war years and was able to get things back on track. He was also instrumental in getting the company to build a modern manufacturing facility in its present location on Roosevelt Ave in Springfield.

This modern factory enabled Smith and Wesson to survive the difficult post-war years that adversely affected a number of other firearms companies. Hellstrom's valuable contributions were rewarded when he became president of the company in 1946.

Hellstrom was well aware of the need to develop new products and it was at his urging that the company began developing handguns like the Model 39 as well as revolvers such as the Model 19 Combat Magnum and the Model 29 44 Magnum, all of which were very successful in the marketplace. Even though the Model 39 was not immediately accepted, it paved the way for Smith & Wesson's extensive line of double-action service pistols.

It is safe to say that not only did Carl Hellstrom save the company in the early war years, but he also ensured its growth and survival in the post-war years as well. He died of a heart attack in 1963.

THE COLT PYTHON 357 MAGNUM REVOLVER

One of Colt's Most Prestigious Double-Action Revolvers

At the end of World War II, the Colt Firearms Company faced a serious financial crisis in spite of obtaining various wartime contracts for military weapons. At the end of the war, orders sharply diminished. In a number of ill-advised budget-saving moves, the company was unable to resume the manufacture of it pre-war handgun line until 1947-48. This was partly due to mismanagement and the loss of tools and machinery. The laying off of experienced staff, who would have been able to reconstruct such machinery and tooling from memory, aggravated the situation.

The financial problems also restricted the development of new designs. Instead, a number of familiar handguns such as the Single-Action Army and New Service revolvers were dropped from the revolver line along with the popular Pocket Auto Pistol.

During the early 1950s, the company did refine some of its target models—the Officer's Model, the National Match and Woodsman—with improved grips and fully adjustable rear sights. In addition, the new Officer's Model, now called the Officer's Model Match, was used as a basis for a new revolver called the 357 Magnum.

The 357 Magnum model in turn was the basis for what became one of Colt's most prestigious double-action revolvers, the "Python" 357. What makes this revolver significant is its unique barrel, deluxe finish and other features.

DESIGN CHARACTERISTICS AND FEATURES

The Python was a solid-frame, swing-out cylinder, double-action revolver chambered for the 357 Magnum cartridge. It had basically the same frame and internal mechanism as the Officer's Model Match and the 357 Magnum. In fact, these frames and mechanism date back to 1908 and the introduction of the Army Special model.

One important change to the action was the use of a floating firing pin set in the frame instead of in the face of the hammer. This was first used in the earlier Colt 357 Magnum. What really set the Python apart from its competitors was its barrel, grips and finish. The Python had a ventilated top rib that incorporated a ramped front sight. This feature followed a trend of some pistolsmiths who built special custom versions of the Officer's Model with a top rib. In addition to the top rib, the barrel had an ejector rod shroud under the barrel. This ran the full length of the barrel and contributed greatly to the revolver's overall appearance and balance.

The company advertised the vented barrel rib as being intended to disperse heat to aid in aiming. Others have claimed the real reason was that the machined slots were just to reduce the revolver's overall weight.

Other features included the full-size checkered wood grips of the same type fitted to the Officer's Model Match, a fully adjustable rear sight assembly and a hammer with a wide spur for easier thumb cocking. The revolver had a specially hand-honed action and a highly polished blue finish that Colt advertised as "Royal Blue".

The new revolver was striking in appearance. This, combined with its smooth action—both single and double—ensured that it was an instant success. It also proved to be extremely accurate with both Magnum and 38 Special ammunition. Although, with an unloaded weight of 44 ounces, which was a bit on the heavy side, it was superbly balanced. These attributes helped considerably in reducing the recoil of Magnum ammunition.

SPECIAL MODELS AND VARIATIONS

Even though it was intended as a luxury target revolver, the Python's accuracy and comfort in handling the 357 Magnum cartridge soon made it a favorite with handgun hunters.

At that time, target revolvers were losing popularity to semi-automatic pistols among American competition shooters. Elsewhere in the world, the Python did enjoy some popularity in the International Center Fire Match.

During the early years of the newly formed sport of Police Practical Pistol Shooting, the Python's balance, accuracy and smooth action made it a popular revolver with some competitors. It remained quite popular in the Distinguished Match that placed restrictions on the highly tuned, bull-barrel revolvers that were dominating the sport.

The Python enjoyed some popularity among law enforcement, which caused Colt to bring out a 4-inch barrel model that was dubbed the "Police" Python. Police use of the revolver remained limited, however, mainly because of the Python's high price.

In 1981, Colt introduced the Python Hunter with rubber grips and an 8-inch barrel to which was mounted a Leupold

When the Python was first introduced, it was Colt's most prestigious double-action revolver in terms of fit and finish. The first revolvers had 6-inch barrels. Later, 4-inch-barreled models like the one shown here were introduced for law enforcement and defensive use.

The Colt Python (bottom) has many similarities to the post-war Officer's Model Match (top). All share similar features such as large target wood grips, flat topstrap with a fully adjustable rear sight and a broad spur hammer. This Python has a bright stainless steel finish.

2X scope. It came in a padded aluminum carrying case and was only made for one year. The Python Silhouette was exactly the same as the Hunter except for the name roll-stamped on the barrel. In addition, the scope was moved slightly to the rear and it came in a black carrying case.

In 1983, the first stainless steel version was introduced. It had a brushed matte finish and was followed two years later by the Python Ultimate, which had a bright, highly polished stainless finish.

In 1996, Colt's financial difficulties forced production of the Python to be terminated from its handgun line.

BARREL LENGTHS, CALIBERS, GRIPS AND FINISHES

The first Python had a 6-inch barrel, which remained the standard length for many years. Later, 4-inch barrel models were introduced followed shortly afterwards by 2 1/2-inch and finally 8-inch versions. The latter length was offered without the scopes of the Hunter and Silhouette models.

The Python's most notable feature was its heavy, full-lug barrel with a ventilated top rib.

actually released for sale.

For many years Pythons could only be had with the Colt Royal Blue finish. Later, nickel-plated guns were offered. During the 1980s, a satin nickel finish known as Royal Coltguard was applied to some Pythons but ceased after the stainless steel models came online.

THE PYTHON ELITE

This was the last Python to be manufactured, being withdrawn in 1998. It has since been reintroduced as a Custom Shop item where it remains in production at the time of writing. It is one of the few double-action revolvers that Colt still makes.

If the Python has a major fault, it is that it is very expensive to make. A considerable amount of hand fitting and honing of parts is required to create a Python that lives up to its reputation of quality. In addition, it requires a skilled polisher to obtain the superb high gloss of the famous Royal Blue or bright stainless that have become the hallmark of the Python. All this costs money and Pythons have always been expensive revolvers, limited to those few who could afford the steep price.

Sadly, in past years, Colt has not always maintained the quality expected of the Python and its reputation has suffered accordingly. In addition, it has faced increasingly stiff competition from revolvers made by other companies. These have often been equipped with heavy, full-lugged barrels

A limited number of Pythons were made with 3-inch barrels. For many years Pythons came with the large target-style checkered grips, although the design was changed slightly to accommodate the use of speed loaders. The first 2 1/2-inch models had the smaller grips usually fitted to the Official Police revolvers for better concealment. Service rubber stocks were first fitted to the Hunter and later to the stainless models. Combat-style rubber grips were offered as an option during the late 1980s.

The 357 Magnum is the most common caliber of the Python, although a limited run of 38 Special models was made with 8-inch barrels. It is said that a very limited number of Pythons have been made in calibers that include 256 Winchester, 41 Magnum and 44 Special. These were probably restricted to factory experimental models. While the Pythons were advertised as being made in 22 LR and 22 WMR, it seems that such revolvers were never

The Python was the first Colt revolver to employ a frame-mounted floating firing pin. It had the same fully ajustable rear sight and large wood grips as those of the Officer's Model Match and the Colt 357 Magnum revolvers.

including some with ventilated top ribs; a tribute to the trend started and set by the Python.

Even though copied and imitated, a quality-made Python can stand on its own in terms of appearance, balance, finish and performance. Lucky are those who have one.

LOADING AND UNLOADING THE PYTHON

Unloading and loading a Python is exactly the same as for the Detective Special described in an earlier chapter. Remember that the cylinder latch is pulled to the rear and not pushed forward to release the cylinder from the frame.

SHOOTING AND HANDLING THE PYTHON

The Python is Colt's premier double-action revolver and as such has a performance that matches its attractive flowing lines. My bright, stainless steel, 6-inch-barreled model is one of my most prized double-action revolvers.

Pythons are capable of excellent accuracy not only with magnums but also 38 Special target wadcutters. In addition to its great inherent accuracy, one of its great attributes is its fine balance.

The heavy, ribbed barrel with all the weight up front just seems to keep the sights as steady as rock. Its excellent sights and superb single-action trigger make it a natural for accurate shooting. A good friend of mine won the Rhodesian National Center Fire Match for some 17 years with a 6-inch-barreled Python.

The heavy barrel also aids in reducing recoil when shooting magnum ammunition. All of these factors also make the Python a popular handgun for hunting, especially when fitted with scope.

A 4-inch-barreled Python makes a fine revolver for defense. It still has above-average accuracy and the heavy barrel helps in minimizing the recoil of magnum ammunition. Its double-action trigger is one of the best of all Colt double actions. It is light and smooth although it does tend to stack near the end of the stroke.

I am not bothered by the stacking, which I find helps in long-range, double-action shooting if a two-stage trigger pull is used. Still, there are Python critics who do not like the Python's double-action trigger.

The fact is there are gunsmiths who specialize in working on the Python who can eliminate the stack and reduce the pull down to 6 or 7 pounds. To be honest, this is far too light for safety or reliability and is best left for seasoned shooters.

As with most revolvers, the Python can be improved by fitting a set of custom grips and replacing the standard rear sight with an Eliason target sight, which is used in the Gold Cup.

COLLECTOR INTEREST

As Colt's top-line revolver, the Pythons were expensive. Surprisingly, used model values have hardly risen at all. A Python, in good condition, is a good candidate for shooting.

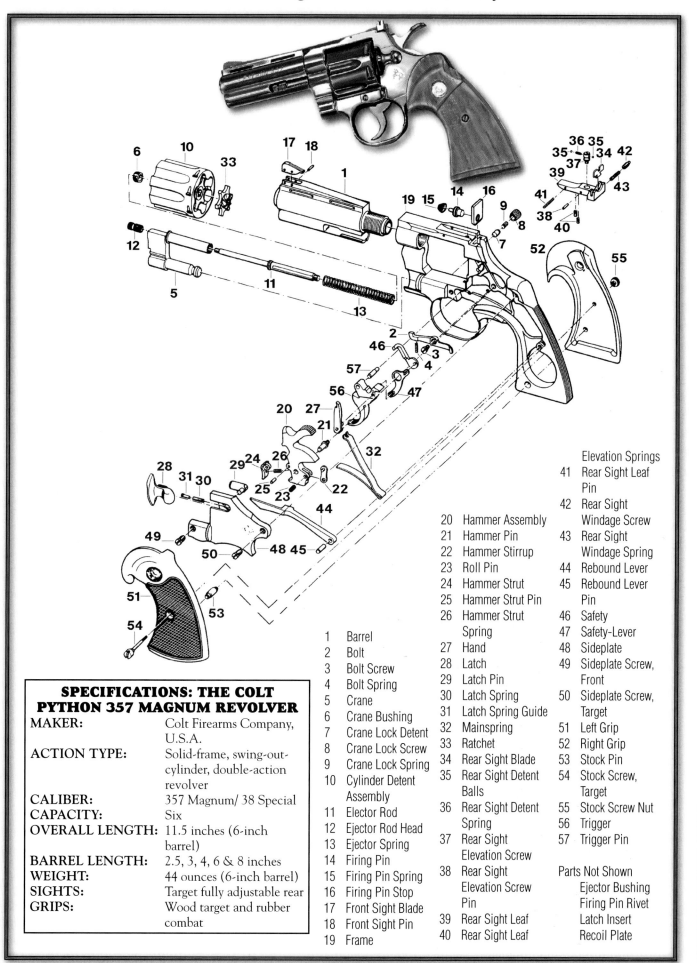

6 10 33 17 18 1 19 15 14 16 36 35 35 34 42 37 39 41 38 40 43 9 8 7 52 55 12 5 11 13 2 46 3 4 57 56 47 20 27 21 32 28 31 30 29 24 26 25 23 22 44 49 50 48 45 51 53 54

20	Hammer Assembly		Elevation Springs
21	Hammer Pin	41	Rear Sight Leaf Pin
22	Hammer Stirrup	42	Rear Sight Windage Screw
23	Roll Pin	43	Rear Sight Windage Spring
24	Hammer Strut	44	Rebound Lever
25	Hammer Strut Pin	45	Rebound Lever Pin
26	Hammer Strut Spring	46	Safety
27	Hand	47	Safety-Lever
28	Latch	48	Sideplate
29	Latch Pin	49	Sideplate Screw, Front
30	Latch Spring	50	Sideplate Screw, Target
31	Latch Spring Guide	51	Left Grip
32	Mainspring	52	Right Grip
33	Ratchet	53	Stock Pin
34	Rear Sight Blade	54	Stock Screw, Target
35	Rear Sight Detent Balls	55	Stock Screw Nut
36	Rear Sight Detent Spring	56	Trigger
37	Rear Sight Elevation Screw	57	Trigger Pin
38	Rear Sight Elevation Screw Pin		Parts Not Shown
39	Rear Sight Leaf		Ejector Bushing
40	Rear Sight Leaf		Firing Pin Rivet
			Latch Insert
			Recoil Plate

1	Barrel
2	Bolt
3	Bolt Screw
4	Bolt Spring
5	Crane
6	Crane Bushing
7	Crane Lock Detent
8	Crane Lock Screw
9	Crane Lock Spring
10	Cylinder Detent Assembly
11	Elector Rod
12	Ejector Rod Head
13	Ejector Spring
14	Firing Pin
15	Firing Pin Spring
16	Firing Pin Stop
17	Front Sight Blade
18	Front Sight Pin
19	Frame

SPECIFICATIONS: THE COLT PYTHON 357 MAGNUM REVOLVER

MAKER:	Colt Firearms Company, U.S.A.
ACTION TYPE:	Solid-frame, swing-out-cylinder, double-action revolver
CALIBER:	357 Magnum/ 38 Special
CAPACITY:	Six
OVERALL LENGTH:	11.5 inches (6-inch barrel)
BARREL LENGTH:	2.5, 3, 4, 6 & 8 inches
WEIGHT:	44 ounces (6-inch barrel)
SIGHTS:	Target fully adjustable rear
GRIPS:	Wood target and rubber combat

THE RUGER BLACKHAWK 357 MAGNUM SINGLE-ACTION REVOLVER

The First Really Modern Single-Action Revolver

The Blackhawk is another example of one of the successful handgun designs of Bill Ruger and his company. While the revolver is based on the design of the original Colt Model "P" Single-Action Army, it has a number of modern improvements that help resolve some of the weaknesses of the old Peacemaker. It continues to be made today with few changes from when it became an instant success after being introduced in 1955.

THE RUGER "SINGLE SIX" 22 REVOLVERS

The Blackhawk was a logical development of Ruger's second handgun venture, a 22 single-action revolver called the "Single Six." It was introduced in 1953, which could not have been timelier, as shooters were still dealing with the fact that the Colt Single-Action Army was no more.

The revolver was slightly smaller in size than the original Frontier revolver because of its chambering for the 22 cartridge. It was both functional and reliable and far more reasonably priced than the few available Colt SAAs. It retained the appearance and handling qualities of the originals, all of which ensured its success in the marketplace.

The first models had a disc-style loading gate, although this was later upgraded to one of the traditional design. The Single Six was joined in 1958 by a similar, slightly smaller revolver called the "Bearcat." Its other difference was a plain un-fluted cylinder.

Following the success of the Single Six, Ruger followed up with a full-size version chambered for the 357 Magnum cartridge. Called the Blackhawk and introduced in 1955, the new revolver was just as successful.

DESIGN CHARACTERISTICS AND FEATURES

While the Blackhawk and Single Six closely resembled the Colt Single-Action Army in appearance and basic design, there were a number of important differences.

Most important was the use of coil springs throughout the action. These are more durable than the flat springs used in the Colt, and they effectively resolved the problem of breakage. Like the Single Six, the Blackhawk has a one-piece grip frame investment cast of an aluminum alloy. This not only simplifies construction, but it also helps in correcting the problem of the backstrap and trigger guard assemblies loosening during firing. The ejector rod housing is also an aluminum alloy casting.

The frame, cylinder and barrel are all made of chrome molybdenum steel, the former being a high-quality investment casting. The frame differs from the Colt SAA in that the topstrap is flat instead of round. This provides a home for a fully adjustable rear sight assembly. The firing pin is of the floating type located in the frame instead of being part of the hammer. This reduced the chance of the primer being driven back into the firing pin hole. This improvement, however, did not resolve the problem of the revolver discharging if dropped on its hammer or struck a heavy blow.

The Blackhawk retained the same method of loading and unloading as the traditional single action.

THE SUPER BLACKHAWK

In 1956, Ruger came out with a Blackhawk chambered for the 44 Magnum cartridge. The revolver was identical in size and appearance to the 357 Magnum versions, and while the revolver had the strength to handle the cartridge, recoil was on the heavy side.

In 1950, a 44 Magnum revolver was introduced that had a larger frame, a square-backed trigger guard and a plain un-fluted cylinder. Called the "Super Blackhawk," it became an instant hit with handgun hunters.

Blackhawks of any vintage used coil springs in the action and have a one-piece grip frame, which helps resolve the old problem of screws loosening during firing.

Both the Blackhawk and Super Blackhawk have the firing pin mounted in the frame as well as modern features like a fully adjustable rear sight set in the rear of a flat top frame. The Super Blackhawk introduced two lugs at the rear of the topstrap to provide protection for the sight.

THE "NEW MODEL" SINGLE ACTIONS

Up until 1973, the Blackhawk underwent very few changes or modifications. Probably the most noticeable of all was a change to the topstrap that consisted of a protective shroud around the rear sight assembly.

The revolver was still susceptible to accidents if carried fully loaded and the hammer was struck a heavy blow. The company resolved this problem by redesigning the action to include a transfer bar safety. This mechanism consists of a sliding bar that rides up between the face of the hammer and the frame-mounted firing pin to enable the former to strike the latter to ignite the primer. This only occurs if the trigger is properly cycled.

This changed the loading operation. No longer does the hammer have to be placed on half-cock. Simply opening the loading gate disconnects the trigger and unlocks the cylinder. The new mechanism was fitted to all Super Blackhawk, Blackhawk and Single Six models that are identified by the prefix "New Model."

Ruger also designed a replacement mechanism that could be retrofitted by the factory to all the earlier single-action models at no cost to the owner. This offer remains in force at the time of writing.

Other changes included adding a sight shroud to the topstrap and replacing the hammer, trigger and cylinder frame screws with two single pins. These pins do not jar loose during firing like screws tend to do.

THE HAWKEYE AND BLACKHAWK SRM

During the early 1960s, Ruger, together with Colt and Smith & Wesson, announced they would be making a handgun chambered for a hot new wildcat cartridge called the 256 Magnum.

All three companies experienced problems with the tapered cartridge case setting back in the chamber during firing. The latter two companies abandoned the project, but Ruger persevered, producing a single-shot pistol called the Hawkeye in 1963.

The Hawkeye was basically a Blackhawk with the cylinder replaced with a unique rotating breechblock. Sales were not as anticipated and production ceased after a year.

The SRM was a New Model Blackhawk with a

lengthened cylinder to chamber the new 357 Maximum cartridge, which was a 357 Magnum with a lengthened case that produced velocities in the region of 1600 fps. The revolver was withdrawn shortly after it was introduced in 1982 because of unresolvable problems caused by excessive gas cutting of the topstrap and erosion of the forcing cone.

THE BISLEY MODELS

In 1986, Ruger introduced a new single action with a Blackhawk upper body and a grip patterned after the Colt Bisley target single actions. It was appropriately called the "Bisley" and the first model was chambered for the 44 Magnum. A smaller version that was based on the Single Six was also made in 32 Magnum and 22 LR. The Bisleys were made with a blue finish only and smooth wood grips. Both fluted and un-fluted cylinders were offered.

CALIBERS, BARREL LENGTHS, GRIPS AND FINISHES

The first Single Six had a 5 1/2-inch barrel, grips of black checkered plastic, an all blue finish and was chambered for the 22 RF cartridge. Later revolvers were chambered for the 22

All the original Blackhawks were loaded and unloaded like the Colt Frontier. The hammer was placed in the second or half-cock notch to free the cylinder and the loading gate opened to access the chambers.

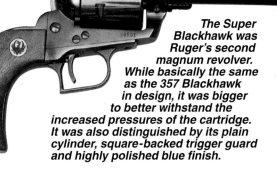

The Super Blackhawk was Ruger's second magnum revolver. While basically the same as the 357 Blackhawk in design, it was bigger to better withstand the increased pressures of the cartridge. It was also distinguished by its plain cylinder, square-backed trigger guard and highly polished blue finish.

WRM Magnum round. A number of revolvers with dual 22 LR and 22 WRM cylinders were also made.

Barrel lengths included 4-5/8, 5-1/2, 6-1/2 and 9-1/2 inches. Single Sixes were generally finished in all blue. Some lightweight, alloy-frame models were offered with a duo-tone finish. These had the frame and grip frame with a gray/silver-anodized finish while the barrel, cylinder and ejector housing had a blue finish.

The introduction of the New Models with the transfer bar system saw the introduction of all stainless steel Single Sixes and Blackhawks. The frame now had a flat top and a fully adjustable rear sight. The plastic grips were replaced with smooth wood ones. Calibers remained the same although revolvers chambered for 32 Magnum were now offered.

The first Blackhawks were chambered for the 357 Magnum cartridge, had 4 5/8-, 6 1/2- and 10-inch barrels. Like the Single Six, grips were of a black checkered material and finishes were all blue.

In the years leading up to the introduction of the New Models, other calibers were added to include 45 Colt, 44 Magnum, 41 Magnum and 30 carbine. Convertible models with dual cylinders in 45 Colt and 45 ACP as well as 357 Magnum and 9mm Luger were also offered.

In 1973, with the introduction of the transfer bar safety, the first stainless steel Blackhawks were introduced. These stainless models had a matte brushed finish. By this time, the black grips had been replaced with smooth wood panels.

THE VAQUERO SINGLE ACTIONS

An important feature of the Blackhawk was its fully adjustable rear sight. While most shooters found this desirable, competitors of the new sport of cowboy action shooting preferred fixed-sight single actions of more traditional lines. Ruger's answer came in 1993 with the introduction of the Vaquero.

The revolver followed the basic design of the Blackhawk, except for a round topstrap that contained the traditional fixed sight. The revolver first appeared chambered for 45 Colt, but since then, most of the other popular calibers have been offered. The revolver can be had with a bright stainless steel finish that resembles nickel plating or the traditional blue barrel, cylinder and simulated color case-hardened frame.

Bisley models have since been added to the line, as well as a model with a rounded birdshead, beak-style grip. There are also Vaqueros in 22 LR and 32 Magnum.

Virtually all of the Single Six, Blackhawk, Bisley and Vaquero revolvers remain in production, clear proof of soundness of their respective designs.

LOADING AND UNLOADING THE BLACKHAWK

Loading and unloading an original Single Six, Blackhawk or Super Blackhawk is exactly the same as for the Colt Peacemaker. The hammer is placed on half-cock and the loading gate swung open. Spent cases are removed using the ejector rod. For safety reasons, the revolver should only be loaded and carried with five rounds so that an empty chamber can be placed under the hammer

Stainless steel versions of all the company's single-action models were introduced at the same time as the New Model Blackhawk.

The Blackhawk was a modern version of the classic Colt Single-Action Army revolver. The New Model that replaced the old version in 1970 differs from the first Blackhawk of the 1950s only in a few respects.

All the New Models are a lot easier to load and unload. Opening the loading gate disconnects the firing mechanism and allows the cylinder to rotate. The only drawback is that the cylinder chambers do not automatically index with the ejector rod as they do with the Colt or early model Rugers. In theory, the transfer bar does allow the New Models to be carried with all chambers filled. Cowboy action shooters, however, are still required to load only five chambers.

SHOOTING AND HANDLING THE RUGER BLACKHAWK

All my shooting with the Blackhawk has been confined to cowboy action shooting. Although I already owned a number of Colt Single-Action Armys, I was reluctant to subject any of them to the rigors of competition and risk reducing their value in any way.

Instead, I selected a stainless steel 357 Magnum New Model Ruger Blackhawk, which has served me very well. It was very accurate with 38 Special, which is the ammunition I chose to use in competition.

Although it did not have the same fine balance that my Colts have, its heft reduced any recoil to an absolute minimum. When shooting the more powerful magnum ammunition, recoil was still quite manageable.

The target adjustable sight provided an excellent sight picture. And while the single-action trigger pull was not perfect, it was greatly improved through some action work.

While many shooters express a marked preference for the older model Blackhawks, claiming they had much better trigger actions, I never found this to be the case. In fact, I prefer the new transfer bar action, because it makes loading and unloading simpler and safer.

More importantly, I feel more comfortable when shooting fast strings knowing that if I fumble cocking back the hammer, no serious consequences will result. This has occurred several times in practice and competition with no damage to the revolver. I shudder to think what would have happened to my Colt single actions in similar circumstances.

I have also fired a number of Ruger Bisley models and Vaqueros. Of the two, I prefer the latter because of its close resemblance to the original Peacemaker. I also much preferred its grip to that of the Bisley. I found the fixed sights quite adequate for cowboy action shooting.

The Blackhawks that I have shot all performed flawlessly. I have shot many thousands of rounds in my own New Model Blackhawk and never experienced a single malfunction. It is still as accurate as it ever was and its action is as tight as when I first removed it from its box.

COLLECTER INTEREST

Rugers have become quite collectible and there is a Ruger Collectors Association. Nevertheless, few of the single actions have attracted high values. Rugers are very strong handguns and there is no reason why they cannot be shot.

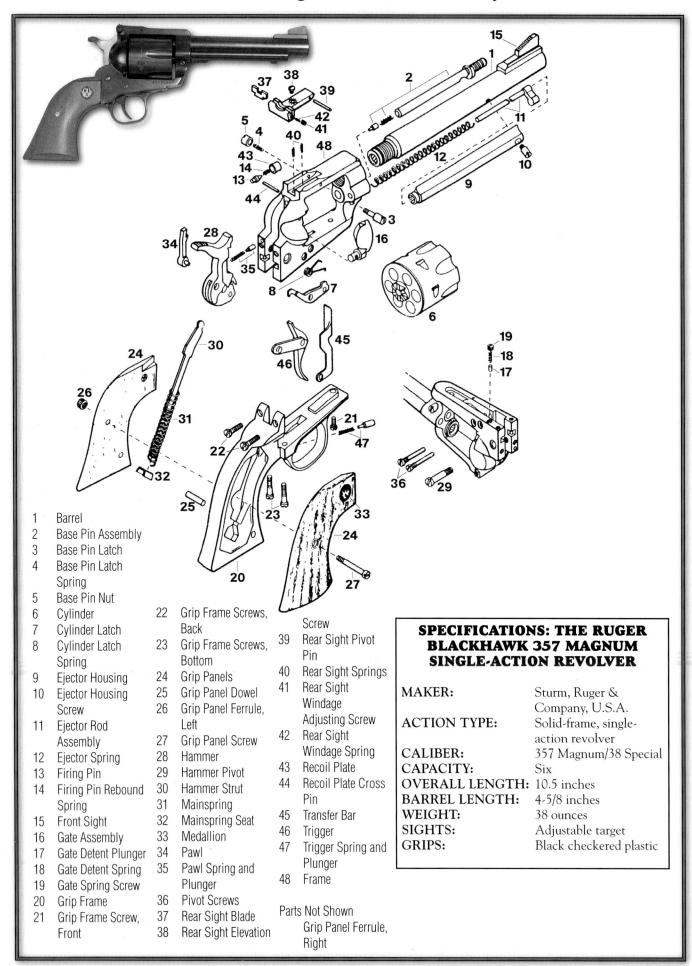

1 Barrel
2 Base Pin Assembly
3 Base Pin Latch
4 Base Pin Latch
  Spring
5 Base Pin Nut
6 Cylinder
7 Cylinder Latch
8 Cylinder Latch
  Spring
9 Ejector Housing
10 Ejector Housing
  Screw
11 Ejector Rod
  Assembly
12 Ejector Spring
13 Firing Pin
14 Firing Pin Rebound
  Spring
15 Front Sight
16 Gate Assembly
17 Gate Detent Plunger
18 Gate Detent Spring
19 Gate Spring Screw
20 Grip Frame
21 Grip Frame Screw,
  Front

22 Grip Frame Screws,
  Back
23 Grip Frame Screws,
  Bottom
24 Grip Panels
25 Grip Panel Dowel
26 Grip Panel Ferrule,
  Left
27 Grip Panel Screw
28 Hammer
29 Hammer Pivot
30 Hammer Strut
31 Mainspring
32 Mainspring Seat
33 Medallion
34 Pawl
35 Pawl Spring and
  Plunger
36 Pivot Screws
37 Rear Sight Blade
38 Rear Sight Elevation

  Screw
39 Rear Sight Pivot
  Pin
40 Rear Sight Springs
41 Rear Sight
  Windage
  Adjusting Screw
42 Rear Sight
  Windage Spring
43 Recoil Plate
44 Recoil Plate Cross
  Pin
45 Transfer Bar
46 Trigger
47 Trigger Spring and
  Plunger
48 Frame

Parts Not Shown
  Grip Panel Ferrule,
  Right

SPECIFICATIONS: THE RUGER BLACKHAWK 357 MAGNUM SINGLE-ACTION REVOLVER

MAKER:	Sturm, Ruger & Company, U.S.A.
ACTION TYPE:	Solid-frame, single-action revolver
CALIBER:	357 Magnum/38 Special
CAPACITY:	Six
OVERALL LENGTH:	10.5 inches
BARREL LENGTH:	4-5/8 inches
WEIGHT:	38 ounces
SIGHTS:	Adjustable target
GRIPS:	Black checkered plastic

THE SMITH & WESSON MODEL 19 COMBAT MAGNUM

A Peace Officer's Dream Revolver

This revolver proved to be one of the most popular 357 Magnum revolvers ever made and a firm favorite with law enforcement. Its popularity was due to the use of the K frame and grip that made it user-friendly for most hand sizes.

One of the objections to the 357 Magnum was that, up until 1955, only large frame revolvers were considered strong enough to handle the high pressures generated by the cartridge. While Colt's use of their .41-size frame in the Python and 357 revolvers did result in a more manageable revolver, it was still on the large side for some.

In 1954, Carl Hellstrom, the company president, asked Bill Jordan what he thought would be an ideal revolver for law enforcement. Jordan, who was a well-known border patrol officer and exhibition shooter, replied that the company should explore the feasibility of a K-frame revolver for the 357 Magnum cartridge.

Hellstrom followed Jordan's advice, and by using improved steels and heat treatment processes, a K-frame 357 Magnum was introduced in November of 1955. Called the Combat Magnum, Bill Jordan referred to it as "the answer to a peace officer's dream."

DESIGN CHARACTERISTICS AND FEATURES

The Combat Magnum was built on a Smith & Wesson K frame that had been lengthened slightly and strengthened in the yoke area to accommodate a slightly longer cylinder chambered to hold six rounds of 357 Magnum cartridges.

The first models had 4-inch heavy barrels that incorporated a top rib and an ejector rod shroud. The revolver came with walnut target stocks and had a fully adjustable rear sight and a ramped front post.

MODIFICATIONS AND UPGRADES

During its life, the Combat underwent relatively few modifications apart from upgrades that were applied to all the company's revolvers at particular points in time.

These included the elimination of the barrel-securing pin, counter-bored cylinders and the fifth screw securing the top of the sideplate.

The first models had a blue finish and a 4-inch barrel. Nickel plating was later offered as an option as were longer and shorter barreled revolvers.

THE STAINLESS MODEL 66

The continuing popularity of the Model 19 (as it became known in 1957) made it an early candidate for a stainless steel version. The first such revolver, designated the Model 66 Combat Magnum Stainless, appeared in 1970.

As the demand for stainless steel revolvers increased, the popularity of the Model 66 soon began to rival that of the Model 19.

The model 19 was a 357 Magnum built on the popular K frame that was specially strengthened to handle the more powerful cartridge. The first revolver had a 4-inch barrel.

THE L-FRAME 357 MAGNUMS

While an argument can be made that these revolvers are different models than the Combat Magnums, there is an association as to why they were developed. Even though the Models 19 and 66 are magnums, the fact is many shooters did most of their shooting with the milder 38 Special than with the more violent 357 ammunition. This reduces considerably the amount of wear and tear the revolver is subjected to if only magnum ammunition be used.

This began to change as concerns about the effectiveness of the 38 Special increased. This resulted in many shooters, especially police officers, shooting a lot more magnum ammunition in their revolvers. In addition, more use was being made of high velocity 38 ammunition such as the +P and +P+ loads. All this placed much more stress on medium-size revolvers like the Model 19/66 and there were reports of the revolvers showing signs of accelerated wear.

While there were no reports of catastrophic blowups or structural failures, Smith & Wesson was concerned enough to seek a remedy. The answer came in a new creation that used a slightly larger frame but retained the same K-size grip. The L frames were released in 1981 in two versions.

The 581 Distinguished Service Magnum had fixed sights and small regular wood grips while the 586 Distinguished Combat Magnum had an adjustable rear sight and the large target grips. Both were made with 4- and 6-inch barrels. Stainless steel versions designated as the 681 and 686 were also introduced.

Apart from its slightly larger frame, the Distinguished Combat Magnum differed from the Model 19 in that it had a heavy barrel with a full-length under lug similar to the Colt Python.

BARREL LENGTHS, GRIPS, FINISHES AND SPECIAL OPTIONS

The first Combat Magnum had a 4-inch barrel, wood target grips and a high polished blue finish. Later, barrel lengths of 6 and 2-1/2 inches were offered. The 2 1/2-inch models had grips with a more rounded back strap and butt for easier concealment. Some 3-inch-barreled guns were also made but these are very rare. Nickel plating was offered as an alternative finish.

The stainless steel Model 66 went through similar changes, as did the 686. The 686 eventually phased out the blue 586 and the fixed-sight 581 models. During the 1990s, Smith & Wesson provided most of the revolvers with Hogue rubber combat grips. The grip frames were also changed from square to round butt. Two rubber grip designs were offered, one a round butt and the other with a slight extension that made it in effect a square butt.

Also, during the 20th century's final decade, Smith & Wesson offered a 6-inch 686 with a ported muzzle and one with a seven-shot cylinder. The Combat Magnum remains in production as the stainless steel Model 66, retaining virtually all of the features that made it such a popular revolver well over 30 years ago.

LOADING AND UNLOADING THE COMBAT MAGNUM

The Model 19 is unloaded and loaded in exactly the same manner as the Military & Police revolver described in an earlier chapter.

The revolver has a heavy un-tapered barrel that has a top rib and a protective shroud underneath for the ejector rod.

SHOOTING AND HANDLING THE COMBAT MAGNUM

I have two Combat Magnums. One is a stainless steel Model 66 with a 4-inch barrel and the other a 6-inch-barreled blue Model 19. Both have above average accuracy and excellent triggers in both single and double action.

Being built on Smith & Wesson's excellent K frame, the trigger is easy to access and control. This, together with the excellent adjustable target sights, almost guarantees good target accuracy. This is especially the case with my 6-inch-barreled Model 19.

Recoil with 357 Magnums is quite mild in my Model 19 and quite controllable in my 4-inch-barreled Model 66. The latter is almost the perfect combat revolver. Its smooth, even, double-action pull is ideally suited for fast accurate shooting at combat distances. Reliability is excellent, as I have yet to experience a single malfunction or misfire with either revolver.

The short 2 1/2-inch-barreled models I have shot have more recoil, especially with magnum ammunition. Recoil, however, can be reduced by fitting a set of aftermarket rubber grips. Like other short-barreled revolvers, these deliver good accuracy and their adjustable rear sight is an asset when sighting them in.

The only thing I have had done to both guns is to fit them with custom rubber grips, which aid in minimizing the effects of recoil. I also have a set of K.N. Nill orthopedic target grips that can convert my Model 19 into an excellent target arm.

As most of my shooting with both revolvers is confined to 38 Special ammunition, shooting loose does not apply to my

Not long after its introduction, the Model 19 was offered with a 6-inch barrel.

revolvers. Both are as tight as the day I first acquired them.

COLLECTOR INTEREST

There appears to be little collector interest and catalog values indicate there has been very little increase in used gun values. Nevertheless, any version of this revolver is an excellent choice for self-defense or for general shooting.

The M66 was the stainless steel version of the Model 19 and proved to be just as popular. This revolver, belonging to the author, has a polished bright finish instead of the standard matte brushed finish.

The revolver has large wood target grips and other features such as a fully adjustable rear sight. The first revolvers also had countersunk chambers.

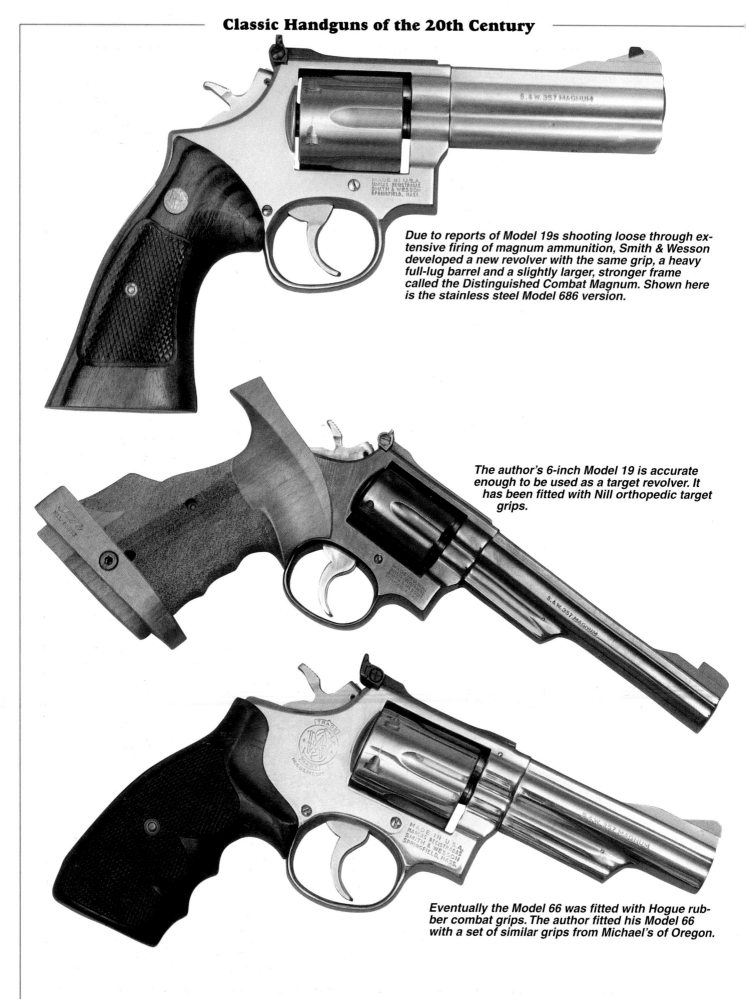

Due to reports of Model 19s shooting loose through extensive firing of magnum ammunition, Smith & Wesson developed a new revolver with the same grip, a heavy full-lug barrel and a slightly larger, stronger frame called the Distinguished Combat Magnum. Shown here is the stainless steel Model 686 version.

The author's 6-inch Model 19 is accurate enough to be used as a target revolver. It has been fitted with Nill orthopedic target grips.

Eventually the Model 66 was fitted with Hogue rubber combat grips. The author fitted his Model 66 with a set of similar grips from Michael's of Oregon.

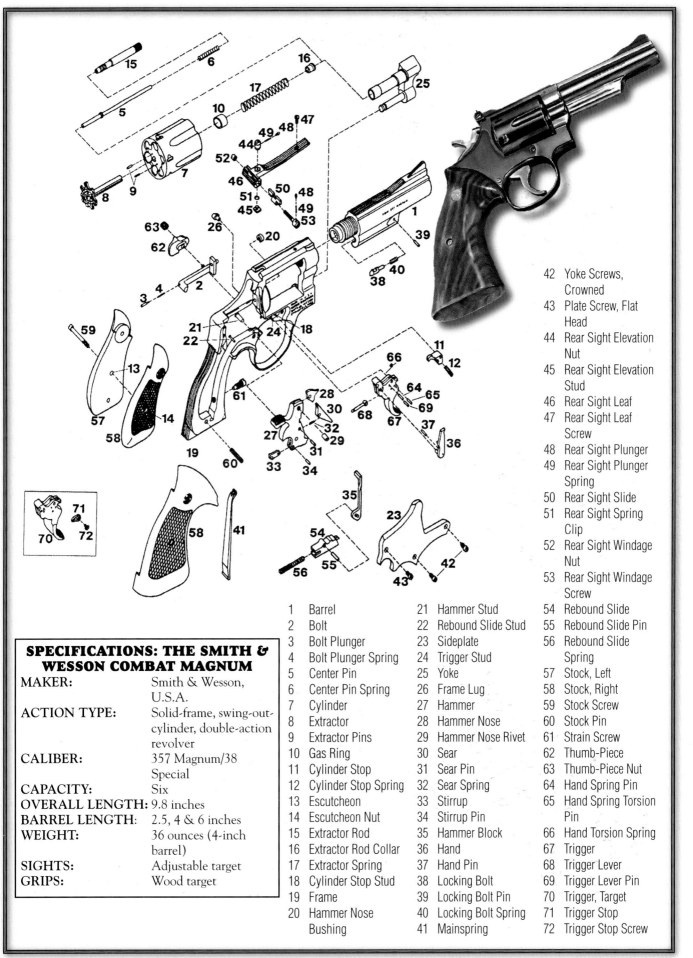

42 Yoke Screws, Crowned
43 Plate Screw, Flat Head
44 Rear Sight Elevation Nut
45 Rear Sight Elevation Stud
46 Rear Sight Leaf
47 Rear Sight Leaf Screw
48 Rear Sight Plunger
49 Rear Sight Plunger Spring
50 Rear Sight Slide
51 Rear Sight Spring Clip
52 Rear Sight Windage Nut
53 Rear Sight Windage Screw
54 Rebound Slide
55 Rebound Slide Pin
56 Rebound Slide Spring
57 Stock, Left
58 Stock, Right
59 Stock Screw
60 Stock Pin
61 Strain Screw
62 Thumb-Piece
63 Thumb-Piece Nut
64 Hand Spring Pin
65 Hand Spring Torsion Pin
66 Hand Torsion Spring
67 Trigger
68 Trigger Lever
69 Trigger Lever Pin
70 Trigger, Target
71 Trigger Stop
72 Trigger Stop Screw

SPECIFICATIONS: THE SMITH & WESSON COMBAT MAGNUM

MAKER:	Smith & Wesson, U.S.A.
ACTION TYPE:	Solid-frame, swing-out-cylinder, double-action revolver
CALIBER:	357 Magnum/38 Special
CAPACITY:	Six
OVERALL LENGTH:	9.8 inches
BARREL LENGTH:	2.5, 4 & 6 inches
WEIGHT:	36 ounces (4-inch barrel)
SIGHTS:	Adjustable target
GRIPS:	Wood target

1 Barrel
2 Bolt
3 Bolt Plunger
4 Bolt Plunger Spring
5 Center Pin
6 Center Pin Spring
7 Cylinder
8 Extractor
9 Extractor Pins
10 Gas Ring
11 Cylinder Stop
12 Cylinder Stop Spring
13 Escutcheon
14 Escutcheon Nut
15 Extractor Rod
16 Extractor Rod Collar
17 Extractor Spring
18 Cylinder Stop Stud
19 Frame
20 Hammer Nose Bushing

21 Hammer Stud
22 Rebound Slide Stud
23 Sideplate
24 Trigger Stud
25 Yoke
26 Frame Lug
27 Hammer
28 Hammer Nose
29 Hammer Nose Rivet
30 Sear
31 Sear Pin
32 Sear Spring
33 Stirrup
34 Stirrup Pin
35 Hammer Block
36 Hand
37 Hand Pin
38 Locking Bolt
39 Locking Bolt Pin
40 Locking Bolt Spring
41 Mainspring

Bill Jordan
and
The Model 19

Bill Jordan was a legendary law officer, an excellent all-around marksman with rifle, shotgun and handgun and exponent of the fast draw with a double-action revolver. In the Border Patrol, he attained the rank of Assistant Chief Inspector.

During his long years of service with this department, he was well acquainted with lethal confrontations with criminal elements along the U.S.-Mexican border.

He was a member of the Border Patrol pistol team and competed in numerous competitions.

During World War II, he served in the Marine Corps, seeing action in most of the major island battles in the Pacific. On his retirement from the Border Patrol, he became a representative of the National Rifle Association, conducting numerous demonstrations of fast double-action shooting and fast draw from a Border Patrol holster; his speed from the holster is what he was most famous for.

A firm advocate of the double-action revolver for law enforcement work, he suggested to Smith & Wesson president Carl Hellstrom that the company examine developing a K-frame-size 357 Magnum revolver.

Hellstrom took his advice and the Combat Magnum was born, the first one off the production line being presented, deservedly, to Bill Jordan.

It was Jordan who coined the description of the Model 19 as "The answer to a Peace Officer's dream" when he was interviewed about the revolver on the television show "You Asked For It."

THE
SMITH & WESSON
44 MAGNUM
(MODEL 29) REVOLVER
The Most Powerful Handgun in the World

This revolver came hot on the heels of the Combat Magnum, being introduced one month later in 1955. It was the company's second magnum revolver, yet another collaborative effort with an ammunition manufacturer to create a new revolver cartridge.

Remington agreed to develop the cartridge while Smith & Wesson worked on a revolver for it. When the project was completed, the revolver was touted as the World's Most Powerful Handgun, a title it was to hold for many years. In many ways, the Model 29 replaced the Model 27 357 Magnum as the company's premier handgun. It also gained immortality at the hands of actor Clint Eastwood in the "Dirty Harry" movies.

HISTORY AND DEVELOPMENT

As with the 357 Magnum, the Model 29 and the 44 Magnum came about thanks to the efforts of a number of civilian shooters who had experimented with improving the performance of the 44 Special through handloading.

One of these shooters was Elmer Keith, who was renowned as a gun writer, hunter and handgun authority. For some years, he had developed high-velocity 44 Special loads that he had successfully used in an N-frame revolver. During the 1950s, he approached Carl Hellstrom of Smith & Wesson and urged him to consider building a dedicated revolver to shoot these high performance loads.

Hellstrom, no doubt remembering how the 357 Magnum had exceeded sales expectations, contacted the Remington ammunition company and got them to agree to develop the cartridge, while Smith & Wesson would work up a revolver for it.

Development of the 44 Magnum began with four specially

heat-treated 44 Hand Ejector revolvers. While these produced favorable results, they did indicate that something slightly heavier was needed. As a result, the production 29 had the diameter of the barrel and frame slightly enlarged and strengthened.

After completion of tests and evaluation, the revolver went into production towards the end of 1955 with one of the first models being presented to Elmer Keith.

DESIGN CHARACTERISTICS AND FEATURES

The Model 29 was a solid-frame, swing-out-cylinder revolver that used the Smith & Wesson large Hand Ejector N frame, which was strengthened, where necessary, to be able to handle the higher pressures developed by the new cartridge. In a similar manner, the barrel and cylinder were also strengthened, and as a result, the revolver had an unloaded weight of 47 ounces.

The revolver's six-shot cylinder was lengthened by 1/8 inch to accommodate the longer 44 Magnum cartridge case. The longer case was not only to contain additional powder but also to prevent the cartridge from being mistakenly loaded in a weaker 44 Special cylinder. The first models had a 6 1/2-inch heavy barrel that incorporated a top rib and a shrouded ejector housing underneath. The revolvers had a ramped front sight blade with colored plastic inserts.

Like the Model 27, the 29 became Smith & Wesson's top-line revolver, and it had all the same deluxe features. These included a highly polished blue finish, large wood target grips, fully adjustable rear sight and a target hammer.

The Model 29 was a large-frame revolver made for the new, powerful 44 Magnum cartridge. It shared many of the characteristics of the Model 27, especially in respect to finish and features.

MODIFICATIONS AND UPGRADES

From the date of its introduction until 1988, the Model 29 underwent relatively few upgrades or improvements other than what was applied to all of the company's revolvers. The most significant occurred in 1960 when the ejector rod thread was changed to one with a left-hand twist to prevent it from loosening during firing. The majority of changes that were made were confined to additional finishes and barrel lengths of special models. A 44 Magnum stainless steel version called the Model 629 was introduced in 1978.

While the Model 29 can be considered a very successful revolver, reports were received that some were shooting loose when fed a steady diet of magnum ammunition or subjected to hot handloaded cartridges, a problem that faces any powerhouse handgun. No matter how powerful factory ammunition may be, there are always those who will try to push the envelope by increasing velocities in handloads. Often this may be done for reasons such as developing more potent ammunition for hunting or higher performance in competition. The 44 Magnum has certainly been subjected to such treatment for many years.

In 1988, the company revised the cylinder lock-up mechanism of the Model 29, making it stronger and less likely to be forced open by the recoil generated by heavy loads. Later, other measures to help reduce the effects of recoil were added such as Hogue rubber grips, full-lugged heavy barrels and un-fluted cylinders. Powerport models were also made with a single compensator placed ahead of the front sight.

THE 41 MAGNUM

Although this is a different model in its own right, it owes its existence to the Model 29. The 41 Magnum cartridge was developed as a cartridge for law enforcement. In the never-ending search for improved stopping power, a few police officers and departments adopted the 44 Magnum over the 38 Special revolver. However, many officers found the excessive recoil hard to handle. A more serious problem was the size of the Model 29, especially in respect to the ability to properly engage the trigger for double-action shooting. This proved to be a real problem for officers with small hands.

A number of gun writers, including Elmer Keith, suggested a milder cartridge of 41 caliber. The idea was that this could be chambered in a medium-size revolver. Smith & Wesson accepted the challenge and collaborated once again with the Remington Ammunition Company to develop a revolver and ammunition. The revolver was introduced in 1963 as the Model 57.

The Model 57 was virtually identical to the Model 29 except for its slightly smaller caliber. It had all the same features including adjustable sights and target grips. Its 41-caliber cartridge was a magnum of slightly less power than the 44 Magnum. This may be why the revolver did not enjoy the success that had been anticipated.

The fact that the Model 57 is no different in size means it is still a difficult revolver to shoot double action for shooters with small hands. To compound the situation, recoil, while less than that of the 44 Magnum, was stiff enough to be intimidating for the unseasoned shooter. It is my opinion that these two aspects are why the revolver was not embraced by law enforcement.

Admittedly, a milder non-magnum load was offered later, and Smith & Wesson did make a fixed-sight 41 Military & Police model called the Model 58. As it was, neither model caught on. Perhaps if they had been introduced together, things might have been different.

A stainless steel version of the 57 known as the 657 was made and the cartridge retains a small but dedicated following. Smith & Wesson continues to make the stainless steel Model 657, having dropped the blue 57 in 1993.

BARREL LENGTHS, GRIPS, FINISHES AND SPECIAL MODELS

The first Model 29s had a 6 1/2-inch barrel, large target grips and a highly polished blue finish. On completion of the first 500 production revolvers, 4-inch barrels were introduced. Very rare are some 500 revolvers made with 5-inch barrels. Although the

The Model 29 used the same large N frame of the Model 27 that was beefed up in the area of the crane. Its barrel was stronger and heavier and did not have the taper of that of the Model 27.

first models were made with a blue finish, nickel-plated models were also available. In 1958, after numerous requests, a new 8-3/8-inch-barreled Model 29 was released. The longest barrel was 10-5/8 inches made for the Model 29 Silhouette models.

In the late 1980s and early 90s, several different grip options were offered. These included wood grips with finger grooves. In keeping with the popular trend of round butt frames, Hogue rubber grips are now fitted that provide the option of having either a square or round butt. Several commemorative 29s and 629s have been made, some of which were engraved, such as the Elmer Keith commemorative edition recognizing his contribution to the creation of the revolver and its cartridge.

The 629 Classic models had all the cylinder locking upgrades, a heavy full-lugged barrel and a bright stainless steel finish.

Other special models include the Classic Hunters with un-fluted cylinders and the Mountain models that have 4-inch tapered barrels for ease of carry.

The Classic Powerport was designed to reduce recoil as much as possible. It had a full-lug barrel with a large port in the muzzle. It also had Hogue grips.

Although the 44 Magnum is no longer the world's most powerful handgun, it remains popular with big bore revolver shooters and hunters and remains in production.

Like the 27, the Model 29 had many of the same deluxe features, like a target hammer and a fully adjustable rear sight.

The first barrels had a ramp front sight with a red plastic insert.

LOADING AND UNLOADING THE MODEL 29

Loading and unloading the 29 is the same as for all the Smith & Wesson revolvers previously described. One thing that those who handload need to be aware of is that any evidence of hard or difficult extraction of spent cases from the chamber may be a warning that pressures are too high.

SHOOTING AND HANDLING THE MODEL 29

Even though the 44 Magnum and the Model 29 can no longer claim to be the world's most powerful handgun, it still has an impressive performance. Because of this, recoil is far greater than that of the 357 and other magnums of a smaller caliber.

In fact, recoil is enough to make the shooting of some models unpleasant and e v e n

painful. In my experience, it is the shorter-barreled versions that have the most recoil. Revolvers with barrels 4 inches or longer are reasonably comfortable to shoot.

Looking at the revolver's other strengths, its deluxe finish is equal to that of any comparable revolver. It is capable of delivering excellent accuracy with both 44 Magnum and 44 Special ammunition. This is complemented by its fine trigger action, excellent target-grade adjustable sights and target wood grips, which all enable it to deliver excellent long-range accuracy. This accuracy and great stopping power is why it has been a popular choice for handgun hunting and long range silhouette shooting.

I have found that my two Model 629s perform best when I shoot them single action. Fast double-action shooting is difficult, even though the 29 has an excellent, smooth DA trigger pull. The problem is that the muzzle lift generated by the recoil, even with

The Model 629 was the stainless steel version of the Model 29. This revolver has been given a custom bright polished finish.

long-barrel models, inhibits fast recovery between shots. This is compounded with short-barrel models because the backstrap tends to be driven back sharply into the web of the hand, making shooting both difficult and painful.

Recoil effects can be reduced by fitting rubber grips and using compensating devices such as porting and Magna-porting. I have used both with some success on my 629. I was concerned that the rubber grips might adversely affect my ability to properly engage the double-action trigger. As it turned out, the grips were thinner and actually improved my trigger reach.

While the revolver can be used for self-defense, there are better choices available. The 29's defensive capabilities are best used as a back-up gun for hunting dangerous game. This is for what the slim-barreled Mountain models were intended. The trouble is that their lighter weight increases their recoil quite substantially, and they are very unpleasant to shoot.

As already mentioned, the later 29s were strengthened to enable them to hold up better when shot extensively with hot-loaded magnums. The older models are still safe enough to handle most factory-grade ammunition. Much depends on how the revolver is shot. Firing the revolver slowly and deliberately is not going to tear it up as much as rapid, double-action shooting will. Careful use of high-velocity, hotly loaded magnums is also advisable.

A good friend of mine was an avid handloader who delighted in developing handloads at the extreme limits of what was considered safe. I can still hear him whooping with delight as his Model 29 kicked viciously in his hand. It was not long before the revolver developed end shake and exhibited signs of gas cutting of the topstrap.

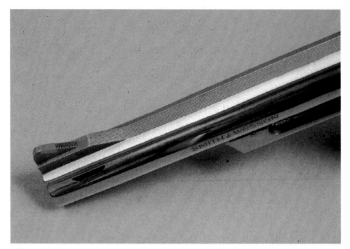

The 44 Magnum develops heavy recoil. The author's bright stainless 629 has been Magna-Ported. This consists of two small slots on the top of the muzzle that deflect gases up to help reduce recoil.

In contrast, my two stainless 44 Magnums are as tight as the day I purchased them. The fact is the Model 29, when used with proper loads, can be an enjoyable and fun gun to shoot for many years.

COLLECTOR INTEREST

As with other Smith & Wesson hand-ejector revolvers, the 44 Magnums do not command high values or collector interest. Exceptions are engraved and presentation models. Being strong revolvers, they are suitable to use and shoot.

During the late 1980s and early 90s, Smith & Wesson revamped the Model 29 and 629 by strengthening the cylinder-locking mechanism and fitting longer, full-lug, heavy barrels. This 7 1/2-inch-barreled 629 has been fitted with an aftermarket scope.

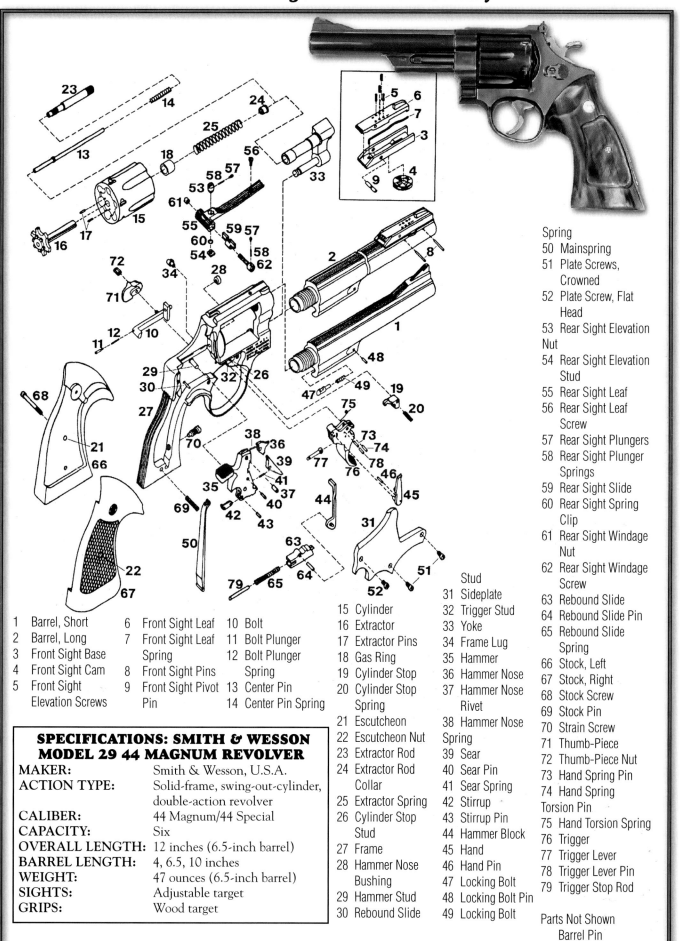

Spring
50 Mainspring
51 Plate Screws, Crowned
52 Plate Screw, Flat Head
53 Rear Sight Elevation Nut
54 Rear Sight Elevation Stud
55 Rear Sight Leaf
56 Rear Sight Leaf Screw
57 Rear Sight Plungers
58 Rear Sight Plunger Springs
59 Rear Sight Slide
60 Rear Sight Spring Clip
61 Rear Sight Windage Nut
62 Rear Sight Windage Screw
63 Rebound Slide
64 Rebound Slide Pin
65 Rebound Slide Spring
66 Stock, Left
67 Stock, Right
68 Stock Screw
69 Stock Pin
70 Strain Screw
71 Thumb-Piece
72 Thumb-Piece Nut
73 Hand Spring Pin
74 Hand Spring Torsion Pin
75 Hand Torsion Spring
76 Trigger
77 Trigger Lever
78 Trigger Lever Pin
79 Trigger Stop Rod

Parts Not Shown
Barrel Pin

1 Barrel, Short
2 Barrel, Long
3 Front Sight Base
4 Front Sight Cam
5 Front Sight Elevation Screws
6 Front Sight Leaf
7 Front Sight Leaf Spring
8 Front Sight Pins
9 Front Sight Pivot Pin
10 Bolt
11 Bolt Plunger
12 Bolt Plunger Spring
13 Center Pin
14 Center Pin Spring

15 Cylinder
16 Extractor
17 Extractor Pins
18 Gas Ring
19 Cylinder Stop
20 Cylinder Stop Spring
21 Escutcheon
22 Escutcheon Nut
23 Extractor Rod
24 Extractor Rod Collar
25 Extractor Spring
26 Cylinder Stop Stud
27 Frame
28 Hammer Nose Bushing
29 Hammer Stud
30 Rebound Slide

31 Sideplate
32 Trigger Stud
33 Yoke
34 Frame Lug
35 Hammer
36 Hammer Nose
37 Hammer Nose Rivet
38 Hammer Nose Stud
39 Sear
40 Sear Pin
41 Sear Spring
42 Stirrup
43 Stirrup Pin
44 Hammer Block
45 Hand
46 Hand Pin
47 Locking Bolt
48 Locking Bolt Pin
49 Locking Bolt

SPECIFICATIONS: SMITH & WESSON MODEL 29 44 MAGNUM REVOLVER

MAKER:	Smith & Wesson, U.S.A.
ACTION TYPE:	Solid-frame, swing-out-cylinder, double-action revolver
CALIBER:	44 Magnum/44 Special
CAPACITY:	Six
OVERALL LENGTH:	12 inches (6.5-inch barrel)
BARREL LENGTH:	4, 6.5, 10 inches
WEIGHT:	47 ounces (6.5-inch barrel)
SIGHTS:	Adjustable target
GRIPS:	Wood target

Elmer Keith

Elmer Keith was born in 1899 in Missouri. In 1905, Keith and his family moved out West to a mining town in Montana. Here, young Elmer witnessed the waning years of American frontier life, growing up among cowboys, miners and other pioneer types. He became acquainted with a few early lawmen and witnessed a gunfight or two. He developed an interest in firearms and hunting at an early age.

As a young man, he became a cowboy in Montana, herding cattle and breaking in horses and participating in rodeos. After he married, he moved to Salmon, Idaho, where he remained until the end of his life. He continued an active outdoor life, working as a hunting outfitter.

His interest in firearms continued, and he had plenty of opportunity to sharpen his shooting skills with handgun, rifle and shotgun. He competed in a number of rifle and handgun competitions with some measure of success. He experimented with developing a number of high performance handgun handloads that he used to take a variety of game.

When he was about 25, he began to write about his hunting and shooting exploits for several firearm publications. His outspoken views on many shooting subjects soon garnered him a loyal following of shooters. He was soon recognized as an authority on handguns. He wrote several books, with his work *Six-guns* being considered a classic.

He was an enthusiastic advocate of both the single- and double-action revolver. He also became an authority on long-range shooting with handguns as well as handgun hunting. His experimentation with various powerful large-caliber handloads caused him to suggest to Carl Hellstrom of Smith & Wesson the possibility of developing an exceptionally powerful 44 revolver.

The result was the creation of the Model 29 44 Magnum of which he was presented the first one off the production line. His hunting exploits included a safari to Africa where he shot specimens of all the major animals.

His long, active life ended sadly when he suffered a stroke in 1981 that left him bedridden and mute. He passed away without recovering in 1984.

THE SMITH & WESSON MODEL 60 REVOLVER

The World's First All–Stainless Steel Handgun

The impact that this small revolver has had on handgun development is completely out of proportion to its size. Introduced in 1965, the Model 60 was the world's first production handgun to be made of stainless steel. It began a trend that has been followed by virtually all of the major handgun manufacturers.

DESIGN CHARACTERISTICS AND FEATURES

The Model 60 was simply a Model 36 Chief's Special, a small, J-frame, 2-inch, 38 Special revolver manufactured of stainless steel instead of blue carbon steel. Its internal mechanism was identical to that in the Model 36.

In the first revolvers, the hammer, trigger and various components of the lockwork were made of un-tempered stainless steel, but these were not entirely successful. The parts were later hardened and eventually hard chrome plated to improve their resistance to wear.

The first models had a highly polished finish, but as this was undesirable for police use, the finish was later changed to a less-reflective satin-brushed appearance.

THE ADVANTAGES AND DRAWBACKS OF STAINLESS STEEL

Smith & Wesson's main objective in introducing the Model 60 was to provide a revolver that had low maintenance and that was resistant to rust and corrosion. As small, short-barreled revolvers are often concealed close to the body, they can be exposed to moisture from perspiration. The salts and acids from this can cause rusting if the revolver is not well cared for on a regular basis. The problem can be aggravated in moist climates, especially near the coast. Stainless guns are, therefore, much more durable and require less maintenance in such conditions.

One downside of stainless steel, however, is that it is difficult to machine. Another problem is that it tends to gall when two surfaces come in contact. This causes rough actions and reliability problems with semi-automatic firearms. Machining can be reduced by lowering the chromium content, while galling can be improved through hardening and tempering processes. The former solution does, however, reduce somewhat resistance to rust and corrosion.

While the introduction of the Model 60 was considered sensational, not everyone welcomed the new revolver with open arms. Traditionalists claimed the revolver's trigger was rougher than the blue Model 36 and that its resistance to rust was not much better than blue steel. In fact, there are still some who claim that stainless guns are not very rust resistant. The fact is, while a Model 60 (or any other stainless gun) will rust in extreme conditions, it is still far superior to what a blue gun can endure.

The Smith & Wesson Model 60 was the world's first handgun to be made of stainless steel. This revolver has custom rubber stocks in place of the smaller factory wood grips.

In developing the Model 60, Smith & Wesson took a bold gamble that has paid off. Before long, the company introduced stainless steel models of all of the company's popular handguns.

DESIGN CHARACTERISTICS AND FEATURES

As already stated, the Model 60 was a stainless steel version of the Model 36 Chief's Special. As such, it is a small, short-barreled, solid-frame, swing-out-cylinder revolver made of stainless steel. The revolver had a round grip frame and wood grips.

The Model 60 is a small J-frame revolver that is virtually a stainless steel version of the popular Model 36 Chief's Special.

As with all J-frame models, the Model 60 had a five-shot cylinder. Sights were fixed. Some internal parts, such as the hammer and trigger, were hard chrome plated.

RELATED MODELS

The enormous success of the Model 60 prompted Smith & Wesson to offer stainless versions of the other J-frame revolvers. In addition, lightweight versions were also made with silver-anodized aluminum frames and barrels and cylinders of stainless steel.

Popular models included the 640, a stainless steel version of the Model 40 Centennial concealed-hammer revolver, and the Model 649, a stainless Bodyguard with a shrouded hammer. The Airweight versions of both revolvers were also offered. Both revolvers had aluminum alloy frames with barrels and cylinders made of stainless steel.

CALIBERS, BARREL LENGTHS AND GRIPS

The first Model 60 was chambered for the 38 Special cartridge, had a 2-inch barrel and wood grips. Initially, like all the other J-frame revolvers, the company did not warrant the Model 60 for use with 38 Special +P loads. Eventually, the Model 60, together with other J-frame revolvers, was rated for +P ammunition.

Later, models chambered for the 357 Magnum were also made. Other calibers included 32 Magnum. A number of Centennial models were chambered for the 9mm Luger cartridge.

A special version of the Model 60 was used for the Ladysmith revolvers that were made for the women's market.

While 2 inches was the most common barrel length, some Centennial, Airweights and 9mm were made with 3-inch barrels. In addition, a number of special order revolvers were made with 3-inch, full-lugged compensated barrels.

While the original grips were the standard round wood type, as more powerful chamberings were added, these were replaced by rubber combat stocks from Hogue and Uncle Mike's.

Today, the Model 60 remains in production. In fact, it survives together with the other stainless steel revolvers that it helped create.

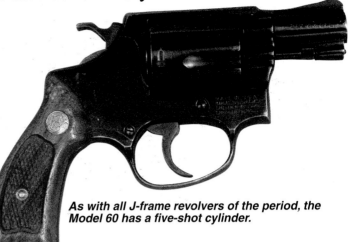

As with all J-frame revolvers of the period, the Model 60 has a five-shot cylinder.

LOADING AND UNLOADING THE MODEL 60

The Model 60 and its progeny are unloaded and loaded just like all the other Smith & Wesson revolvers described in earlier chapters. One point needs to be mentioned, however. The ejector rod has a short stroke and needs to be rapped quite smartly if all the chambers are to be cleared properly.

SHOOTING AND HANDLING
THE MODEL 60

Before commenting on my impression of shooting the Model 60, I must first say that I am not a great fan of short-barreled, five-shot revolvers. I find most of them have sharp recoil and excessive muzzle blast. Their hard kick is difficult to control because of their small slim grips and this also makes it difficult to obtain a proper engagement of the double-action trigger. This gives me the impression that the trigger pull is harder and heavier than it really is.

In spite of these detractions, I have to admit that I was very impressed with the Model 60 when I first handled one and shot it. Like most short-barrel revolvers, it had good accuracy.

Its small size made it very concealable and its stainless steel construction reduced maintenance to an absolute minimum. In addition, it removed the concerns of rust and corrosion if carried close to the body.

Its small fixed sights are quite adequate. As with other Smith & Wesson revolvers, it has a very good trigger, although as I already stated, the double-action pull is compromised by its small grips and sharp recoil.

The good news is that most of these faults can be resolved by fitting a good set of aftermarket custom grips of wood or rubber. The latter are the best for reducing recoil. In addition, these grips provide me with a firmer hold that enables me to exercise better control of the double-action trigger.

The downside is that these grips, being larger, do somewhat compromise its very compact size. Nevertheless, for me this is a small sacrifice to pay for the improvement in performance. This is all I need to turn what is a very fine revolver into a fine shooter.

COLLECTOR INTEREST

The M60 and its progeny have little collector interest and prices of used specimens are not overly high. They are, therefore, still a viable choice for concealed carry.

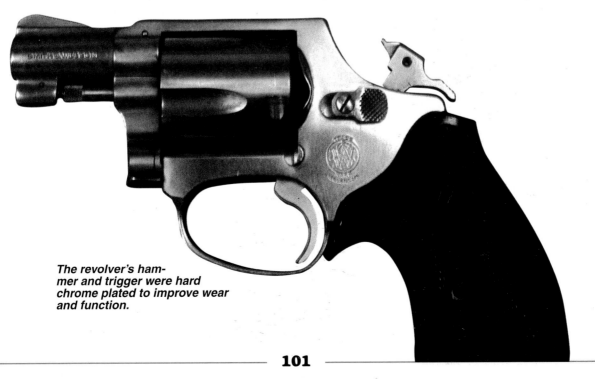

The revolver's hammer and trigger were hard chrome plated to improve wear and function.

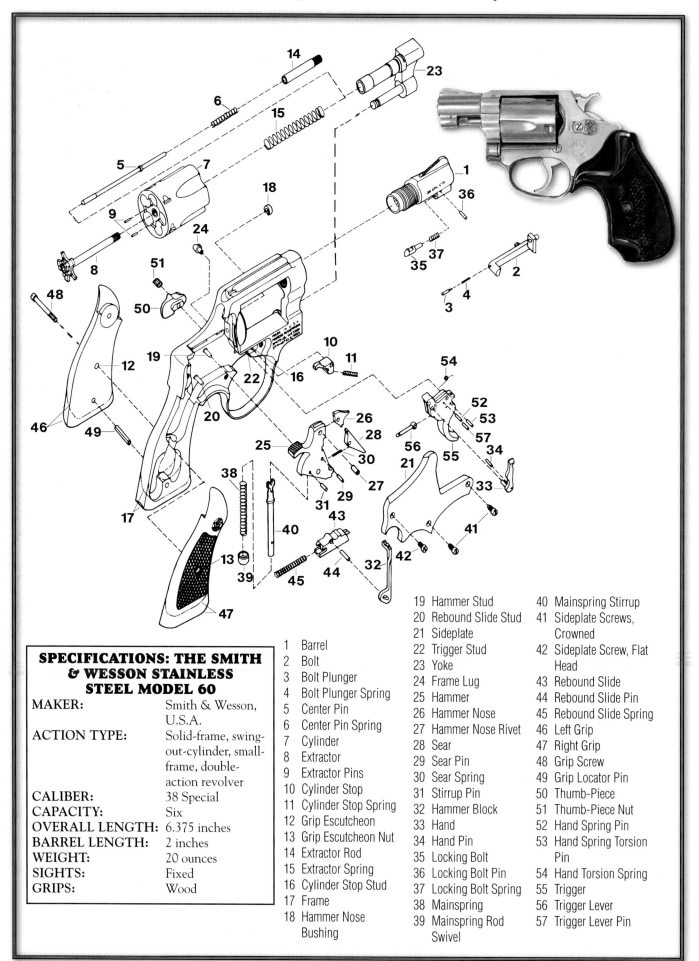

SPECIFICATIONS: THE SMITH & WESSON STAINLESS STEEL MODEL 60

MAKER:	Smith & Wesson, U.S.A.
ACTION TYPE:	Solid-frame, swing-out-cylinder, small-frame, double-action revolver
CALIBER:	38 Special
CAPACITY:	Six
OVERALL LENGTH:	6.375 inches
BARREL LENGTH:	2 inches
WEIGHT:	20 ounces
SIGHTS:	Fixed
GRIPS:	Wood

1 Barrel
2 Bolt
3 Bolt Plunger
4 Bolt Plunger Spring
5 Center Pin
6 Center Pin Spring
7 Cylinder
8 Extractor
9 Extractor Pins
10 Cylinder Stop
11 Cylinder Stop Spring
12 Grip Escutcheon
13 Grip Escutcheon Nut
14 Extractor Rod
15 Extractor Spring
16 Cylinder Stop Stud
17 Frame
18 Hammer Nose Bushing

19 Hammer Stud
20 Rebound Slide Stud
21 Sideplate
22 Trigger Stud
23 Yoke
24 Frame Lug
25 Hammer
26 Hammer Nose
27 Hammer Nose Rivet
28 Sear
29 Sear Pin
30 Sear Spring
31 Stirrup Pin
32 Hammer Block
33 Hand
34 Hand Pin
35 Locking Bolt
36 Locking Bolt Pin
37 Locking Bolt Spring
38 Mainspring
39 Mainspring Rod Swivel

40 Mainspring Stirrup
41 Sideplate Screws, Crowned
42 Sideplate Screw, Flat Head
43 Rebound Slide
44 Rebound Slide Pin
45 Rebound Slide Spring
46 Left Grip
47 Right Grip
48 Grip Screw
49 Grip Locator Pin
50 Thumb-Piece
51 Thumb-Piece Nut
52 Hand Spring Pin
53 Hand Spring Torsion Pin
54 Hand Torsion Spring
55 Trigger
56 Trigger Lever
57 Trigger Lever Pin

THE BERETTA MODEL 92

The U.S. Military's New Service Pistol

While this pistol has not introduced anything radically new to handgun design, the fact that it replaced the Colt Government Model 45 Pistol of 1911 as the official U.S. Military sidearm is reason enough for its inclusion in this book. This had a profound effect on the acceptance of the 9mm Luger cartridge and the high-capacity double-action pistol as a viable option for service and self-defense.

HISTORY AND DEVELOPMENT

The Italian company of Beretta can boast of being one of the world's oldest firearms manufacturer. It is generally accepted that the Beretta family started in the gun making business in 1680 (there are claims of an even earlier date). Initially, the company started making gun barrels, but this was later broadened to include complete firearms.

Beretta began pistol manufacture under the leadership of Pietro Beretta (1870-1957). Pietro Beretta, who is considered the father of the modern Beretta company, decided to enter the handgun business in 1903. The company's first pistol was the Model 1915, a military semi-automatic pistol chambered for the 9mm Gilisenti cartridge.

The 1915 was a marked improvement over the Italian service pistol, the Gilisenti pistol of 1910. The military was quick to appreciate its advantages and quickly adopted it during World War I.

In the years that followed, the company produced a number of subsequent semi-automatic pistols. Among the best known is the Model 1934, which established a reputation for great reliability and saw service as the official sidearm of the Italian army during World War II. It became a favorite souvenir of allied troops in Italy.

In the post-war years, Beretta refined the 1934, using it as the platform for a number of newer models. Beretta designers were very much influenced by the Walther P38 pistol used by the German military during World War II, and Beretta subsequently used a number of its features in its double-action models that eventually culminated in the Model 92.

The post-war period also saw Beretta begin developing a 9mm pistol. Initially, attempts were made to develop a blowback design based on the Model 1934. Excessive recoil made the pistol difficult to shoot, however, and excessive wear problems were experienced.

Eventually, a locked-breech model using the Walther locking system was developed called the Model 951. This pistol had a single-action trigger and was successful enough to be adopted by Italy, Israel, Iraq and Egypt, where it was made under license and known as the "Helwan" pistol.

The 951 was used as a platform for the company's first double-action service pistol. A design team comprised of Carlo Beretta, Giuseppe Mazzetti and Vittorio Valle began working on the project sometime in 1970, and some five years later, they had completed the task. The new pistol had a Walther-style double-action trigger and a high capacity 15-shot magazine—the first Model 92. It differed from the final 92 version adopted by the U.S. military in that it had a sear blocking safety and a button magazine catch positioned in the bottom left side of the grip.

While the frame-mounted sear-blocking safety gave the 92 the capability of being carried in "condition one" (chamber loaded, hammer cocked and safety applied), it was not in keeping with the current military thinking of the time, which was to have a safety that would safely place the pistol in the double-action mode when applied.

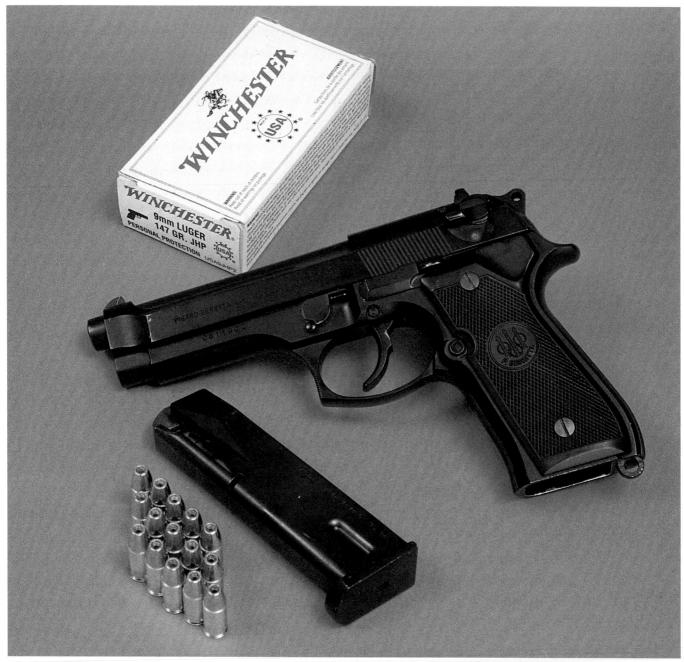

The Beretta 92 was a 15-shot, 9mm, double-action pistol selected to replace the Colt 45 Government Model 1911 pistol as the U.S. military's official sidearm.

Nevertheless, the 92 quickly gained a reputation for being a rugged, reliable pistol with good shooting characteristics. While it was not adopted by the armies of any of the major powers, it was accepted by a number of military forces, notably in South America.

Beretta did not rest with the original design, however, but worked on improving the pistol by eliminating its perceived faults. Late in 1978, the Model 92 S-1 appeared with a revised safety and magazine catch. The former was now positioned in the slide and safely lowered a cocked hammer when applied, as well as disconnecting the trigger. The new button-style magazine catch was moved to the favored position behind the trigger.

The 92 S-1 competed in the U.S. Air Force test conducted at Elgin AFB in 1979-80 and won handsomely. After being awarded the contract, further changes were made and the

Model 92SB appeared soon afterwards.

The 92SB had an ambidextrous safety and magazine catch (reversible) and an internal passive firing pin lock and was basically the pistol that the company submitted for the U.S. military trials of 1979 and 1981.

THE U.S. TRIALS FOR A NEW MILITARY PISTOL

As early as the end of World War II, the United States military began to consider replacing the Colt Government Model 45 with a 9mm pistol. Anticipating this, both Colt and Smith & Wesson submitted 9mm pistols for consideration. Smith & Wesson's submission was the Model 39 while Colt produced a compact, lightweight version of the 1911 that later enjoyed good commercial sales as the "Commander."

The military rejected both pistols after deciding there were

The Model 92 used the same dropping locking block system of the Walther P38 to lock the action during firing.

The pistol retains the open top slide of the company's earlier designs to provide for more positive ejection of spent cases.

sufficient numbers of 1911s in inventory. No further action was taken until after the Air Force had tested and selected the Model 92SB. By this time, the pistol inventory was dangerously low and those still in service were beginning to show signs of wear. Compounding the problem was the fact that there were quantities of nonstandard handguns, including revolvers, in service with various branches of the military.

At the urging of Congress, the Defense Department was ordered to decide on a suitable 9mm for use by all services. The Model 92SB had to compete against service pistols submitted by other companies that included Colt, Smith & Wesson, Heckler & Koch, SIG-Sauer and Walther.

In what eventually became three separate trials that were marked with controversy involving inter-service rivalry and disputes over the methodology employed, Beretta was eventually declared the winner. Close behind were pistols submitted by SIG and Smith & Wesson.

In spite of accusations that Beretta received favorable treatment—because of an agreement for the U.S. to have missile bases in Italy—there is no evidence that the 92 was selected for reasons other than it had the best performance in the trials. Nevertheless, this did nothing to appease the opponents of the 9mm.

After the military's acceptance of the 92SB (now designated as the M9 pistol), lawsuits against the results were brought by Heckler & Koch and Smith & Wesson. While both suits were unsuccessful, they simply fueled the acrimonious debate over the adoption of the Beretta that still continues today.

DESIGN CHARACTERISTICS AND FEATURES

Instead of employing one of the Browning-type breech-locking systems, the 92 used the same locking block system employed in the Walther P38. This had the advantage of not titling the barrel during the unlocking process. The pistol had an open top slide like that of the earlier Beretta pistols.

The pistol's double-action trigger system and hammer-lowering safety were also typical Walther. The ambidextrous safety was mounted on the left rear of the slide. Depressing the lever disconnected the trigger and safely lowered the hammer. Pushing the lever up put the pistol in the double-action firing mode. The pistol also had a passive firing pin safety.

The pistol retained the open top slide of the company's pre-war designs and had a high-capacity double-column magazine that held 15 rounds. The pistol magazine catch was in the American-favored position of behind the frame. Other controls included a slide stop and a takedown lever. The frame was made of an aircraft quality aluminum alloy, while the slide, barrel and some other components were made of carbon steel.

The pistol's field stripping procedure

The pistol's controls are all on the left side and include a takedown latch, slide stop, magazine catch and hammer-lowering safety.

was greatly simplified by a frame-mounted takedown catch. Rotating it down releases the slide/barrel assembly, permitting its removal from the frame.

The initial order of pistols came from Beretta in Italy, but as the company already had a plant in Maryland, subsequent pistols were manufactured in the United States by Beretta USA.

SERVICE RECORD

By most accounts, the 92 has been well received by the military. The only exception was the navy. Ironically, the coast guard has been an enthusiastic user of the pistol.

The fact that Beretta's pistol was adopted as this country's official military sidearm had a dramatic effect on law enforcement's acceptance of the high-ammunition-capacity double-action pistol and the 9mm cartridge. No doubt impressed by the 92's passing of the stringent military trials, a number of departments have since adopted the 92SB. These include the Connecticut State Police and the Los Angeles Police and Sheriff's Departments to name but a few.

By all accounts, the policemen have been quite satisfied with the pistol. Thanks to the 92, Beretta is now a major supplier of law enforcement handguns. Commercial sales have also been good, as civilians are greatly influenced by what the military and police use.

This is not to imply that the Model 92 is beyond criticism. In the author's opinion, most criticism has been unsubstantiated claims of lack of stopping power and unreliability originating from 1911 and 45 ACP adherents. Both the Government Model and its cartridge have garnered an almost cult-like following among many handgun enthusiasts who cannot accept its replacement by a double-action auto—and a 9mm one at that.

THE SLIDE FAILURES

The most serious complaint against the M92 came when the U.S. Navy reported a number of slide failure incidents. These occurred to members of SEAL units firing the M92. According to the reports, slides fractured unexpectedly causing injuries to some shooters when the rear of the slide was driven off the frame into a shooter's face and chest. In addition, there were some reports of frame cracks being discovered.

The reports were serious enough that the navy, apparently never really happy with the adoption of the M92,

When the takedown catch is rotated down, it releases the slide/barrel assembly so that the same can be removed from the frame.

suspended accepting any more pistols into service. There were even threats of possibly canceling the navy order.

Both the army and Beretta conducted an investigation, which revealed no defects in the basic design or the quality of materials used. There were, however, suggestions that the cause was due to the use of abnormally high-pressure ammunition used by the navy. Beretta did make modifications that solved the frame cracking and prevented the slide from coming off the frame.

The Model 92's critics focused upon this report to validate their case against it. In passing, it is worth mentioning that frame and slide cracking is a fairly common occurrence in self-loading pistols, especially after extensive firing. Another important point is that apart from these military reports, there have been no similar reports from other users, such as civilians of law enforcement, who probably put more rounds through their handguns than does the military.

In the author's opinion, if the Beretta 92 has a fault, it is the size of its grip, which can be problematic for small-handed users.

MODEL 92 VARIATIONS

In addition to the changes required by the military, Beretta has responded to market demands, usually from law enforcement, by introducing a variety of versions of the Model 92.

The Model 92F has a conventional double-action trigger and is a civilian version of the military M92 pistol.

The Model 92G looks just like the 92F but has a de-cocking lever instead of the hammer-dropping safety. The lever looks just like the safety on the F model except it does not disconnect the trigger when applied. Instead, it safely lowers the hammer when depressed and then returns to the horizontal position when released, putting the trigger in the double-action mode.

The Model 92D has a double-action-only trigger that requires the same long heavy pull for each firing cycle. It is easily identified by what is termed a "slick" slide, so called because of its plain, flat side and an absence of safety or de-cocking levers. It also has a spurless hammer.

The 92M has a single-column 6-shot magazine that provides a narrower grip to accommodate shooters with small hands.

Beretta has also made a number of compact versions of the 92 that have shorter barrels and grips. The reduction of grip size resulted in a magazine capacity reduction. These culminated in the Centurion, which has a 4-inch barrel but a full-size grip and the standard 15-shot magazine for sales to military and police forces.

The growing popularity of the 40 S&W cartridge prompted the company to bring out models in this caliber. Fortunately, the strength of the 92 enabled this to be done on the same 92 platform. Both full and compact versions were made and designated as the Model 96 and 96 Centurion, respectively.

In terms of other calibers, 30 Luger versions have been made for those countries where civilians are prohibited from having larger caliber pistols.

Several competition 92s have been made with longer barrels, compensators and target sights. The Brigadier is a 92 with a beefed up slide for sustained shooting.

The standard finish for the 92 and most of its variants has generally been blue steel barrels and slide with alloy frame that have a matching "Bruiton" finish. Optional finishes have included stainless as well as some specially enhanced and engraved commemorative models.

THE 92 TODAY

The latest version of the 92 is the Vertex. It has a straight backstrap to better accommodate small-handed shooters, without a reduction in magazine capacity.

The 92 pistol remains in production today with it still being the official service pistol of America's military and many of the country's police forces. It has performed satisfactorily in Panama, Desert Storm and Afghanistan. In spite of its earlier trials and tribulations and the claims of its critics, it has proved to be a worthy successor to the Colt Government Model 45.

FIELD STRIPPING THE MODEL 92

First apply the safety, remove the magazine and check that the chamber is unloaded. Then unlock the takedown latch by pushing in the locking plunger positioned on the right side of the frame and rotate the latch down as far as it will go. This releases the slide/barrel assembly, allowing it to be removed from the front of the frame. With the slide removed, take out the recoil spring assembly from under the barrel. The barrel can then be removed from the bottom of the slide to complete the stripping procedure. Assembly is done in reverse order.

SHOOTING AND HANDLING
THE BERETTA MODEL 92

While I do not own a 92, I have evaluated a fair number over the past 20 or so years. I have been impressed with the pistol in respect to the high quality of the fit, finish and reliability.

All of the 92s I have shot have had above-average accuracy. Most shot sub-3-inch groups when shot from a seated bench rest at 25 yards. The fixed sights are good at presenting a nice clear sight picture.

Recoil with 9mm ammunition is quite mild and the pistol is very pleasant to shoot. As far as reliability is concerned, I have yet to experience a malfunction with any of the many 92s that have passed through my hands.

The single-action trigger pull is relatively light and crisp. The double action has an even, relatively smooth stroke that is a trifle on the long side. The latter has not adversely affected my double-action shooting with the pistol at the closer distances, although it does tend to slow down the speed of my shots at ranges over 10 yards.

The pistol's biggest detraction is the size of its grip. While I have no difficulty in accessing the trigger and all its controls, I have seen shooters with smaller hands experience trouble doing either.

Apart from this observation, my opinion of the 92 is that it is an excellent service auto pistol that is a worthy replacement to the Colt Government Model 45.

COLLECTOR INTEREST

There is little apparent collector interest in the Model 92, except, perhaps, in some of the commemorative models. A used 92 in good condition is certainly suitable as a self-defense arm.

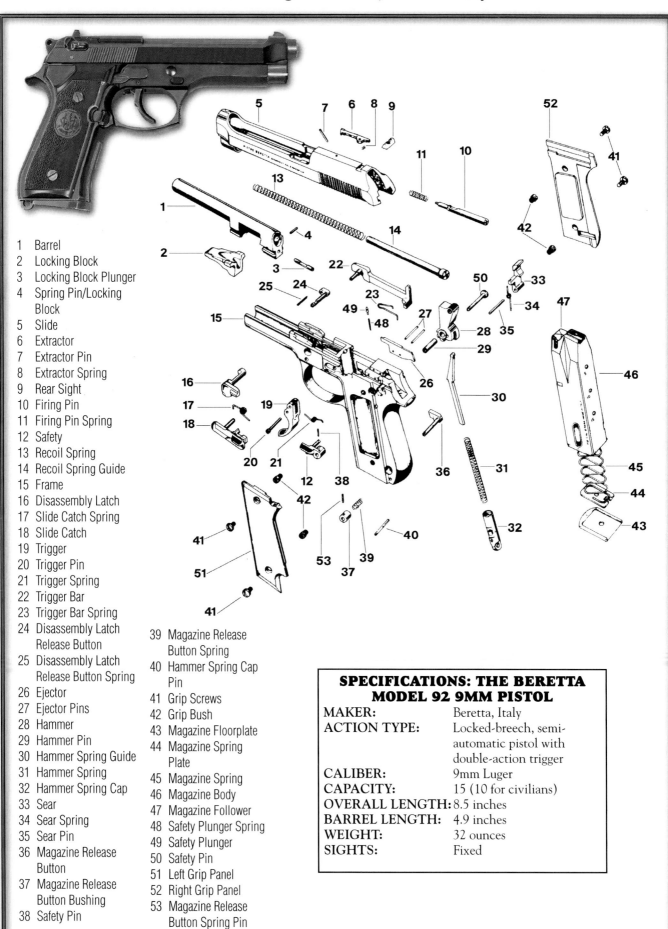

1 Barrel
2 Locking Block
3 Locking Block Plunger
4 Spring Pin/Locking Block
5 Slide
6 Extractor
7 Extractor Pin
8 Extractor Spring
9 Rear Sight
10 Firing Pin
11 Firing Pin Spring
12 Safety
13 Recoil Spring
14 Recoil Spring Guide
15 Frame
16 Disassembly Latch
17 Slide Catch Spring
18 Slide Catch
19 Trigger
20 Trigger Pin
21 Trigger Spring
22 Trigger Bar
23 Trigger Bar Spring
24 Disassembly Latch Release Button
25 Disassembly Latch Release Button Spring
26 Ejector
27 Ejector Pins
28 Hammer
29 Hammer Pin
30 Hammer Spring Guide
31 Hammer Spring
32 Hammer Spring Cap
33 Sear
34 Sear Spring
35 Sear Pin
36 Magazine Release Button
37 Magazine Release Button Bushing
38 Safety Pin

39 Magazine Release Button Spring
40 Hammer Spring Cap Pin
41 Grip Screws
42 Grip Bush
43 Magazine Floorplate
44 Magazine Spring Plate
45 Magazine Spring
46 Magazine Body
47 Magazine Follower
48 Safety Plunger Spring
49 Safety Plunger
50 Safety Pin
51 Left Grip Panel
52 Right Grip Panel
53 Magazine Release Button Spring Pin

SPECIFICATIONS: THE BERETTA MODEL 92 9MM PISTOL	
MAKER:	Beretta, Italy
ACTION TYPE:	Locked-breech, semi-automatic pistol with double-action trigger
CALIBER:	9mm Luger
CAPACITY:	15 (10 for civilians)
OVERALL LENGTH:	8.5 inches
BARREL LENGTH:	4.9 inches
WEIGHT:	32 ounces
SIGHTS:	Fixed

Tullio Marengoni
(1881-1965)

Much of the success of the Beretta pistol can be attributed to this man who was hired by Pietro Beretta in 1904. A man who had little formal education and no university degree, Marengoni was something of an engineering genius.

Marengoni was not afraid to borrow ideas from foreign designs or use his ability to improve on them, which he did with the Model 1915 pistol. He effectively headed the Beretta design team until his retirement in 1957, by which time the company was a well-established international firearms manufacturer.

Marengoni was involved in the design of the Model 951, the precursor of the 92, and its use of Walther features such as the breech locking system.

Marengoni designs were not confined to handguns but also encompassed military semi-automatic rifle and machineguns. Although the Model 92 was introduced long after Marengoni had died, many of its features can be traced back to the ideas of this brilliant firearms designer.

THE HECKLER & KOCH P7 SQUEEZE–COCKING AUTO PISTOL

A Most Promising Design That Did Not Quite Live Up To Expectations

Even though its sales have been disappointing after what began as a very promising start, the P7 is significant in that it is the only really radically new handgun design to appear after World War II.

HISTORY AND DEVELOPMENT

The P7 was created to compete in the German police pistol trials of 1977. These trials came about as the result of the disastrous massacre of Israeli athletes by Arab terrorists at the Munich Olympics in 1972.

A subsequent investigation of the incident concluded that the failure of the police to save the athletes was largely due to inadequate training and equipment. The West German government therefore established criteria for the type of handgun police should arm themselves with. Heckler & Koch (HK), together with other companies like Walther and SIG-Sauer, submitted pistols for testing and evaluation.

The criteria set by the government was stringent in terms of dimensions, safety and performance. To meet these, HK created a pistol that featured a radically new cocking and trigger action as well as an equally unique breech gas-retarding system.

In subsequent trials to select a police pistol, no single winner was determined. Instead, HK's pistol was one of three authorized for use by German police and given the official designation of P7.

It took some time before the P7 began to enjoy respectable

sales in the U.S., probably partly due to its 9mm caliber and the fact that the magazine capacity was only eight rounds. Another minor factor may have been the magazine catch, which was positioned in the bottom of the grip. This changed after HK submitted a high-capacity P7 to compete in the U.S. military service pistol trials that had the magazine catch located in the favored position of in the frame behind the trigger.

These changes made the pistol more acceptable to U.S. shooters. As a result, the company offered two models for the American market called the P7 M8 and the P7 M13. The former had an 8-shot magazine, while the M13's magazine held 13 rounds.

DESIGN CHARACTERISTICS AND FEATURES

The P7 M8 was a 9mm striker-fired semi-automatic pistol that employed a gas-operated retarding action that delayed the opening of the action until such time as chamber pressures were safe enough.

On firing, gases were bled off into a piston under the barrel by means of a gas port in the bottom of the chamber. In the piston, the gases operated against a piston rod that was connected to the slide. This force against the piston rod kept the action closed until chamber pressure reached a safe level. At this point, the slide was permitted to move back to eject the spent case, cock the striker and chamber a fresh round.

Heckler & Koch's P7 was a remarkably simple design with only one control consisting of two levers on either side of the trigger guard—the magazine catch—which was made especially for American shooters who do not like the magazine catch in the bottom of the grip.

In addition to cushioning the effects of recoil, this also allowed the barrel to be permanently pinned to the frame, which provided enhanced accuracy.

The continuous motion firing system consisted of a pivoting lever attached to the front of the grip. This in turn was connected to the striker by means of a lever that cocked the same when it was compressed by the fingers taking a normal hold on the grip. The cocked striker was released in the normal manner by applying pressure to the trigger.

This unique system had many attributes that included enhanced safety. The pistol could only fire when the cocking lever was fully compressed. As soon as it was released, the pistol was rendered safe. Some 8 pounds of pressure were needed to fully cock the striker but only a few pounds were needed to keep the lever compressed. In addition, the pistol had a relatively light trigger release, unlike the long heavy pull of most conventional double-action pistols. The striker protrudes out of the rear of the slide to indicate when it is fully cocked and ready to fire.

The P7 had two basic controls—a magazine catch comprised of two small levers on either side of the trigger guard and a button-type takedown catch positioned at the rear of the frame.

Upon firing the last cartridge in the magazine, the slide was locked open. The cocking lever performed double-duty as a slide release as releasing it and then compressing it allowed the slide to close.

The P7 employed a radical squeeze-cocking, continuous-motion ignition system. Compressing the front of the grip cocks the striker ready to be released by the trigger.

The P7 M8 and M13 were pretty much identical except for their magazine capacities. The M13's had a wider grip to accommodate the double-column magazine. The magazine catch consisted of two small levers positioned at the bottom rear of the trigger guard. Depressing either of these released the magazine. Having a lever on either side of the trigger guard allowed for ambidextrous operation of the catch.

SUBSEQUENT P7 MODELS AND VARIATIONS

In addition to the original P7, the P7 M8 and the P7 M13, there have been two other production models. The P7 K3 was a version chambered for either the 380 or the 22 LR cartridges. There was also a 22-conversion unit made for the 380 P7 K3.

The P7 M10 was a slightly enlarged version made for the 40 S&W cartridge. It was obviously made with the law enforcement market in mind. There were rumors that consideration was given to producing a P7 chambered for the 45 ACP. A prototype was actually made but production models were not. In order to be able to handle the bigger cartridge, the 45 P7 was slightly enlarged.

Apart from the models already described, the P7 had no significant changes in respect to barrel lengths or grips. In terms of finish, the pistol always had black plastic grips and a black oxide finish. Heckler & Koch did, however, provide a service whereby U.S. customers could have a nickel-plated finish applied to their P7s.

SERVICE RECORD

After a promising start in both Germany and the United States, sales of the P7 suddenly began to decline. It is hard to

The gas-retarding system allows gases to bleed off into a piston under the chamber where they engage a piston rod that is attached to the front of the slide. The action of the gases against the piston rod prevent the slide from moving back until chamber pressures have reached a safe level.

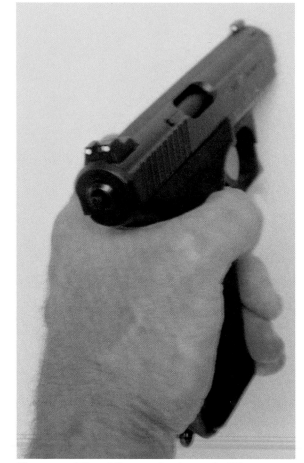

The rear of the striker protrudes out of the rear of the slide when it is cocked.

determine the exact reason for this. The pistol had no glaring defects, was reliable and extremely well made, which, ironically, may be one of the reasons for its decline. The P7's high quality of workmanship made it an expensive pistol to manufacture. It was also made of forged and machine construction. Unlike HK's previous pistols that use pressed and stamped metal parts, both these construction methods added to the cost of manufacture.

Thus the P7 was more expensive than many of its competitors in the United States. To compound the problem, an increase in the exchange rate between the U.S. dollar and the West German mark drove the price even higher. This occurred just as P7 sales in America were beginning to surge.

Another problem was the uniqueness of the pistol's shooting and handling characteristics, which usually occurred with shooters used to conventional pistols and revolvers. When under stress, one could forget to keep the cocking lever compressed to fire or fail to release it when re-holstering or covering a suspect.

Apparently there were a number of incidents of accidental discharges occurring in Germany that cast some doubt on the pistol's suitability as a police sidearm. This was unfortunate because, if handled correctly, the P7 was, in the author's opinion, one of the safest pistols made. It was also found that shooters with little prior handgun experience generally mastered the pistol better than those experienced with more conventional handguns.

Heckler & Koch continue to market the 8-shot P7 M8 in the United States, although their main handgun is the polymer-framed USP. It is sad that the P7 has not enjoyed the success that it deserves. Nevertheless, it was a fine pistol of high quality and a classic design, one of the very few to appear late in the last century.

The pistol employs a unique gas-retarding system to lock the action during firing. This permits the use of a fixed barrel that enhances accuracy and also reduces the effects of recoil.

FIELD STRIPPING THE P7

The pistol is simple to takedown for cleaning. As usual, the first task is to remove the magazine and retract the slide to ensure the chamber is unloaded. Next, push in the disassembly button on the left rear of the slide. This releases the slide from the frame, permitting it to be pulled back, up and pushed forward off the frame. The recoil spring can then be removed

The front of the grip incorporates a pivoting lever. The top of the lever engages the striker in the slide and moves back to cock it as the lever is compressed.

from the barrel to complete the procedure.

With the slide removed, the barrel can be cleaned via the chamber. The piston can also be cleaned of any fouling build up using a small wire brush provided with the pistol.

SHOOTING AND HANDLING THE P7

I have no hesitation in admitting that I like the P7 and the high quality of its construction. I also like its compact size and unique handling qualities. All of its few controls are easy and simple to access and operate.

My P7 delivers excellent accuracy, has good fixed sights and possesses a very nice trigger. Its gas-retarding locking system keeps recoil to a minimum. All these attributes help considerably in fast, accurate shooting.

I have also found the P7 to be completely reliable. It is

The slide is locked open after the last shot in the magazine has been fired. Releasing and compressing the cocking lever allows the slide to close.

worth mentioning, however, that it is important to shoot only jacketed or semi-automatic ammunition in any P7 as lead bullets can foul the gas port in the chamber and cause malfunctions.

While I have not experienced any problems with the unusual firing system, I have to admit that all my shooting has been confined to the calm and structured atmosphere of the shooting range, engaging targets that don't shoot back.

I have noticed, however, that I don't have to think so much when I shoot my P7 one-handed. When I use a two-handed hold, I find that releasing the cocking lever requires a conscious effort. It is almost a case of having too many fingers in the way. I cannot help but wonder if this is not the cause of the problems with unintentional discharges experienced by the German police officers.

As I have already stated, I like my P7 and have no problems in shooting it. My only regret is that this promising design was not developed further.

COLLECTOR INTEREST

The P7 is of too recent vintage to attract much collector interest. It has always been a highly priced handgun and catalog values indicate only a marginal drop in price for used pistols.

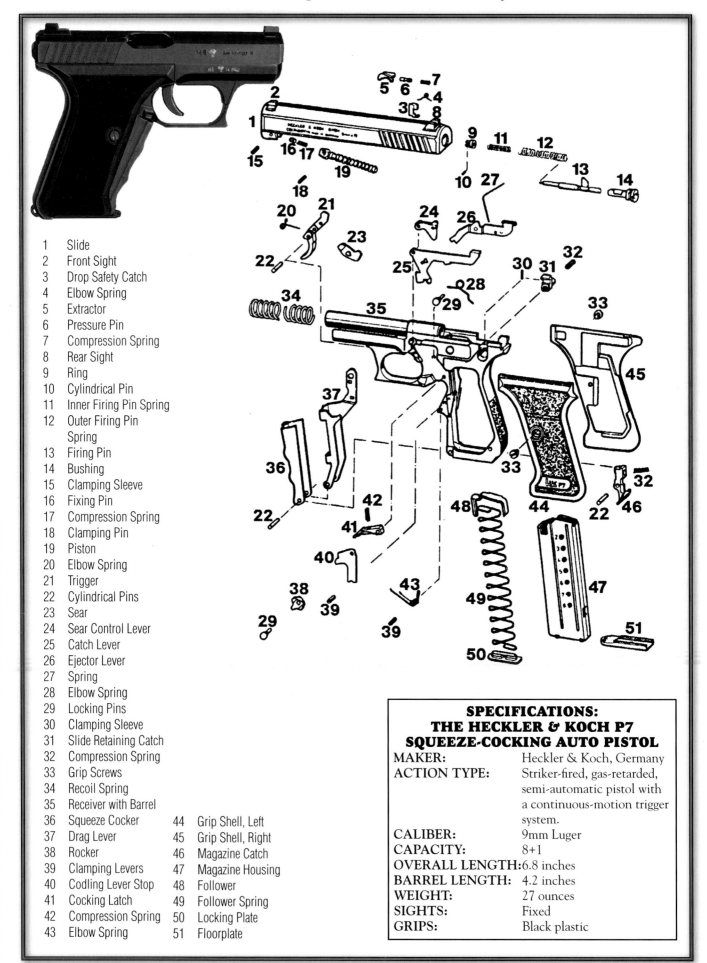

1   Slide
2   Front Sight
3   Drop Safety Catch
4   Elbow Spring
5   Extractor
6   Pressure Pin
7   Compression Spring
8   Rear Sight
9   Ring
10 Cylindrical Pin
11 Inner Firing Pin Spring
12 Outer Firing Pin
      Spring
13 Firing Pin
14 Bushing
15 Clamping Sleeve
16 Fixing Pin
17 Compression Spring
18 Clamping Pin
19 Piston
20 Elbow Spring
21 Trigger
22 Cylindrical Pins
23 Sear
24 Sear Control Lever
25 Catch Lever
26 Ejector Lever
27 Spring
28 Elbow Spring
29 Locking Pins
30 Clamping Sleeve
31 Slide Retaining Catch
32 Compression Spring
33 Grip Screws
34 Recoil Spring
35 Receiver with Barrel
36 Squeeze Cocker
37 Drag Lever
38 Rocker
39 Clamping Levers
40 Codling Lever Stop
41 Cocking Latch
42 Compression Spring
43 Elbow Spring

44 Grip Shell, Left
45 Grip Shell, Right
46 Magazine Catch
47 Magazine Housing
48 Follower
49 Follower Spring
50 Locking Plate
51 Floorplate

SPECIFICATIONS:
THE HECKLER & KOCH P7
SQUEEZE-COCKING AUTO PISTOL

MAKER:	Heckler & Koch, Germany
ACTION TYPE:	Striker-fired, gas-retarded, semi-automatic pistol with a continuous-motion trigger system.
CALIBER:	9mm Luger
CAPACITY:	8+1
OVERALL LENGTH:	6.8 inches
BARREL LENGTH:	4.2 inches
WEIGHT:	27 ounces
SIGHTS:	Fixed
GRIPS:	Black plastic

Heckler & Koch

This German arms company, better known as HK, is a relative newcomer to the world of firearms manufacturing. Nevertheless, they quickly gained a well-deserved reputation, making a line of military rifles, pistols and sub-machineguns that were well made, reliable and innovative.

The company started as a machine tool operation, occupying the empty Mauser factory at the end of World War II. When Germany was permitted to resume the manufacture of military arms in the 1950s, HK developed a semi-automatic rifle based on the Spanish CETME. The rifle employed a large number of stamped and pressed parts in its construction and was adopted by the German military as the G3 rifle. This gun was followed by the very successful MP5 submachine gun.

The company's first handgun was a pocket-sized semi-automatic that came with a multi-choice of barrels and magazines that enabled calibers to be changed. This was followed by an innovative 9mm service pistol called the P9, which had a unique roller-breech locking system and used a lot of metal pressings and stampings in its construction.

The company then embarked on development of the P7. The company's latest handgun is the Universal Service Pistol (USP), a polymer-framed, large-caliber, semi-automatic with a choice of several trigger options. A pistol based on the USP platform and chambered for the 45 ACP cartridge was selected by the U.S. Special Forces.

Just before the reunification of Germany, the Company was working on an ambitious military rifle that used caseless ammunition. HK was anticipating a substantial contract with the German military for this weapon. Just as the project was nearing completion, Germany was unified and suddenly inherited large quantities of brand-new AK 74 rifles. This ended any hopes of a military contract and the company found itself in financial difficulties.

In 1990, it was announced that HK had been purchased by GIAT of France, but the sale was later cancelled. The company was subsequently sold to Royal Ordnance of Great Britain and it continues to operate in Europe and the U.S.

THE SIG-SAUER P226 DE-COCKING DOUBLE-ACTION AUTO PISTOL

Considered by Many to be the Best of the 9mm Double-Action Pistols

The P226 introduced a hammer-lowering system that considerably simplified the operation of double-action auto pistols. While not the first of such pistols made by the company, it was the first to introduce the concept to American shooters. The pistol was enthusiastically received in the U.S. by both civilians and law enforcement, many of whom claim that it is one of the best of the modern high-capacity auto loaders.

HISTORY AND DEVELOPMENT

The P226 is a high-magazine-capacity version of the earlier SIG Model P220 that first appeared in 1976. The P220 was developed as SIG's first double-action pistol and was adopted by the Swiss army.

The P225 was a more compact version of the 220 and was one of the pistols authorized by the West German government for use by the various police forces of that country.

One of the P220/225's most significant features was the replacement of the Walther-style hammer-dropping safety with a frame-mounted lever that simply and safely lowered the hammer when depressed. The advantage of this system was that it simplified the pistol's operation. With the conventional hammer-lowering safety, the pistol was deactivated until such time as the safety was disengaged. It was reasoned that in the stress of combat, an officer may forget to deactivate the safety.

With these SIG pistols, lowering the hammer did not deactivate the pistol but simply put the pistol in a first-shot double-action mode. As this required a long heavy pull on the trigger, it was reasoned that a safety was not needed.

The pistols also employed a number of state-of-the-art manufacturing methods intended to keep costs down. These included the use of high quality metal forming technology to fabricate many components that are usually machine forged.

While the pistol was very well received in Europe, it did not really create much interest in the United States, even though it was later chambered for 45 ACP and 38 Super cartridges. American interest only began when the P226 appeared in the 1980s.

The P226 was developed to compete in the U.S. military trials for a new service pistol. While basic design and caliber was unchanged, the pistol had a high-capacity 15-shot magazine and a button-style magazine catch in the favored position behind the trigger.

The P226 performed very well in the trials, only to lose out to the Beretta 92 by a narrow margin. This, combined with an increased demand for high-capacity double-action 9mm pistols, boded well for the P226. Consequently, it did extremely well in the commercial and law enforcement markets.

The alloy frame has another machined steel block that engages the barrel cam during firing.

DESIGN CHARACTERISTICS AND FEATURES

The P226 was a locked-breech double-action semi-automatic pistol. It employed the Browning cam-operated tilting-barrel locking system to lock the action after firing.

To reduce weight, the pistol had an aluminum frame with the barrel and slide made of steel. There was a steel locking block within the slide. Its purpose was to engage the barrel cam and prevent wear to the softer aluminum frame.

The slide was formed from thick steel plate that was then welded and machined. This was so well done it gave the impression of being a totally machined component. The firing pin mechanism was contained within a forged steel block that was secured to the slide by means of a cross pin.

The pistol uses the Browning cam-operated tilting-barrel system to lock the action during firing.

The controls were all on the left side and included a takedown latch, magazine catch, a slide stop and a decocking lever that was connected to a double-action lock. Depressing this lever safely lowered the hammer when cocked to put the pistol in the double-action mode.

While there was no external safety catch, there was a passive firing pin lock that blocked the same until the trigger was properly cycled. The de-cocking system was very similar to that of an earlier Sauer pistol, the Model 38H, although it differed in that it could not cock the hammer when at rest as could be done with the 38H.

The slide is fabricated of pressed heavy-gauge steel plate welded together. The firing pin and mechanism is contained in a machined steel block.

The pistol had fixed low-profile sights that had a ramped post with a white dot and rear sight notch with a white bar at the bottom for low-light shooting. The grips were made of a black plastic material that covered the backstrap.

The P226 was simple to field strip for cleaning. The slide is locked back on an empty magazine and the takedown lever is rotated down. This releases the slide/barrel assembly, allowing it to be taken off the frame.

The pistol's controls include a disassembly latch, magazine catch, de-cocking lever and slide stop, all positioned on the left side of the frame.

ASSOCIATED MODELS AND VARIATIONS

As the demand for the P226 grew, SIG-Sauer introduced a number of new models. Among the first of these was a more compact version with a shortened barrel and slide called the P228. It was followed shortly by the P229, which was identical

The SIG-Sauer P226 has built up an enviable reputation for being an accurate, reliable and very well made service pistol. In addition, it introduced the concept of a de-cocking lever as opposed to a hammer-lowering safety.

that there have been very few changes or modifications. Barrel lengths have only changed with the models already described, while grips and finish have remained basically unchanged.

The standard grips are a molded black plastic with a roughened surface with more fancy wood grips being offered as an option or for presentation models. The standard finish is matte black oxide for steel parts with a matching black anodizing applied to the aluminum frame.

Some two-tone pistols with matte silver stainless slides and black frames have been made, while an all stainless steel model was recently added to the line.

The P226 and most of its variants remain in production at the time of writing and are still popular with shooters who demand a reliable pistol of very high quality.

except for its caliber of 40 S&W and the fact its slide was machined from stainless steel instead of being fabricated from steel plate. The slide had a matte black finish and was made in SIG-Sauer's U.S. facility. The rest of the pistol including the frame was manufactured in Germany.

As some police departments showed an interest in double-action-only pistols, additional versions of the P226 and the P228/9 were offered with this feature. The P239 was an even more compact version with a single-column seven-shot magazine intended for shooters with small hands.

In the last years of the century, the Sig Pro and the P245 Compact appeared. The former is similar to the P226 except that it has a polymer frame. The latter pistol is considerably reduced in size and, as its name implies, is a very compact version of the P226, but chambered for the 45 ACP cartridge.

Generally, the overall design of the P226 has been so sound

FIELD-STRIPPING THE P226

After removing the magazine and pulling back the slide to ensure that the chamber is unloaded, lock it open using the slide stop. Then rotate the takedown latch down. The slide can now be removed forward off the frame.

With slide removed, take out the recoil spring assembly followed by the barrel. This completes the field-stripping. The pistol is assembled in reverse order.

SHOOTING AND HANDLING THE P226

This is such an excellent pistol that there is very little negative than can be said about it. All the ones I have handled and shot have been very well made and absolutely reliable as well as being simple and easy to operate.

When the de-cocking lever is depressed, the hammer, when cocked, is safely lowered, putting the pistol in the double-action mode.

Rotating the disassembly latch down enables the slide assembly to be removed from the frame.

The pistol's grip provides a comfortable hold for my hand, although it may be a bit of a handful for those with small hands and short fingers. Recoil is mild and easy to control when shooting fast multi-shot strings. The controls are well positioned for easy access without having to alter one's grip on the pistol.

I have always found the pistol to have above-average accuracy. The sights are prominent and easy to acquire quickly and the pistol has a very good single-action pull.

The double-action pull is equally good, having a relatively light, smooth, even, short stroke, which is achieved by the fact the de-cocking lever lowers the hammer to what is in effect an almost pre-cocked position, thus reducing the distance it has to be cocked before the point of release.

Having personally experienced times when I have forgotten to disengage the safety of some conventional double-action pistols, I particularly like the simplicity of operation that the de-cocking lever provides.

After shooting a P226, it is easy to understand why it is so popular.

COLLECTOR INTEREST

The P226 is of such recent manufacture that it does not qualify as a collector item. The pistol was always a high-priced handgun and the prices of used pistols do not exceed that of the new models of today.

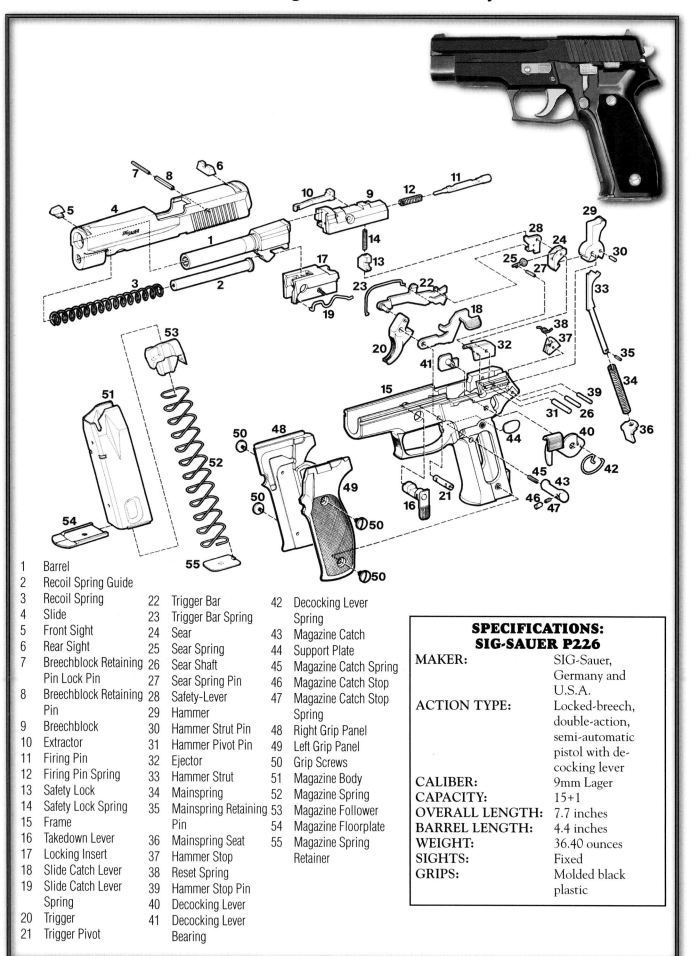

1 Barrel
2 Recoil Spring Guide
3 Recoil Spring
4 Slide
5 Front Sight
6 Rear Sight
7 Breechblock Retaining
  Pin Lock Pin
8 Breechblock Retaining
  Pin
9 Breechblock
10 Extractor
11 Firing Pin
12 Firing Pin Spring
13 Safety Lock
14 Safety Lock Spring
15 Frame
16 Takedown Lever
17 Locking Insert
18 Slide Catch Lever
19 Slide Catch Lever
   Spring
20 Trigger
21 Trigger Pivot

22 Trigger Bar
23 Trigger Bar Spring
24 Sear
25 Sear Spring
26 Sear Shaft
27 Sear Spring Pin
28 Safety-Lever
29 Hammer
30 Hammer Strut Pin
31 Hammer Pivot Pin
32 Ejector
33 Hammer Strut
34 Mainspring
35 Mainspring Retaining
   Pin
36 Mainspring Seat
37 Hammer Stop
38 Reset Spring
39 Hammer Stop Pin
40 Decocking Lever
41 Decocking Lever
   Bearing

42 Decocking Lever
   Spring
43 Magazine Catch
44 Support Plate
45 Magazine Catch Spring
46 Magazine Catch Stop
47 Magazine Catch Stop
   Spring
48 Right Grip Panel
49 Left Grip Panel
50 Grip Screws
51 Magazine Body
52 Magazine Spring
53 Magazine Follower
54 Magazine Floorplate
55 Magazine Spring
   Retainer

SPECIFICATIONS: SIG-SAUER P226

MAKER:	SIG-Sauer, Germany and U.S.A.
ACTION TYPE:	Locked-breech, double-action, semi-automatic pistol with de-cocking lever
CALIBER:	9mm Lager
CAPACITY:	15+1
OVERALL LENGTH:	7.7 inches
BARREL LENGTH:	4.4 inches
WEIGHT:	36.40 ounces
SIGHTS:	Fixed
GRIPS:	Molded black plastic

The Sig-Sauer
Firearms Company

The P226 series of pistols are the creation of a collaboration of a Swiss and a German firearms company—Schweizerische Industrie Gesellschaft or SIG of Neuhasen, Switzerland, and J.P. Sauer & Son of Eckernfoerde, Germany.

Both companies had a reputation for producing firearms of high quality and good design. SIG had produced a number of excellent designs that ranged from machineguns to handguns, a number of which had been adopted by the Swiss military. Many claim one SIG product, the P210 9mm semi-auto pistol, is one of the world's finest service 9mm pistols. J.P. Sauer had a number of well-designed pistols under its belt as well, including an excellent pocket pistol designated the Model 38H.

Being a Swiss company, SIG was restricted by that country's laws from selling its firearms to foreign nations. To circumvent these restrictions, SIG entered an agreement with J.P. Sauer for that company to manufacture their designs so that they could be sold on the international market. The guns of the two companies were marketed under the name of SIG-Sauer. Their first effort was the Model P220, which was one of three 9mm pistols authorized by the West German government for use by that country's police forces. Although SIG played a dominant role in the design of the P220, Sauer also made a contribution with the de-cocking system that was similar to that employed in the Model 38H.

The P226 competed in the U.S. military service pistol trials in the early 1980s. Even though it lost out to the Beretta 92 by a narrow margin, its stellar performance was enough for it to secure a sizable share of the U.S commercial and law enforcement market.

The growing sales of the P226 caused SIG-Sauer to open a subsidiary in the United States known as SigArms. SIG also entered into another collaborative relationship with the Swiss sporting arms company of Hammerli.

Although SIG-Sauer was recently sold, the company continues to manufacture firearms and operate in the United States through SigArms.

THE GLOCK 17 "SAFE ACTION" PISTOL

The Pistol that has Taken Police by Storm

This remarkable pistol is a classic not only because of the success of its design but also for the materials used in its construction. Its extensive use of synthetic plastic or polymer materials has resulted in a revolution in firearms manufacture and design that has gradually been followed by most of the company's competitors.

Nicknamed "Drastic Plastic" and "Combat Tupperware," no other series of self-defense pistols had the impact on the American law enforcement or armed self-defense scene like those from Glock, Inc. Estimates run that more than 60 percent of American law enforcement officers are armed with Glock handguns in a variety of calibers and sizes.

Glock pistols are chosen for a variety of reasons, but all of these reasons point to an extremely successful design that has established a solid reputation for accuracy, ease of control and most importantly in a defensive pistol—reliability.

HISTORY AND DEVELOPMENT

Gaston Glock is the driving force behind these guns and the design genius responsible for this incredibly successful product. In 1963, he established his firm in Deutsch-Wagram, a community near Vienna, Austria.

Although Glock had worked as an engineer for Steyr, his new company first made such mundane items as plastic curtain rods. During the 1970's, he secured contracts with the Austrian military for items ranging from entrenching tools to military knives and machinegun ammunition belt links.

It wasn't until the Austrian military announced they were interested in purchasing a new military pistol that Glock got serious about making a handgun. It is readily apparent that Gaston Glock in his first attempt to manufacture a serious military-style service pistol scored a long ball hit the first time at bat. The pistol achieved success and its designer's initial goal almost immediately because the Austrian military adopted the Glock 17 in 1982 as their P80 service pistol.

The next Glock conquest following the adoption by the Austrian military was the Norwegian military service pistol contract in 1984. This was the first major sale of the pistol outside of Austria and it was noticed by handgun manufacturers around the world.

Two years later, the Glock pistol came to America where there was some initial resistance to the "plastic" gun and more than one comparison was made to a cheap, throwaway plastic ink pen. The performance of this handgun soon overcame the naysayers and sales increased beyond expectation. In addition, anti-gun American politicians claimed this plastic gun was invisible to airport metal detectors. That simply isn't true, nor was it ever. The slide, barrel and recoil spring are all steel components and together comprise more than 80% of the gun's total weight. These steel components are easily recognizable by all security devices in use over the past 20 years.

Law enforcement agencies interested in converting to auto-pistols favored the Glock for several reasons. Transition to the Glock Safe Action was easier than any other contemporary design. The pistol had only one external operating lever and was less confusing to the individual used to the simple operation of the swing-out cylinder revolver. Another persuasive factor was the pistol's simplicity. This dispensed with the need for extensive gunsmith knowledge and police armorers were trained in as little as one day.

DESIGN CHARACTERISTICS AND FEATURES

The Glock 17 offered a number of innovations when first introduced, but by far the most notable was its one-piece polymer frame. Other manufacturers had previously experimented and attempted to make handguns with polymer parts, sometimes major polymer parts, but none had created such a solid design.

The result was a pistol that was considerably lighter than most of its contemporaries, and it also had a grip that came closer to fitting that elusive "one size fits all" category. Additionally, the double-stack magazine on the original Glock 17 was also made from polymer and held 17 rounds of 9x19mm ammunition! With one round loaded in the chamber, the Glock 17 was an 18 shooter.

According to various sources outside the company, the

The Glock 17 was an Austrian-made service pistol that revolutionized handgun design by its extensive use of plastic materials in its construction.

Glock pistol frames are molded from a proprietary derivative of Nylon 6 polymer. Nylon 6 polymer is chemically stable in a wide range of conditions and chemical environments. It will degrade very, very slightly over time when subjected to long periods of ultraviolet exposure, but Nylon 6's greatest weakness occurs when submersed in water in excess of 120 degrees. However, few bathers have been attacked in sulfur spring baths, so this is a small concern for most Glock owners and operators.

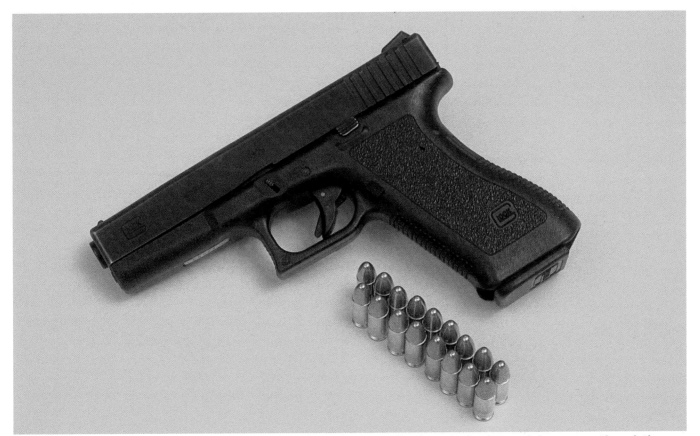

The use of polymer to construct the frame has enabled weight and grip size to be kept to a minimum even though the pistol has a 17-shot magazine.

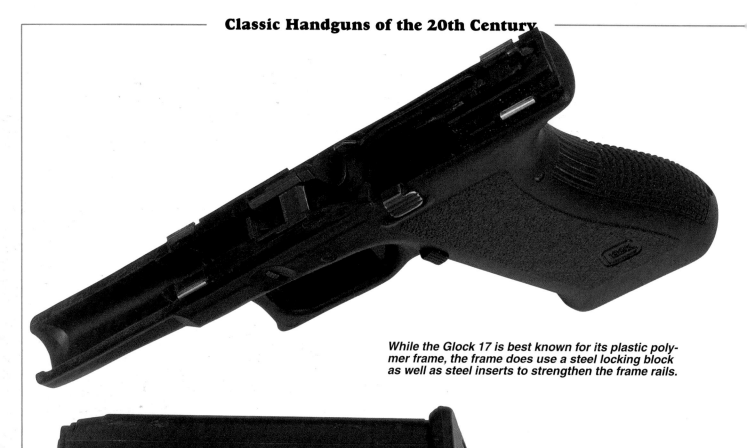

While the Glock 17 is best known for its plastic polymer frame, the frame does use a steel locking block as well as steel inserts to strengthen the frame rails.

The pistol's slide and barrel were forged of steel, and Glock used the Browning cam-operated, tilting-barrel system to lock the action during firing.

The Glock's controls were all on the left side of the frame and included a takedown latch, magazine catch, slide stop and a trigger that incorporated a safety. The latter is part of the pistol's trigger mechanism that the company classified as a "SAFE Action" system.

The system has three independent safety systems. The first is the trigger safety, which is located in the center of the trigger pad itself and is the most non-conventional of all the Glock safety systems. This trigger safety has to be deliberately depressed in order for the trigger to move. There is the firing pin lock that blocks movement of the firing pin or striker assembly until action from the trigger bar disengages it. The third and final safety system is the drop safety and it works off the rear part of the trigger bar, which has a cruciform shape. While sounding somewhat complicated on the printed page, the truth is it is simple in operation and works extremely reliably.

Another big plus to the design of the Glock 17 was its simplicity and the relatively low number of parts. When there are fewer parts, there is a significantly reduced opportunity for things to break or go wrong. The parts count varies according to how the parts are counted. Some commentators state the Glock design features 29 separate parts, while some authorities list 34. The main reason there is a discrepancy is due to the differences found in the rear sight, and whether or not the Glock in question has the extra pin in the locking block. This pin is not found on the Glock 17, 17L, 18, 19, 25 and 34 models. Regardless, the part count for this design remains low in comparison to other designs and the reliability factor has proven to be high.

In spite of the use of plastic, Glock pistols are remarkably rugged and durable. During the Austrian military pistol trials, one Glock 17 ran through 15,000 rounds without a single malfunction. Before they adopted the Glock 22 and 23 in 40

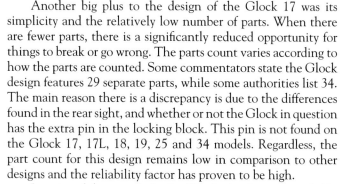

The pistol uses the Browning cam-operated tilting-barrel system to lock its action during firing.

S&W, the FBI ran higher round counts with even better results. At a recent IWA show, the company had a pistol on display that had run through an amazing 348,210 rounds. This specific pistol had been used by Hirtenberger for functional and durability tests of their 9mm ammunition and the only parts replaced throughout their testing was a recoil spring assembly and a firing pin spring. After the 348,210 rounds had been fired, an inspection revealed a crack in the barrel and it was replaced. But it is well to note that 65 percent of the rounds fired were stress level proof rounds, and another five percent of this total round count was high-pressure military combat ammunition.

SUBSEQUENT GLOCK MODELS

The next pistol to be born into the Glock family was the Glock 18. It appeared in 1986 and was a select-fire or full-auto pistol in 9x19mm caliber. Most experts of full-auto machine pistols have little positive to say on their behalf, other than the fact they are easier to conceal than a larger submachine gun. Nevertheless, if the target distances are limited to those of the average room in a home, the Glock 18 is effective with regard to the number of rounds placed on target. The Glock 18 operates at its best efficiency when it is fired in short two or three round bursts. Yet, it must be said the Glock 18 is a rather exotic member of the Glock family due to its restricted availability. It is sold only to military and law enforcement agencies.

The next two models to appear were the Glock Model 17L and the Glock 19 in 1988. The Glock 17L was the first 'Long Slide' Glock and was intended strictly for competition use. It featured a barrel of 6 inches and a slide to match. The early Glock 17L pistol barrels all featured compensator ports, but problems with these forced the factory to discontinue the barrel porting and later versions have all featured non-ported barrels.

The Glock 17L was also the first Glock pistol to feature the "Minus" trigger connector. The Minus trigger connector is sometimes mistakenly referred to as the 3.5 pound connector, which it is not. The trigger pulls on a 17L are between 4.5 pounds and 5.5 pounds, but the "Minus" connector does lighten the felt trigger pull significantly on a Glock pistol. Unfortunately, Glock feels it is too good at this task and could create a dangerous situation for those armed personnel who routinely hold people at gunpoint. The trigger pull is so light they could unintentionally discharge the pistol without realizing they are pulling the trigger.

The Glock 19 is a reduced-size Glock 17. This new pistol has a shorter height grip and a shortened slide, but the big advantage is its magazine capacity of 15 rounds, which matches that of many far larger 9mm service pistols.

In 1988, changes were made to the surface pattern on the grip of all Glock pistols. The original Glock 17 had a polymer grip with a "pebbled" surface texture, but starting in 1988, a serrated pattern was added to the front of the grip and a combination serrated/checkered pattern was found at the rear of the grip. These serrations aided in the shooter's purchase of the gun, especially so if the shooter's hand was moist from either perspiration or any sort of water or other liquid.

In 1990, Glock scored another coup when it initially announced the introduction of the Glock 20 and Glock 21 handguns. The Glock 20 is the large-frame Glock pistol chambered for the 10mm Auto cartridge and the Glock 21 is another large-frame pistol built

One of the attractions of all Glock pistols is their simplicity. Controls consist of a takedown catch, a unique trigger safety, a magazine catch and a slide stop.

The Glock "Safe Action" has a small lever set in the face of the trigger. When the chamber is loaded and the action partially cocked, the lever is set to lock the trigger. It is released when the trigger is properly engaged.

to handle the 45 ACP cartridge.

These guns were introduced at the SHOT Show of that year, but Smith & Wesson and Winchester made bigger news with the introduction of the 40 S&W-caliber cartridge and the prototype S&W Model 4006, which chambered the round. Gaston Glock took the technical information about the cartridge back to Austria with him and actually beat Smith &

Wesson into production with Glock's own 40 S&W pistols—the Glock 22 and Glock 23.

The Glock 22 is the same size as the original Glock 17, while the Glock 23 is a companion pistol to the Glock 19 in size and shape. The Glock 22, after 11 years of existence, has gone on to become the single-most popular sidearm in American law enforcement. Much of this success can be credited to the Glock's design and the compromise offered by the 40-caliber chambering. The 40 S&W cartridge offers big-bore terminal ballistics while at the same time maintaining the ability to stay within the size package of a conventional 9x19mm pistol.

It would be 4 more years before another pistol was added to the Glock family of handguns, and this time it was a pistol designed solely for competition called the Glock 24. Essentially, the Glock 24 is similar to the previous Glock 17L, but now it is chambered for the 40 S&W cartridge.

The year 1995 saw the introduction of the Glock 25. This pistol is chambered for the 380 ACP and is the same size and shape as the previous Glock 19 and Glock 23. The big difference here is the unlocked action. It operates via a straight blow-back design and the magazine, holding 15 rounds of 380 ammo, has a recessed wall in the back to take up the space not needed by the shorter 380 Auto cartridges.

The Glock 25 was created for sale in those countries that prohibit private citizens from owning any military- or police-caliber handgun. Apparently, it has proven to be a popular pistol in South America, but due to the lack of sufficient import points, it is prohibited from import and sale to the general public in this country.

In 1996, the Mini-Glocks were introduced. They are the Glock 26 in 9x19mm caliber and the Glock 27 in 40 S&W. Both are small, easy to carry and accurate.

A 380 Auto version of the Glock 26 was introduced the following year, and it was appropriately labeled the Glock 28. Also introduced in 1997 were the Glock 29 and the Glock 30.

The 1994 Crime Bill outlawing the possession of "ammunition feeding devices capable of holding more than 10 rounds of ammunition" fostered the development of and interest in guns holding 10 rounds or less.

While the Glocks 26, 27 and 28 can truly be called Mini-Glocks, the Glock 29 and 30 were mid-size versions of the large-frame Glock 20 and Glock 21 in 10mm and 45 ACP, respectively. Again, the magazine capacity is limited to 10 rounds in the Model 29 and nine rounds in the Model 30. (The Model 30 has an option of a slightly extended magazine holding 10 rounds, but it adds length to the butt of the pistol.)

During this same time period, a new law enforcement cartridge was developed by SigArms called the 357 SIG. In lighter projectile weights, this round offers not only the performance of a 357 Magnum revolver but also the ability to be combined with the high magazine capacity of a law enforcement auto-pistol.

As a result, in 1998 Glock introduced the 357 SIG-chambered Glock 31, 32, and 33 models. The Glock 31 is equivalent in size, shape and balance to the 17 while the 32 mimics the Glock 19 and 23. The Glock 33 is another Mini-Glock and the same size and shape as the Glock 26 and 27.

Also introduced that same year were two more models aimed for both competition and tactical team use by law enforcement agencies. The Glock 34 was a 9x19mm-caliber pistol featuring a 5.32 inch barrel and a longer slide than that found on the Glock 17. It employed the same frame as the

Glock 17, but the slide featured a prominent cutout on the top forward portion.

The Glock 35 was essentially the same pistol built on the Glock 22 frame, but chambered for the 40 S&W cartridge. These pistols were built to fit inside the box mandated by the freshly created IDPA shooting association and to meet the needs of different law enforcement emergency response teams that wanted a pistol with a longer sight radius, but with the proven reliability of the Glock pistol design.

The last member to join the Glock line-up was the Glock 36. Introduced in 1999, the Glock 36 is significant because it is the first Glock to feature an originally designed single-column magazine to provide an even narrower grip profile than that found on the previous Glock 30. The Glock 36 is a 45 Auto pistol and the single-column magazine holds six rounds. Although its overall shape and size is approximately the same as the Glock 30, the slide is narrower so the two pistols do not have interchangeable parts.

Gaston Glock may not appreciate the nicknames given his products, but in truth, the term "Combat Tupperware" has come to signify the respect so many military, law enforcement and armed civilians have developed over the years for the many different Glock products. The legacy of the Glock 17 is a long line of pistols that have earned a solid reputation for accuracy and reliability.

FIELD STRIPPING THE GLOCK

Begin by removing the magazine and checking that the chamber is unloaded and then un-cock the striker by pulling the trigger, making sure the muzzle points in a safe direction.

The barrel latch has two serrated edges that protrude out of grooves on both sides of the frame just above the trigger. Pull the slide back about 1/8 inch and grasp both of these protrusions and pull them down to release the barrel. The slide can then be removed off the front of the frame.

With the barrel removed, take out the recoil spring assembly followed by the barrel to complete the field strip. The pistol is assembled in reverse order.

SHOOTING AND HANDLING THE GLOCK 17

I must confess that I have never been a great fan of the Glock pistol. I also have to admit that much of my prejudice is rooted in the fact the Glock is a handgun with absolutely no aesthetic appeal. For me, it is just plain ugly when compared to other handguns like a Peacemaker, Model 19 or a Luger. The Glock does not give me the "pride of ownership" feeling that is associated with wearing a quality-made Swiss watch.

My antipathy towards the Glock is not based on aesthetics alone. I have never felt comfortable with the Safe Action trigger system. Muscular coordination is not my strong suit. When I was active in action shooting, I found my finger often inadvertently came in contact with the trigger when making a fast draw. My concern is, should this happen to me with a Glock, I might compress the first light take-up and end up releasing the striker. My other concern is that the only way to release the striker when it is partially cocked is to pull the trigger. If there were some de-cocking control, I would feel much more comfortable with the pistol.

Nevertheless, my shooting experience with Glock pistols over the past 20 years has resulted in a grudging respect and appreciation of its merits. All have performed well and made me realize that the Glock is actually a remarkable design.

It is the extensive use of plastic that gives the impression that the Glock is a cheap product. A closer examination of the pistol, however, reveals it is actually very well made. The steel parts like the barrel and slide exhibit a high quality of forging and machining, while the polymer frame is very well executed.

With only two controls (a magazine catch and slide stop), operating the Glock is simplicity itself. The well-designed grip provides good access to the trigger. The grip also places the barrel axis low in relation to the hand, giving the pistol excellent pointing characteristics as well as reducing recoil to a minimum.

The pistol has very good fixed sights that are easy to acquire quickly and the unique Safe Action trigger is very easy to control—perhaps too easy for uncoordinated individuals such as myself.

The trigger action needs some elaboration. While officially designed as a double-action-only, my immediate impression was that it was more like that of a single action that has a lot of pre-travel.

After the unlocking lever in the face of the trigger is compressed, there is a relatively light, long pull until the final stage where the striker is about to be released. At this point, depending upon the type of trigger, pulls vary from between as light as 3.5 pounds to 12 pounds. The latter pull is known as the New York Plus trigger and is often installed for police departments that want a heavier pull.

It is imperative when shooting a Glock to keep your finger off the trigger until you have to shoot. Under stress, one can inadvertently press the trigger to the point where the striker is to be released without being conscious of having done so. In truth, this applies to virtually all firearms.

Another point to stress is that the only way to un-cock the striker is to pull the trigger. As this has to be done in a number of handling and operating procedures, it is essential to double-check that the pistol's chamber is unloaded and, as an extra measure of safety, to keep the pistol pointing a safe direction.

While the Glock has great reliability, it is important to always retain a strong, firm grip on the pistol. If not, the slide will not cycle back far enough to load a fresh round in the chamber. This occurrence is known as "limp wristing" and usually happens with one-handed shooting. It is not just confined to Glocks, however, but can occur with any lightweight semi-automatic pistol.

The fact is Glocks are in use with thousands of police officers and civilians throughout the nation. All the officers and trainers to whom I have spoken have had high praise for the pistol. So putting my personal feelings and prejudices aside, I have to admit the Glock is an excellent service pistol and one of the classic handguns of the century.

COLLECTOR INTEREST

The Glock 17 is of such recent manufacture that it does not qualify as a collector item. Used pistol values do not exceed the price of the new models.

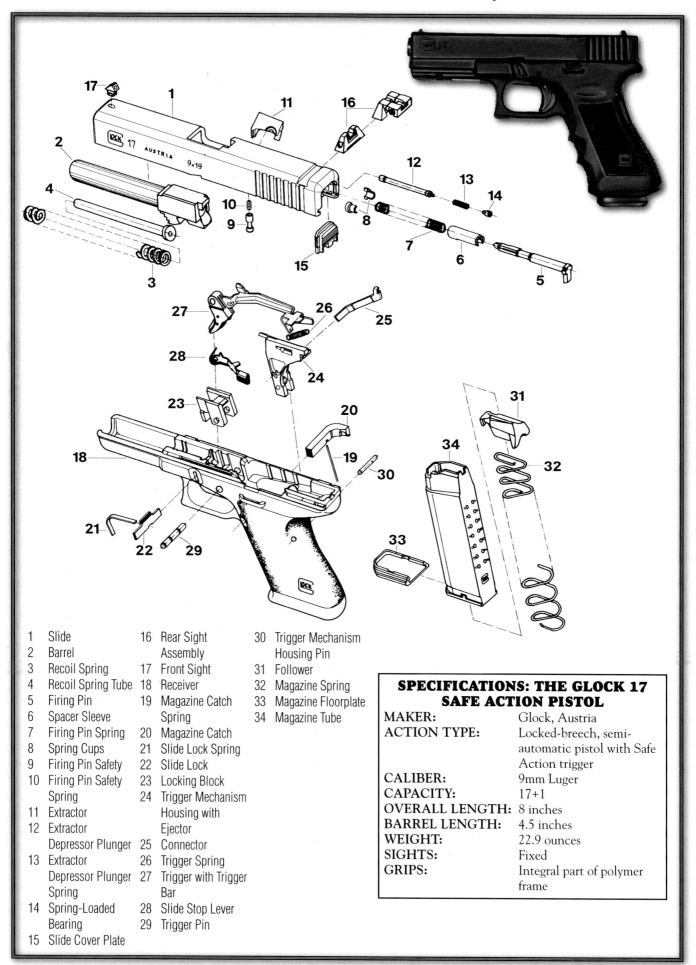

1	Slide	16	Rear Sight
2	Barrel		Assembly
3	Recoil Spring	17	Front Sight
4	Recoil Spring Tube	18	Receiver
5	Firing Pin	19	Magazine Catch
6	Spacer Sleeve		Spring
7	Firing Pin Spring	20	Magazine Catch
8	Spring Cups	21	Slide Lock Spring
9	Firing Pin Safety	22	Slide Lock
10	Firing Pin Safety	23	Locking Block
	Spring	24	Trigger Mechanism
11	Extractor		Housing with
12	Extractor		Ejector
	Depressor Plunger	25	Connector
13	Extractor	26	Trigger Spring
	Depressor Plunger	27	Trigger with Trigger
	Spring		Bar
14	Spring-Loaded	28	Slide Stop Lever
	Bearing	29	Trigger Pin
15	Slide Cover Plate		

30	Trigger Mechanism
	Housing Pin
31	Follower
32	Magazine Spring
33	Magazine Floorplate
34	Magazine Tube

SPECIFICATIONS: THE GLOCK 17 SAFE ACTION PISTOL

MAKER:	Glock, Austria
ACTION TYPE:	Locked-breech, semi-automatic pistol with Safe Action trigger
CALIBER:	9mm Luger
CAPACITY:	17+1
OVERALL LENGTH:	8 inches
BARREL LENGTH:	4.5 inches
WEIGHT:	22.9 ounces
SIGHTS:	Fixed
GRIPS:	Integral part of polymer frame

Collecting
CLASSIC HANDGUNS
Can They be Fired and What Are They Worth?

It is sometimes hard for me, as a shooter who grew up with the classic handguns that are described in this book, to accept that many are fast becoming vintage and, in some cases, antiques. The Colt Single-Action Army and the P08 Luger pistol obviously are in the latter category. It won't be long before these two are joined by others such as the Smith & Wesson M&P and Colt Detective Special.

All the classic handguns that have been described in this book are very well made. They can remain functional for many years and be safe to shoot, provided they are properly cared for. Even though a vintage handgun may be safe to shoot, there is the question of its value, and it is best not to fire handguns that have high collector interest. While safe, shooting may adversely mar the finish and lower the gun's value. Although I have briefly touched on the matter of potential collector interest in previous chapters, this must be viewed as only a rough guide.

Many of these classic handguns still exist, probably stored in home drawers and closets. In addition, quite a few are circulating as used handguns in gun shops and other places where firearms are legally sold. Except for specimens that have a high collector's value, most are reasonably priced.

IDENTIFICATION

The first task is to find out exactly what handgun you have. Hopefully, this book will help in such identification. Unfortunately, identification can be confusing with some handguns like the Colt Single-Action Army and the 45 Government Pistol. The difficulty is due to the number of clones of both these guns that are in circulation.

Generally, handguns have the maker's name roll-stamped somewhere, often on the right side of the barrel or slide. The gun's caliber is also roll-stamped here as well, but this may also be the source of some confusion as the caliber designation may be mistaken as the manufacturer's name. A case in point is the 45 Colt cartridge. Many non-gun people have sought

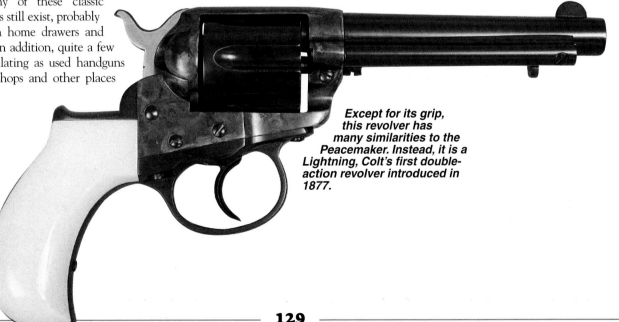

Except for its grip, this revolver has many similarities to the Peacemaker. Instead, it is a Lightning, Colt's first double-action revolver introduced in 1877.

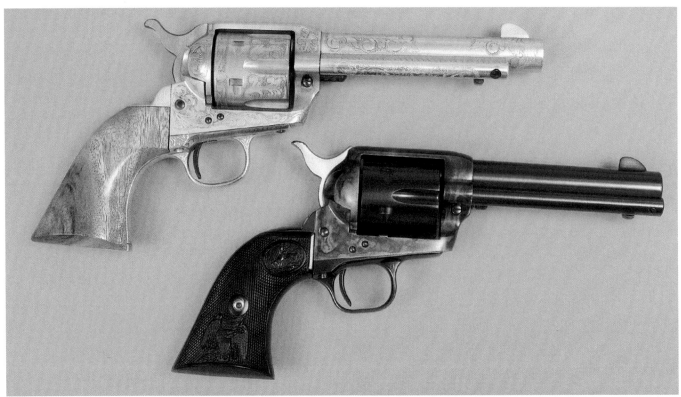

Identification can be problematical with guns that have been cloned by other manufacturers. The top revolver has all the appearance of a silver-plated, engraved model of the famous Colt Single Action like the one below it. It is in fact a clone from EMF.

my assistance in identifying an old family heirloom that they are sure is a vintage Colt. I often find the gun has been misidentified simply due to the barrel being marked 45 Colt.

Major manufacturers often have a distinctive company logo that will appear somewhere on the handgun. Colt has a rampart horse, while Smith & Wesson has a scroll logo made up of the letters S and W intertwined.

COLLECTOR CLASSICS

The Colt Single-Action Army and the Luger are obvious collector items. This is especially so in the case of the former, where one is lucky to find any model, irrespective of condition, under $600. Even Third Generation models are priced at over $700. With Lugers, models of World War I vintage usually have some collector value. Later models of World War II vintage generally have less value.

An increasing number of Colt 1911s are becoming collector items. This applies to almost all the 1911 models. Certain 1911 A1 pistols are also sought by collectors. These include pistols made by other manufacturers such as Singer Sewing Machine and the Signal Switch companies.

Many of the other classics have certain models that have collector value. There are many factors that affect this and are too numerous to cover here. In general, numbers made, vintage and special models are common factors, but not always.

Finally, condition, especially finish, is important in any estimate of value. Any pre-World War II pistol or revolver in mint condition and in its original box with documents such as manual and warranties may have collector potential. Highly engraved models may also command high values.

Any handgun that can be shown to have been carried by a notable personality can be valuable. For example, a Smith & Wesson M&P Victory Model by itself is probably worth under $400. The value can soar if it can be proved to have been carried by a highly decorated soldier or famous high-ranking officer.

There are used-gun catalogs that are useful in identifying and determining a handgun's potential value. Two that I use regularly are the *Standard Catalog of FIREARMS* by Ned Schwing (published by Krause Publications) and the *BLUE BOOK OF GUN VALUES* by S.P. Fjestad (published by Fjestad). The former has many photos that help in identification.

SHOOTING CLASSIC HANDGUNS

Virtually all of the classics in this book were intended for military, police or civilian self-defense. Most are still suitable for self-protection. Handguns of recent vintage are obvious candidates, but many of the earlier vintage handguns are still more than suitable.

Any Colt Government Model, Detective Special, Python, or S&W Model 10, 27 or 19 will serve one as well as anything available today for normal self-protection. In the end, the key question is "Is the gun safe to shoot with modern ammunition?" If the gun in question is in good mechanical condition, a quick answer is "Yes."

Even so, a handgun that is over 50 years old may have some hidden defects that are not easily seen. In addition, there is no way of knowing just how much use and abuse an old gun has had. Even though handguns are generally strong and very well made, parts do break or wear out with use.

Parts that tend to break are springs and the like. Larger components such as frames, barrels, slides and cylinders are much more durable. Any evidence of cracks, excessive play or looseness is an indication that a gun may not be safe to fire and should be checked by a qualified gunsmith.

Any German military handgun must be treated with caution because manufacturing standards deteriorated as the

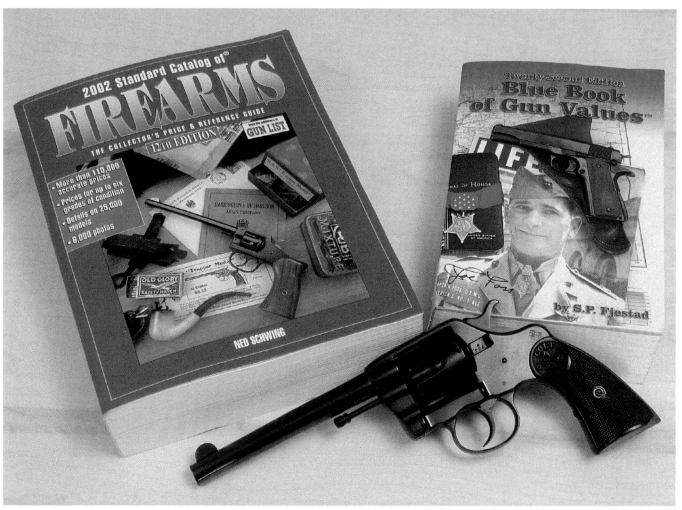

Used-gun price catalogs like these are a good reference for identification.

war progressed. As previously mentioned, some were made using slave labor that often sabotaged critical parts. Such guns should also be checked by a gunsmith

Some handguns have a history of accelerated wear. As discussed previously, the post-war Walther P38s with alloy frames are likely to experience slide cracking. Some of the magnum revolvers can shoot loose after continued firing of magnum ammunition. With such handguns, it is a good idea to limit the amount of ammunition fired in them and to constantly check them for any signs of wear. With the P38, the frame cracks are quite easy to spot. Magnum revolvers must be checked for signs of excessive movement in the cylinder/crane fit.

Finally, it is important to select the right ammunition for a classic handgun. Just as the handguns described have undergone various changes and upgrades, the same applies to much of the ammunition for which such guns are chambered. A good example is the 38 Special. During the last 40 years of the previous century, there were numerous attempts to increase the effectiveness of this ammunition. In most cases, this involved increasing the cartridge's velocity. The same applies to the 9mm Luger.

This does not mean that these classic handguns cannot handle such ammunition and are in danger of blowing up. What is more likely is that these high-pressure loads will accelerate

wear and cause fatigue cracks. Because of this, 38 Special +P and +P+ as well as 9mm +P loads should be avoided or at least used sparingly. By so doing, you can ensure that your classic handgun continues to function efficiently and reliably.

Most of the classics can still be shot, if in good condition. Shown here are a Colt 1911 (top right) and S&W Military & Police (bottom left).

CLASSIC HANDGUN AMMUNITION OF THE 20TH CENTURY

In Chapter 1, it was mentioned that there were few radically new handgun designs introduced after World War II. During the second half of the 20th century there were, however, many dramatic improvements made in respect to handgun ammunition.

AMMUNITION DEVELOPMENT AT THE TURN OF THE CENTURY

During the 19th century, significant ammunition advances included the invention of the percussion cap, self-contained cartridge and smokeless powder, which paved the way for the development of self-loading or semi-automatic firearms.

By the turn of the century, popular American handgun cartridges tended to be large calibers like 44 and 45, while Europeans were content with smaller calibers like 6.5mm, 7.72mm, 8mm and 9mm. An exception was England, where the 45 was the favored military cartridge, although some European armies did use calibers larger than 10mm.

During the 19th century, there had been little or no scientific ballistic studies about the effectiveness of caliber and velocity in respect to stopping power. Cartridges that were reputed to be good man stoppers generally tended to be the larger calibers. The reputation came from verbal reports and accounts from soldiers and others who had been involved in gunfights.

The first real scientific examination on wound effects from bullets occurred during the first decade of the new century. This was prompted by reports of the failure of the smaller Colt 38 to stop determined attackers. The study, which has become known as the Thompson/Lagarde tests, was quite exhaustive and involved shooting at animal and human cadavers as well as live animals in slaughter houses. The conclusion arrived at was that cartridge size was more important than velocity in terms of stopping power.

The study eventually led to the adoption by the U.S. military of the Colt 45 automatic pistol and its cartridge, the 45 ACP. The Thompson/Lagarde test was generally accepted as being the definitive examination of stopping power.

To some extent, the validity of the study was supported by reports of the superiority of the 45 ACP over smaller caliber cartridges. Most of these reports were unsupported anecdotal accounts and have given the 45 a somewhat inflated reputation.

THE RELIABILITY FACTOR

By the turn of the century, reliability affected revolver and pistol ammunition in two ways. Revolvers had been developed to a point where they could shoot any type of self-contained ammunition. In fact, the self-contained cartridge actually solved most of the revolver's functioning problems.

The situation with the new self-loading pistols was very different. Their ability to function could be adversely affected by various factors such as dirt, bullet material and shape. The latter two factors could cause feeding problems.

Soft lead bullets or ones with sharp edges could stick on the feed ramp causing a jam. Revolvers, not having feed ramps, were unaffected and could take advantage of the perceived, better stopping power of lead and irregularly shaped bullets. The problem of semi-automatic reliability was resolved by using only round-nose jacketed bullets.

International law, as dictated by various conventions such as those held in Geneva and Hague, also influenced ammunition by restricting military forces to use only round-nose fully jacketed ammunition.

At the beginning of the last century, revolver ammunition generally had lead bullets (back row) while semi-automatics were restricted to ammunition with fully cased bullets (front row) to ensure reliable feeding.

The 1980s saw the introduction of the very successful 40 S&W pistol cartridge (center) that split the difference in performance between the 45 ACP (left) and the 9mm Luger (right).

THE STOPPING POWER CONTROVERSY

The situation regarding handgun ammunition, as already described, remained unchanged for much of 20th century. Revolvers could shoot pretty much anything, while auto pistols were restricted to cartridges with jacketed round-nose bullets. Caliber was considered to be the deciding factor in stopping power.

Throughout the rest of the century, the question of bullet performance never went away. The gang era of the late 1920s and 30s raised concerns, not just of stopping power, but also of a bullet's ability to penetrate the body and vehicle armor being used by some criminal gangs. This led to the development of high velocity rounds like the 357 Magnum and the 38 Super.

The first three decades after World War II saw concerns about the effectiveness of the 38 Special. This led to the

(Left) The magnum cartridge appeared in the 1930s and was a revolver round called the 357 Magnum. Initially, semi-jacketed bullets were used to prevent the build-up of lead in the rifling grooves in the barrel. (Right) After World War II, high velocity ammunition with hollow-point bullets was developed in an attempt to enhance stopping power. This is a 38 Special +P with a 158-grain semi-wadcutter hollow-point bullet.

By the 1980s, ammunition development included reliable hollow-point ammunition for all the major semi-automatic pistol calibers.

development of the 41 Magnum. More importantly, it also led to improvements to the 38 special. This was achieved by increasing velocities and using hollow and softpoint bullets. The theory was that the latter would expand or mushroom on impact. The result would be a larger caliber, which created a bigger wound channel and more stopping power. While this high-velocity expanding ammunition seemed to provide better knockdown performance, there were some who were concerned about bullets failing to expand or penetrate deeply enough.

By this time, police departments were switching to high-capacity semi-automatic pistols. Advances were made in ammunition that included greatly enhanced reliability. More significantly, these improvements allowed autos to work reliably with expanding soft and hollow-point ammunition.

This was achieved by using semi-jacketed bullets where a copper or gilded jacket partially covered the bullet. The front of the bullet had a small cavity that exposed the softer lead core. The jacket enhanced feeding, yet pealed away on impact to expose the softer lead core that mushroomed to a greater diameter.

The effectiveness of this ammunition was also questioned and culminated in a single incident involving a shootout in Miami. This was to have a dramatic effect on future ammunition design.

The incident involved a violent shootout between several agents and two robbers. The agents were armed with a variety of firearms that included shotguns, revolvers and 9mm semi-automatic pistols. The robbers were armed with a mixture of weapons as well including handguns and a 223 semi-automatic carbine. The shootout began when the agents attempted to

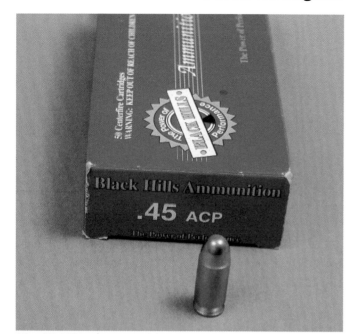

The 45 ACP was created for the Colt Government Model pistol of 1911. It established a formidable reputation as an effective fight-stopper.

The 9mm Parabellum was specially created for the P08 Luger pistol. It was to become the most widely used military pistol cartridge.

apprehend the robbers. In the gun battle that followed, both robbers were killed, but not before they had killed two agents and seriously wounded several others.

An autopsy examination revealed that the most aggressive of the robbers had sustained several wounds, one of which would have eventually been fatal. The concern was the fact that he had continued shooting even after sustaining the potentially fatal wound.

The incident raised concerns by the FBI about the effectiveness of the ammunition they were using. A full investigation of the incident was conducted, followed by various symposiums, which involved presentations from a variety of ammunition, medical and ballistic experts. At the conclusion of both, criteria in respect to caliber, penetration and expansion for police ammunition were compiled.

As a result of this investigation, the FBI requested a new 10mm cartridge and a pistol to arm its agents. Smith & Wesson was asked to develop a pistol to FBI specifications. The company had already been working on a similar 40-caliber cartridge and pistol.

The 40-caliber cartridge had several advantages over the 10mm. It could be used in 9mm-size pistols without a significant reduction of magazine capacity. The 10mm needed a larger pistol and had a smaller ammunition capacity.

The FBI passed on Smith & Wesson's 40 pistol and stayed with the 10mm. Smith & Wesson persevered with the new cartridge and pistol and "struck gold" when it was eagerly accepted by many police agencies. In fact, demand was so great that other pistol manufacturers began making 40 S&W pistols of their own.

The acceptance of the 40 S&W cartridge caused SigArms to develop a new cartridge called the 357 SIG. The cartridge used a 40-caliber cartridge case necked down to accept a

The 357 Magnum (right) was made to provide a cartridge with great penetration performance. It used a lengthened 38 Special (left) case.

The 38 Special was made for the Smith & Wesson M&P revolver. It was to become one of the most versatile and popular revolver cartridges of the century.

The 41 Magnum (right) had slightly less power than the 44 Magnum (left) and was an attempt to provide a replacement for the 38 Special.

Like the 357, which used a lengthened 38 Special case, the 44 Magnum (right) was developed by using a lengthened case of a 44 Special (left). For many years it reigned as the world's most powerful handgun cartridge.

357-caliber bullet. The result was a round that came close to matching the ballistic performance of the 357 Magnum. The new cartridge was well received and a number of departments decided to adopt it.

Great strides had been made in handgun ammunition design during the 1970s and 80s, especially in respect to reliability and performance. In fact, self-loading pistols were no longer restricted to only jacketed bullets but could take full advantage of high-velocity expanding ammunition.

A better understanding of the terminal effects of soft and hollow-point ammunition resulted in a number of very successful self-defense cartridges. Another concern that was successfully addressed was that of lead contamination caused by the firing of ammunition in confined areas such as indoor firing ranges, which could result in serious health issues for shooters and employees. By using better primers and fully encasing bullets (including hollow points) with a thin non-toxic metal jacket, ammunition makers have successfully reduced airborne lead contamination to a minimum.

Another ammunition improvement has been the reduction of muzzle flash, which can be of concern when shooting in low light conditions. Apart from giving the shooter's position away, excessive muzzle flash can have a temporary blinding effect. By using special powders this problem has largely been resolved.

To sum up, the advances in ammunition design has resulted in cartridges that are safer, more reliable and more effective than ever before.

CLASSIC 20TH-CENTURY CARTRIDGES

The following is a list of significant 20th-century ammunition listed in a rough chronological order. Most have been briefly described in the chapters that discuss the first handguns for which they were chambered.

THE 9MM LUGER (PARABELLUM)

This cartridge was specifically made for the DWM P08 Luger pistol because many felt that its original chambering of the 7.65mm was too puny. After its introduction in 1902, the 9mm Luger has become one of the most popular military cartridges of all time.

While the Europeans appear to have been content with the

The 10mm pistol round (right) was made to the specifications of the FBI. It is shown here next to a 45 ACP (left) for comparison.

9mm's performance, American's have not. Much of the reason for this is the formidable reputation that the 45 ACP gained for its fight-stopping ability.

The fact is that when properly loaded with good expanding bullets, the 9mm Luger is quite acceptable for most defense situations. The adoption by our military of the cartridge in 1980 has done much to make it more acceptable to American shooters.

THE 45 ACP

This cartridge and the Colt 1911 have an almost cult-like following. Adopted by the U.S. military in 1911, it remained in service until replaced by the 9mm in 1980. During its 70 years of service, it acquired a legendary reputation as a man stopper.

The 45 ACP's ability as a fight stopper has been somewhat exaggerated by its many supporters. This is especially so in respect to the full-metal-jacket cartridge. In this loading, it was superior to most of the ammunition carried by the opposing Axis forces including possibly the 9 mm.

The 45 also has great accuracy potential and can compete on the target ranges with any other cartridge. Recent developments in high velocity expanding bullets have greatly enhanced the cartridge in respect to stopping power.

The 45 seems to be as popular today as it ever was. While its fight-stopping reputation has been somewhat exaggerated in

The 40 S&W (right) was a pistol cartridge with very similar performance to the FBI 10mm cartridge (left). Its shorter case enabled it to be chambered in 9mm-size pistols and magazine capacity, compared to the 9mm, was only marginally reduced.

The 357 SIG (right) was intended to create a pistol cartridge with similar performance to the 357 Magnum. It was a bottleneck design that used a 40 S&W case necked down for a 357 bullet.

the past, there is no denying it is one of the world's truly classic handgun cartridges.

THE 38 S&W SPECIAL

Introduced in 1902, this cartridge was developed for the Smith & Wesson Military and Police revolver. Smith & Wesson had hopes that both would be accepted by the U.S. military to replace the Colt 38 revolver and its cartridge.

The 38 Special used a slightly longer case than the 38 Colt and it was a more accurate and versatile cartridge. In spite of this, the military did not adopt it as their service sidearm, choosing instead the Colt 45 auto.

The cartridge got a much better reception from others, however, because of its accuracy, mild recoil and reasonable stopping power. It remained the standard cartridge of American police until the 1980s when semi-automatic pistols began replacing revolvers in police holsters.

At various times, law enforcement has expressed concerns about the stopping performance of the cartridge. Eventually, this was partially resolved with 38 ammunition being loaded to higher velocities with expanding bullets.

The 38 Special has always been highly regarded for its accuracy, especially when loaded with wadcutter bullets, which were, for many years, very popular with target shooters throughout the world.

The widespread adoption by police of semi-automatic pistols has reduced the demand for the 38 Special. Nevertheless, it remains in production, and with all the improvements in bullet design, is even more versatile than ever.

THE 357 S&W MAGNUM

This was the world's first magnum handgun cartridge and was created in 1935 because of police concerns about the increased use of automobiles and bulletproof vests by criminal gangs. Something was called for that could defeat both. Smith & Wesson responded by producing stronger revolvers that could handle special 38 ammunition of far greater power and performance. Eventually, this led to the development of the 357 Magnum.

The cartridge had a case that was longer than the 38 Special to provide extra space for powder. Together with its Smith & Wesson revolver, the cartridge had a very impressive performance. In terms of penetration, stopping power and

long-range accuracy, it was far superior to the 38 Special. The cartridge was an instant hit, not just with police, but with civilians as well. Revolvers chambered for the cartridge could also chamber and shoot the milder 38 Specials. Sportsmen also discovered that the 357 Magnum was well suited for hunting small- and medium-sized game.

Demand for the 357 Magnum was enough for Colt to chamber the Single-Action Army and the big New Service revolvers for it. Although the cartridge was an immediate success, its law enforcement use was generally limited to special situations and Highway Patrol officers. It was also felt that the cartridge had too much penetration for use in urban areas. Other drawbacks were its heavy recoil and the fact that only large-frame revolvers could handle it.

In the years following World War II, the popularity of the cartridge increased as more revolvers were chambered for it. The fact these were not as big as the pre-war 357 Magnum revolvers also helped in making the cartridge more acceptable.

With the introduction of the 44 and 41 Magnums, the 357 lost some of its appeal to the handgun hunting community. This was mitigated by increased police use of the cartridge because of dissatisfaction with the performance of the 38 Special. Stopping power of the cartridge was also enhanced by the use of expanding bullets.

Nevertheless, universal replacement of the 38 Special by the 357 never occurred mainly because of concerns that it might over-penetrate. Its recoil was also a concern even though it was less than the larger magnums. Increased use of the cartridge began to cause accelerated wear in some revolvers.

Manufacturers responded by strengthening their revolvers, fitting better rubber grips and providing heavier barrels. The latter two features helped greatly in controlling recoil.

By the 1980s, it was generally agreed that the 357 Magnum had the best stopping power of any handgun cartridge, including the 44 Magnum. The cartridge is still in production and is still the yardstick to which others are compared when it comes to stopping effectiveness.

THE S&W 44 MAGNUM

When introduced in 1955, this cartridge displaced the 357 Magnum as the world's most powerful handgun cartridge. It used a lengthened 44 Special case and revolvers chambered for it could also shoot the 44 Special.

The 44 Magnum was an instant success with sport shooters and handgun hunters. It was accurate and hard hitting but had violent recoil, which limited its use for self-protection, although a few police officers did adopt it. But police use was restricted because of fears of excessive penetration. The fact that only big revolvers could handle the cartridge also presented difficulties for officers with small hands.

More powerful handgun cartridges have since superseded the 44 Magnum. It remains in production, however, and is still popular with sportsmen and handgun hunters.

THE 41 S&W MAGNUM

During the early stages of the stopping-power controversy, a number of noted handgun authorities suggested the answer lay in a new cartridge of greater power than the 38 Special and loaded with a bullet of 40 caliber or more.

Smith & Wesson and Remington stepped up to the plate with a new 41-caliber cartridge and revolver that was released in 1964. The revolver was really just a Model 29 chambered for the new cartridge. The 41 Magnum was similar to the 44 Magnum except for caliber. It also was not as powerful. While the cartridge's recoil was not as violent as the 44's, it was still enough to be intimidating to some. A non-magnum 41 was also made.

Neither of these cartridges, nor the revolver, received the acceptance from law enforcement that had been anticipated. Part of the reason was that the 41 revolvers were as big as the 44 Magnums. This, combined with the heavy recoil, made them difficult to shoot well.

The 41 Magnum did find some acceptance with handgun hunters. It has managed to survive mainly because it has a band of dedicated shooters.

THE 40 S&W

This is a pistol cartridge that was developed by Smith & Wesson in the 1980s. Ironically, it was introduced just as the company was developing a 10mm pistol for the FBI.

The Bureau was concerned about the poor performance of the 9mm in a Miami shootout and had set out specifications for a new 10mm-caliber round. The cartridge was a down-loaded version of an earlier 10mm that had been specially created for an earlier pistol. The latter, known as the Bren Ten never went into full production and the cartridge was left without a home.

The 40 S&W was basically the same caliber but had a shorter case, which enabled the pistols made for it to be similar in size to the 9mm models. Even more importantly, magazine capacities were only reduced by a few rounds. In contrast, the Bureau's 10mm needed a larger pistol and had a greater loss of ammunition capacity.

The ballistic performance of both cartridges was basically the same.

Even though the FBI rejected the 40 S&W in favor of their 10mm, the latter was not as well received by police and civilians. It survives today but only with a limited following. In complete contrast, the 40 S&W has enjoyed excellent sales in the general police market with a number of agencies adopting it over the 9mm.

The 40 S&W has successfully split the difference between the vaunted 45 ACP and the 9mm Luger. By all accounts, the agencies that use it are more than satisfied with its overall performance.

THE 357 SIG

This is a bottleneck cartridge developed by SIG-Sauer's American subsidiary SigArms. The cartridge uses a 40 S&W necked down to accept a smaller diameter 357 bullet. Being a bottleneck design, it provides positive feeding and it has a ballistic performance that is close to that of the 357 Magnum revolver cartridge.

Another of the cartridge's assets is that there is no reduction in magazine capacity. The pistols chambered for it are the same in almost all respects as the 40 S&W models.

The 357 SIG has been very well received by law enforcement, and at one stage, it seemed it might even surpass the 40 S&W in popularity. In fact, it may very well do so in this century.

The Directory of Handgun
Manufacturers, Importers & Distributors

Accu-Tek
4510 Carter Ct.
Chino, CA 91710
909-627-2404
FAX: 909-627-7817
www.accu-tekfirearms.com

AcuSport Corporation
One Hunter Place
Bellefontaine, OH 43311
513-593-7010
FAX: 513-592-5625

American Derringer Corp.
127 N. Lacy Drive
Waco, TX 76715
254-799-9111
FAX: 254-799-7935
www.amderringer.com

American Frontier Firearms
40725 Brook Trails Way
Aguanga, CA 92536
909-763-0014
FAX: 909-763-0014

Armscorp USA Inc.
4424 John Avenue
Baltimore, MA 21227
410-247-6200
FAX: 410-247-6205

Autauga Arms
Pratt Plaza Mall No. 13
Pratville, AL 36067
800-262-9563
FAX: 334-361-2961

Auto-Ordnance Corp.
P.O. Box 220
Blauvelt, NY 10913
845-735-4500
FAX: 845-735-4610
www.auto-ordnance.com

Benelli U.S.A.
17603 Indian Head Highway
Accokeek, MD 20607
301-283-6981
FAX: 301-283-6988
www.benelliusa.com

Beretta U.S.A. Corp.
17601 Beretta Drive
Accokeek, MD 20607
301-283-2191
FAX: 301-283-0435
www.berettausa.com

Bernardelli Vincenzo, S.P.A.
25030 Torbole Casaglia
Gardone, V.T., Brescia, Italy
+39 030 215 1094
FAX: +39 030 215 0963

Briley Mfg. Company
1230 Lumpkin Road
Houston, TX 77043
800-331-5718
FAX: 713-932-1043

Brown, Ed Products
P.O. Box 492
Perry, MO 63462
573-565-3261
FAX: 573-565-2791

Browning
One Browning Place
Morgan, UT 84050
801-876-2711
Parts & Service
800-322-4626
www.browning.com

Caspian Arms, Ltd.
75 Cal Foster Dr.
Wolcott, VT 05680
802-472-6454
FAX: 802-472-6709

Casull Arms Company, Inc.
P.O. Box 1629
Afton, WY 83110
307-886-0200
www.casullarms.com

Charter 2000, Inc.
273 Canal Street
Shelton, CT 06484
203-922-1652
FAX: 203-922-1469

Cimarron Arms
P.O. Box 906
105 Winding Oak Road
Fredericksburg, TX 78624
830-997-9090
FAX: 830-997-0802
www.cimarron-firearms.com

Cobra Enterprises
1960 S. Milestone Dr., Suite
Salt Lake City, UT 84104
801-908-8300
FAX: 801-908-8301
www.cobrapistols.com

Colt Firearms
P.O. Box 1868
Hartford, CT 06144
800-962-COLT
FAX: 860-244-1449
www.colt.com

Colt Blackpowder Arms Co.
110 8th Street
Brooklyn, NY 11215
212-925-2159
FAX: 212-966-4986

Connecticut Valley Arms, Inc. (CVA)
5988 Peachtree Corners East
Norcross, GA 30071
770-449-4687
FAX: 770-242-8546
www.cva.com

CZ-U.S.A.
P.O. Box 171073
Kansas City, KS 66117- 0073
913-321-1811
FAX: 913-321-2251
www.cz-usa.com

Daly, Charles Inc.
P.O. Box 6625
Harrisburg, PA 17112
866-325-9486
FAX: 717-540-8567
www.charlesdaly.com

Ellett Bros.
P.O. Box 128
Chapin, SC 29036
803-345-3751
FAX: 803-345-1820

EMF Co., Inc.
1900 E. Warner Ave. Suite 1-D
Santa Ana, CA 92705
949-261-6611
FAX: 949-756-0133

Enterprise Arms Inc.
15861 Business Center Dr.
Irwindale, CA 91706
626-962-8712
FAX: 626-962-4692
www.entreprise.com

Euro-Imports
605 Main Street E
El Cajon, CA 92020
619-442-7005
FAX: 619-442-7005

European American Armory
P.O. Box 1299
Sharpes, FL 32959
321-639-4842
FAX: 321-639-7006
www.eacorp.com

Freedom Arms
314 Hwy. 239
Freedom, WY 83120
307-883-2468
FAX: 307-883-2005
www.freedomarms.com

Gamba, U.S.A.
P.O. Box 60452
Colorado Springs, CO 80960
719-578-1145
FAX: 719-444-0731

Glock, Inc.
6000 Highlands Parkway
Smyrna, GA 30082
770-432-1202
FAX: 770-433-8719
www.glock.com

Hammerli USA
19296 Oak Grove Circle
Groveland, CA 95321
209-962-5311
FAX: 209-962-5931
www.hammerliusa.com

Heckler & Koch, Inc.
21480 Pacific Boulevard
Sterling, VA 20166
703-450-1900
FAX: 703-450-8160
www.hecklerkoch-usa.com

Heritage Manufacturing, Inc.
4600 NW 135th St.
Opa Locka, FL 30054
305-685-5966
FAX: 305-687-6721

High Standard Manufacturing Co.
5200 Mitchelldale Suite E-17
Houston, TX 77092
713-462-4200
FAX: 713-681-5665

Horton, Lew, Distributing Co., Inc.
15 Walkup Drive
Westboro, MA 01581
508-366-7400
FAX: 508-366-5332

Kahr Arms
P.O. Box 220
Blauvelt, NY 10913
845-735-4500
FAX: 845-735-4610
www.kahr.com

Kel-Tec CNC, Inc.
1475 Cox Rd.
Cocoa, FL 32926
321-631-0068
FAX: 321-631-1169

Kimber
1 Lawton Street
Yonkers, NY 10705
800-880-2418
www.kimberamerica.com

L.A.R. Manufacturing
4133 West Farm Road
West Jordan, UT 84088
801-280-3505
FAX: 801-280-1972

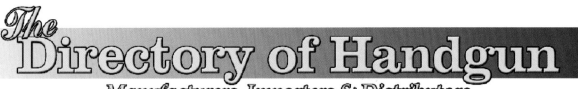

The Directory of Handgun
Manufacturers, Importers & Distributors

Les Baer Custom Inc.
29601 34th Ave.
Hillsdale, IL 61257
309-658-2716
FAX: 309-658-2610
www.lesbaer.com

Magnum Research, Inc.
7110 University Avenue N.E.
Minneapolis, MN 55432
763-574-1868
FAX: 763-574-0109
www.magnumresearch.com

M.O.A. Corp.
2451 Old Camden Pike
Eaton, OH 45320
937-456-3669
www.moaguns.com

Navy Arms Co.
219 Lawn St.
Martinsburg, WV 25401
304-262-9870
FAX: 304-262-1658
www.navyarms.com

North American Arms
2150 South 950 East
Provo, UT 84606
801-374-9990
FAX: 801-374-9998

Nowlin Manufacturing Co.
20622 South 4092 Road
Claremore, OK 74019
918-342-0689
FAX: 918-342-0624

Olympic Arms, Inc.
624 Old Pacific Highway SE
Olympia, WA 98513
360-459-7940
FAX: 360-491-3447
www.olyarms.com

Para-Ordnance
980 Tapscott Rd.
Toronto, Ontario M1X 1C3
416-297-7855
FAX: 416-297-1289
www.paraord.com

Pedersoli Davide & Co.
Via Artigiani, 57-25063
Gardone Val Trompia, Brescia
Italy 25063

Phoenix Arms
1420 South Archibald Ave.
Ontario, CA 91761
909-947-4843
FAX: 909-947-6798

Reeder, Gary Custom Guns
2601 7th Avenue East
Flagstaff, AZ 86004
928-526-3313
FAX: 928-526-1287
www.reedercustomguns.com

Rock River Arms Inc.
1042 Cleveland Road
Colona, IL 61241
309-792-5780
FAX: 309-792-5781
www.rockriverarms.com

Savage Arms
100 Springdale Road
Westfield, MA 01085
413-568-7001
FAX: 413-568-8386

Seecamp, L.W.C.
301 Brewster Rd.
Milford, CT 06460
203-877-3429

SGS Importers International
1750 Brielle Ave., Unit B-1
Wanamassa, NJ 07712
732-493-0302
FAX: 732-493-0301
www.firestorm-sgs.com

SigArms, Inc.
18 Industrial Drive
Exeter, NH 03833
603-772-2302
FAX: 603-772-9082
www.sigarms.com

Smith & Wesson
2100 Roosevelt Road
Springfield, MA 01104
800-331-0852
FAX: 413-747-3317
www.smith-wesson.com

Springfield Armory, Inc.
420 West Main Street
Geneseo, IL 61254
309-944-5631
FAX: 309-944-3676
www.springfield-armory.com

SSK Industries
590 Woodvue Lane
Wintersville, OH 43953
740-264-0176
FAX: 740-264-2257
www.sskindustries.com

S.T.I. International, Inc.
114 Halmar Cove
Georgetown, TX 78628
800-959-8201
FAX: 512-819-0465
www.stiguns.com

Stoeger Industries
17603 Indian Head Highway
Accokeek, MD 20607
301-283-6300
FAX: 301-283-6986

Sturm Ruger & Co., Inc
10 Lacey Place
Southport, CT 06890
203-259-7843
FAX: 203-256-3367
www.ruger-firearms.com

Taurus International
16175 NW 49th Av.
Miami, FL 33014
305-624-1115
FAX: 305-623-1126
www.taurususa.com

Thompson/Center Arms Co.
Farmington Road
P.O. Box 5002
Rochester, NH 03867
603-332-2394
FAX: 603-332-5133
www.tcarms.com

Tristar Sporting Arms
P.O. Box 7496
1814-16 Linn
North Kansas City, MO 64116
816-421-1400
FAX: 816-421-4182
www.tristarsportingarms.com

Turnbull, Doug Restoration, Inc.
6680 Route 5 & 20
P.O. Box 471
Bloomfield, NY 14469
585-657-6338
FAX: 585-657-6338
www.turnbullrestoration.com

United States Fire Arms Manufacturing Co.
55 Van Dyke Av.
Hartford, CT 06106
877-277-6901
FAX: 860-724-6809
www.usfirearms.com

Valtro U.S.A.
24800 Mission Blvd.
Hayward, CA 94544
510-489-8477
FAX: 510-489-8477

Volquartsen Custom
24276 240th Street
Carroll, IA 51401
712-792-4238
FAX: 712-792-2542
www.volquartsen.com

Walther
2100 Roosevelt Avenue
Springfield, MA 01102
800-372-6454
FAX: 413-747-3682
www.waltheramerica.com

Wesson, Dan Firearms
5169 Highway 12 South
Norwich, NY 13815
607-336-1174
FAX: 607-336-2730
www.danwessonfirearms.com

Wichita Arms
923 E. Gilbert
Wichita, KS 67211
316-265-0061
FAX: 316-265-0760

Wildey, Inc.
P.O. Box 1038
Warren, CT 06754
860-355-9000
FAX: 860-354-7759
www.wildeyguns.com

Wilson Combat
2234 CR 719
P.O. Box 578
Berryville, AR 72616
870-545-3635
FAX: 870-545-3310

FOR COLLECTOR ◆ HUNTER ◆ SHOOTER ◆ OUTDOORSMAN
IMPORTANT NOTICE TO BOOK BUYERS

Books listed here may be bought from Ray Riling Arms Books Co., 6844 Gorsten St., P.O. Box 18925, Philadelphia, PA 19119, Phone 215/438-2456; FAX: 215-438-5395. E-Mail: sales@rayrilingarmsbooks.com. Larry Riling is the researcher and compiler of "The Arms Library" and a seller of gun books for over 32 years. The Riling stock includes books classic and modern, many hard-to-find items, and many not obtainable elsewhere. These pages list a portion of the current stock. They offer prompt, complete service, with delayed shipments occurring only on out-of-print or out-of-stock books.

Visit our web site at **www.rayrilingarmsbooks.com** and order all of your favorite titles on line from our secure site.

NOTICE FOR ALL CUSTOMERS: Remittance in U.S. funds must accompany all orders. For your convenience we now accept VISA, MasterCard & American Express. For shipments in the U.S. add $7.00 for the 1st book and $2.00 for each additional book for postage and insurance. Minimum order $10.00. International

Orders add $13.00 for the 1st book and $5.00 for each additional book. All International orders are shipped at the buyer's risk unless an additional $5 for insurance is included. USPS does not offer insurance to all countries unless shipped Air-Mail please e-mail or call for pricing.

Payments in excess of order or for "Backorders" are credited or fully refunded at request. Books "As-Ordered" are not returnable except by permission and a handling charge on these of 10% or $2.00 per book which ever is greater is deducted from refund or credit. Only Pennsylvania customers must include current sales tax.

A full variety of arms books also available from Rutgers Book Center, 127 Raritan Ave., Highland Park, NJ 08904/908-545-4344; FAX: 908-545-6686 or I.D.S.A. Books, 1324 Stratford Drive, Piqua, OH 45356/937-773-4203; FAX: 937-778-1922.

Age of the Gunfighter; Men and Weapons on the Frontier 1840-1900, by Joseph G. Rosa, University of Oklahoma Press, Norman, OK, 1999. 192 pp., illustrated. Paper covers. $21.95

Stories of gunfighters and their encounters and detailed descriptions of virtually every firearm used in the old West.

Beretta Automatic Pistols, by J.B. Wood, Stackpole Books, Harrisburg, PA, 1985. 192 pp., illus. $24.95

Only English-language book devoted to the Beretta line. Includes all important models.

Colt: An American Legend, by R.L. Wilson, Artabras, New York, 1997. 406 pages, fully illustrated, most in color. $35.00

A reprint of the commemorative album celebrates 150 years of the guns of Samuel Colt and the manufacturing empire he built, with expert discussion of every model ever produced, the innovations of each model and variants, updated model and serial number charts and magnificent photographic showcases of the weapons.

The Colt Model 1905 Automatic Pistol, by John Potocki, Andrew Mowbray Publishing, Lincoln, RI, 1998. 191 pp., illus. $28.00

Covers all aspects of the Colt Model 1905 Automatic Pistol, from its invention by the legendary John Browning to its numerous production variations.

Colt Peacemaker British Model, by Keith Cochran, Cochran Publishing Co., Rapid City, SD, 1989. 160 pp., illus. $35.00

Covers those revolvers Colt squeezed in while completing a large order of revolvers for the U.S. Cavalry in early 1874, to those magnificent cased target revolvers used in the pistol competitions at Bisley Commons in the 1890s.

Colt Peacemaker Encyclopedia, by Keith Cochran, Keith Cochran, Rapid City, SD, 1986. 434 pp., illus. $60.00

A must book for the Peacemaker collector.

Colt Peacemaker Encyclopedia, Volume 2, by Keith Cochran, Cochran Publishing Co., SD, 1992. 416 pp., illus. $60.00

Included in this volume are extensive notes on engraved, inscribed, historical and noted revolvers, as well as those revolvers used by outlaws, lawmen, movie and television stars.

COLT PRESENTATIONS: FROM THE FACTORY LEDGERS 1856-1869, by Herbert G. Houze. Lincoln, RI: Andrew Mowbray, Inc. , 2003. 112 pages, 45 b&w photos. Softcover. $21.95

Samuel Colt was a generous man. He also used gifts to influence government decision makers. But after Congress investigated him in 1854, Colt needed to hide the gifts from prying eyes, which makes it very difficult for today's collectors to document the many revolvers presented by Colt and the factory. Using the original account journals of the Colt's Patent Fire Arms Manufacturing Co., renowned arms authority Herbert G. Houze finally gives us the full details behind hundreds of the most exciting Colts ever made.

Colt Revolvers and the Tower of London, by Joseph G. Rosa, Royal Armouries of the Tower of London, London, England, 1988. 72 pp., illus. Soft covers. $15.00

Details the story of Colt in London through the early cartridge period.

Colt's SAA Post War Models, by George Garton, The Gun Room Press, Highland Park, NJ, 1995. 166 pp., illus. $39.95

Complete facts on the post-war Single Action Army revolvers. Information on

calibers, production numbers and variations taken from factory records.

Colt Single Action Army Revolvers: The Legend, the Romance and the Rivals, by "Doc" O'Meara, Krause Publications, Iola, WI, 2000. 160 pp., illustrated with 250 photos in b&w and a 16 page color section. $34.95

Production figures, serial numbers by year, and rarities.

Colt Single Action Army Revolvers and Alterations, by C. Kenneth Moore, Mowbray Publishers, Lincoln, RI, 1999. 112 pp., illustrated. $35.00

A comprehensive history of the revolvers that collectors call "Artillery Models." These are the most historical of all S.A.A. Colts, and this new book covers all the details.

Colt Single Action Army Revolvers and the London Agency, by C. Kenneth Moore, Andrew Mowbray Publishers, Lincoln, RI, 1990. 144 pp., illus. $35.00

Drawing on vast documentary sources, this work chronicles the relationship between the London Agency and the Hartford home office.

The Colt U.S. General Officers' Pistols, by Horace Greeley IV, Andrew Mowbray Inc., Lincoln, RI, 1990. 199 pp., illus. $38.00

These unique weapons, issued as a badge of rank to General Officers in the U.S. Army from WWII onward, remain highly personal artifacts of the military leaders who carried them. Includes serial numbers and dates of issue.

Colts from the William M. Locke Collection, by Frank Sellers, Andrew Mowbray Publishers, Lincoln, RI, 1996. 192 pp., illus. $55.00

This important book illustrates all of the famous Locke Colts, with captions by arms authority Frank Sellers.

Colt's Dates of Manufacture 1837-1978, by R.L. Wilson, published by Maurie Albert, Coburg, Australia; N.A. distributor Madis Books, TX, 1997. 61 pp. $7.50

An invaluable pocket guide to the dates of manufacture of Colt firearms up to 1978.

Cowboy Hero Cap Pistols, by Rudy D'Angelo, Antique Trader Books, Dubuque, IA, 1998. 196 pp., illus. Paper covers. $34.95

Aimed at collectors of cap pistols created and named for famous film and television cowboy heros, this in-depth guide hits all the marks. Current values are given.

The Derringer in America, Volume 1, The Percussion Period, by R.L. Wilson and L.D. Eberhart, Andrew Mowbray Inc., Lincoln, RI, 1985. 271 pp., illus. $48.00

A long awaited book on the American percussion deringer.

The Derringer in America, Volume 2, The Cartridge Period, by L.D. Eberhart and R.L. Wilson, Andrew Mowbray Inc., Publishers, Lincoln, RI, 1993. 284 pp., illus. $65.00

Comprehensive coverage of cartridge deringers organized alphabetically by maker. Includes all types of deringers known by the authors to have been offered to the American market.

The Dutch Luger (Parabellum) A Complete History, by Bas J. Martens and Guus de Vries, Ironside International Publishers, Inc., Alexandria, VA, 1995. 268 pp., illus. $49.95

The history of the Luger in the Netherlands. An extensive description of the Dutch pistol and trials and the different models of the Luger in the Dutch service.

'51 Colt Navies, by Nathan L. Swayze, The Gun Room Press, Highland Park, NJ, 1993. 243 pp., illus. $59.95.

THE HANDGUNS LIBRARY

The Model 1851 Colt Navy, its variations and markings.

Fine Colts, The Dr. Joseph A. Murphy Collection, by R.L. Wilson, Sheffield Marketing Associates, Inc., Doylestown, PA, 1999. 258 pp., illustrated. Limited edition signed and numbered. $99.00.

This lavish new work covers exquisite, deluxe and rare Colt arms from Paterson and other percussion revolvers to the cartridge period and up through modern times.

The French 1935 Pistols, by Eugene Medlin and Colin Doane, Eugene Medlin, El Paso, TX, 1995. 172 pp., illus. Paper covers. $25.95.

The development and identification of successive models, fakes and variants, holsters and accessories, and serial numbers by dates of production.

The Government Models, by William H.D. Goddard, Andrew Mowbray Publishing, Lincoln, RI, 1998. 296 pp., illustrated. $58.50.

The most authoritative source on the development of the Colt model of 1911.

The Handgun, by Geoffrey Boothroyd, David and Charles, North Pomfret, VT, 1989. 566 pp., illus. $50.00.

Every chapter deals with an important period in handgun history from the 14th century to the present.

The History of Colt Firearms, by Dean Boorman, Lyons Press, New York, NY, 2001. 144 pp., illus. $29.95

Discover the fascinating story of the world's most famous revolver, complete with more than 150 stunning full-color photographs.

THE HISTORY OF SMITH & WESSON FIREARMS, by Dean Boorman, Lyons Press, New York, NY, 2002. 144 pp., illus. $29.95

The definitive guide to one of the world's best-known firearms makers. Takes the story through the years of the Military & Police .38 & of the Magnum cartridge, to today's wide range of products for law-enforcement customers. 144 pages, illustrated in Full color. Hardcover. New in New Dust Jacket. (8677)

The Kentucky Pistol, by Roy Chandler and James Whisker, Old Bedford Village Press, Bedford, PA, 1997. 225 pp., illus. $60.00

A photographic study of Kentucky pistols from famous collections.

The Luger Handbook, by Aarron Davis, Krause Publications, Iola, WI, 1997. 112 pp., illus. Paper covers. $9.95.

Quick reference to classify Luger models and variations with complete details including proofmarks.

Lugers at Random, by Charles Kenyon, Jr., Handgun Press, Glenview, IL, 1990. 420 pp., illus. $59.95.

A new printing of this classic, comprehensive reference for all Luger collectors.

The Luger Story, by John Walter, Stackpole Books, Mechanicsburg, PA, 2001. 256 pp., illus. Paper Covers $19.95.

The standard history of the world's most famous handgun.

The Navy Luger, by Joachim Gortz and John Walter, Handgun Press, Glenview, IL, 1988. 128 pp., illus. $24.95.

The 9mm Pistole 1904 and the Imperial German Navy. A concise illustrated history.

Parabellum: A Technical History of Swiss Lugers, by Vittorio Bobba, Priuli & Verlucca, Editori, Torino, Italy, 1996. Italian and English text. Illustrated. $100.00.

The first of a two-volume set of the most complete history and guide for all small arms ammunition used in the Civil War. The information includes data from research and development to the arsenals that created it.

The Scottish Pistol, by Martin Kelvin. Fairleigh Dickinson University Press, Dist. By Associated University Presses, Cranbury, NJ, 1997. 256 pp., illus. $49.50.

The Scottish pistol, its history, manufacture and design.

U.S. Handguns of World War 2: The Secondary Pistols and Revolvers, by Charles W. Pate, Andrew Mowbray, Inc., Lincoln, RI, 1998. 515 pp., illus. $39.00.

This indispensable new book covers all of the American military handguns of World War 2 except for the M1911A1 Colt automatic.

U.S. Martial Single Shot Pistols, by Daniel D. Hartzler and James B. Whisker, Old Bedford Village Pess, Bedford, PA, 1998. 128 pp., illus. $45.00.

A photographic chronicle of military and semi-martial pistols supplied to the U.S. Government and the several States.

U.S. Naval Handguns, 1808-1911, by Fredrick R. Winter, Andrew Mowbray Publishers, Lincoln, RI, 1990. 128 pp., illus. $26.00.

The story of U.S. Naval Handguns spans an entire century—included are sections on each of the important naval handguns within the period.

Walther: A German Legend, by Manfred Kersten, Safari Press, Inc., Huntington Beach, CA, 2000. 400 pp., illustrated. $85.00.

This comprehensive book covers, in rich detail, all aspects of the company and its guns, including an illustrious and rich history, the WW2 years, all the pistols (models 1 through 9), the P-38, P-88, the long guns, .22 rifles,

centerfires, Wehrmacht guns, and even a gun that could shoot around a corner.

Walther Pistols: Models 1 Through P99, Factory Variations and Copies, by Dieter H. Marschall, Ucross Books, Los Alamos, NM. 2000. 140 pages, with 140 b & w illustrations, index. Paper Covers. $19.95.

This is the English translation, revised and updated, of the highly successful and widely acclaimed German language edition. This book provides the collector with a reference guide and overview of the entire line of the Walther military, police, and self-defense pistols from the very first to the very latest. Models 1-9, PP, PPK, MP, AP, HP, P.38, P1, P4, P38K, P5, P88, P99 and the Manurhin models. Variations, where issued, serial ranges, calibers, marks, proofs, logos, and design aspects in an astonishing quantity and variety are crammed into this very well researched and highly regarded work.

The Walther Handgun Story: A Collector's and Shooter's Guide, by Gene Gangarosa, Steiger Publications, 1999. 300., illustrated. Paper covers. $21.95.

Covers the entire history of the Walther empire. Illustrated with over 250 photos.

Walther P-38 Pistol, by Maj. George Nonte, Desert Publications, Cornville, AZ, 1982. 100 pp., illus. Paper covers. $12.95.

Complete volume on one of the most famous handguns to come out of WWII. All models covered.

Walther Models PP & PPK, 1929-1945 – Volume 1, by James L. Rankin, Coral Gables, FL, 1974. 142 pp., illus. $40.00

Complete coverage on the subject as to finish, proofmarks and Nazi Party inscriptions.

Walther Volume II, Engraved, Presentation and Standard Models, by James L. Rankin, J.L. Rankin, Coral Gables, FL, 1977. 112 pp., illus. $40.00.

The new Walther book on embellished versions and standard models. Has 88 photographs, including many color plates.

Walther, Volume III, 1908-1980, by James L. Rankin, Coral Gables, FL, 1981. 226 pp., illus. $40.00.

Covers all models of Walther handguns from 1908 to date, includes holsters, grips and magazines.

SHOOTING COLT SINGLE ACTIONS, by Mike Venturino, MLV Enterprises, Livingston, MT 1997. 205 pp., illus. Softcover. $25.00

A complete examination of the Colt Single Action including styles, calibers and generations. Black and White photos throughout.

Shooting Sixguns of the Old West, by Mike Venturino, MLV Enterprises, Livingston, MT, 1997. 221 pp., illus. Paper covers. $26.50.

A comprehensive look at the guns of the early West: Colts, Smith & Wesson and Remingtons, plus blackpowder and reloading specs.

Firearms Assembly/Disassembly Part VI: Law Enforcement Weapons, The Gun Digest Book of, by J.B. Wood, DBI Books, a division of Krause Publications, Iola, WI, 1981. 288 pp., illus. Paper covers. $16.95.

Step-by-step instructions on how to completely dismantle and reassemble the most commonly used firearms found in law enforcement arsenals.

Firearms Assembly 4: The NRA Guide to Pistols and Revolvers, NRA Books, Wash., DC, 1980. 253 pp., illus. Paper covers. $13.95.

Text and illustrations explaining the takedown of 124 pistol and revolver models, domestic and foreign.

Gunsmithing: Pistols & Revolvers, by Patrick Sweeney, DBI Books, a division of Krause Publications, Iola, WI, 1998. 352 pp., illus. Paper covers. $24.95.

Do-it-Yourself projects, diagnosis and repair for pistols and revolvers.

Home Gunsmithing the Colt Single Action Revolvers, by Loren W. Smith, Ray Riling Arms Books, Co., Phila., PA, 2001. 119 pp., illus. $29.95.

Affords the Colt Single Action owner detailed, pertinent information on the operating and servicing of this famous and historic handgun.

Pistolsmithing, by George C. Nonte, Jr., Stackpole Books, Harrisburg, PA, 1974. 560 pp., illus. $34.95.

A single source reference to handgun maintenance, repair, and modification at home, unequaled in value.

The Tactical 1911, by Dave Lauck, Paladin Press, Boulder, CO, 1998. 137 pp., illus. Paper covers. $20.00.

Here is the only book you will ever need to teach you how to select, modify, employ and maintain your Colt.

Advanced Master Handgunning, by Charles Stephens, Paladin Press, Boulder, CO., 1994. 72 pp., illus. Paper covers. $14.00.

Secrets and surefire techniques for winning handgun competitions.

ADVANCED TACTICAL MARKSMAN More High Performance Techniques for Police, Military, and Practical Shooters, by Lauck, Dave M. Paladin Press, Boulder, CO 2002. 1st edition. 232 pages, photos, illus Softcover $35.00

Lauck, one of the most respected names in high-performance shooting and gunsmithing, refines and updates his 1st book. Dispensing with

THE HANDGUNS LIBRARY

overcomplicated mil-dot formulas and minute-of-angle calculations, Lauck shows you how to achieve superior accuracy and figure out angle shots, streamline the zero process, hit targets at 2,000 yards, deal with dawn and dusk shoots, train for real-world scenarios, choose optics and accessories and create a mobile shooting platform. He also demonstrates the advantages of his custom reticle design and describes important advancements in the MR-30PG shooting system.

American Beauty: The Prewar Colt National Match Government Model Pistol, by Timothy Mullin, Collector Grade Publications, Canada, 1999. 72 pp., 69 illus. $34.95

69 illustrations, 20 in full color photos of factory engraved guns and other authenticated upgrades, including rare 'double-carved' ivory grips.

The BELGIAN BROWNING PISTOLS 1889-1949, by Vanderlinden, Anthony. Wet Dog Publications, Geensboro, NC 2001. Limited edition of 2000 copies, signed by the author. 243 pages, plus index. Illustrated with black and white photos. Hardcover. $65.00

Includes the 1899 compact, 1899 Large, 1900,01903, Grand Browning, 1910, 1922 Grand Rendement and high power pistols. Also includes a chapter on holsters.

BIG BORE HANDGUNS, by Taffin, John, Krause Publishing, Iola, WI: 2002. 1st edition. 352 Pages, 320 b&w photos with a 16-page color section. Hardcover. $39.95

Gives honest reviews and an inside look at shooting, hunting, and competing with the biggest handguns around. Covers handguns from major gunmakers, as well as handgun customizing, accessories, reloading, and cowboy activities. Significant coverage is also given to handgun customizing, accessories, reloading, and popular shooting hobbies including hunting and cowboy activities. Accessories consist of stocks, handgun holster rigs, and much more. Firearms include single-shot pistols, revolvers, and semi-automatics.

Big Bore Sixguns, by John Taffin, Krause Publications, Iola, WI, 1997. 336 pp., illus. $39.95.

The author takes aim on the entire range of big bores from .357 Magnums to .500 Maximums, single actions and cap-and-ball sixguns to custom touches for big bores..

The Browning High Power Automatic Pistol (Expanded Edition), by Blake R. Stevens, Collector Grade Publications, Canada, 1996. 310 pages, with 313 illus. $49.95

An in-depth chronicle of seventy years of High Power history, from John M Browning's original 16-shot prototypes to the present. Profusely illustrated with rare original photos and drawings from the FN Archive to describe virtually every sporting and military version of the High Power. The numerous modifications made to the basic design over the years are, for the first time, accurately arranged in chronological order, thus permitting the dating of any High Power to within a few years of its production. Full details on the WWII Canadian-made Inglis Browning High Power pistol. The Expanded Edition contains 30 new pages on the interesting Argentine full-auto High Power, the latest FN 'MK3' and BDA9 pistols, plus FN's revolutionary P90 5.7x28mm Personal Defence Weapon, and more!

Browning Hi-Power Pistols, Desert Publications, Cornville, AZ, 1982. 20 pp., illus. Paper covers. $11.95.

Covers all facets of the various military and civilian models of the Browning Hi-Power pistol.

Canadian Military Handguns 1855-1985, by Clive M. Law, Museum Restoration Service, Bloomfield, Ont. Canada, 1994. 130pp., illus. $40.00.

A long-awaited and important history for arms historians and pistol collectors.

Collecting U. S. Pistols & Revolvers, 1909-1945, by J. C. Harrison. The Arms Chest, Okla. City, OK. 1999. 2nd edition (revised). 185 pages, illus. Spiral bound. $35.00

Valuable and detailed reference book for the collector of U.S. Pistols & Revolvers. Identifies standard issue original military models of the M1911, M1911A1 and M1917Cal .45 Pistols and Revolvers as produced by all manufacturers from 1911 through 1945. Plus .22 ACE Models, National Match Models, and similar foreign military models produced by Colt or manufactured under Colt license. Plus Arsenal repair, refinish and Lend-Lease Models. 185 pages, illustrated with pictures and drawings.

The Colt .45 Auto Pistol, compiled from U.S. War Dept. Technical Manuals, and reprinted by Desert Publications, Cornville, AZ, 1978. 80 pp., illus. Paper covers. $11.95.

Covers every facet of this famous pistol from mechanical training, manual of arms, disassembly, repair and replacement of parts.

Colt Automatic Pistols, by Donald B. Bady, Pioneer Press, Union City, TN, 1999. 368 pp., illustrated. Softcover. $19.95.

A revised and enlarged edition of a key work on a fascinating subject.

Complete information on every Colt automatic pistol.

Combat Handgunnery, 5th Edition, by Chuck Taylor, Krause Publications, Iola, WI, 2002. 256 pp., illus. Paper covers. $21.95.

This all-new edition looks at real world combat handgunnery from three different perspectives—military, police and civilian.

Combat Revolvers, by Duncan Long, Paladin Press, Boulder, CO, 1999, 8 1/2 x 11, soft cover, 115 photos, 152 pp. $21.95

This is an uncompromising look at modern combat revolvers. All the major foreign and domestic guns are covered: the Colt Python, S&W Model 29, Ruger GP 100 and hundreds more. Know the gun that you may one day stake your life on.

Complete Guide to Compact Handguns, by Gene Gangarosa, Jr., Stoeger Publishing Co., Wayne, NJ, 1997. 228 pp., illus. Paper covers. $22.95.

Includes hundreds of compact firearms, along with text results conducted by the author.

Complete Guide to Service Handguns, by Gene Gangarosa, Jr., Stoeger Publishing Co., Wayne, NJ, 1998. 320 pp., illus. Paper covers. $22.95.

The author explores the revolvers and pistols that are used around the globe by military, law enforcement and civilians.

CONCEALABLE POCKET PISTOLS: HOW TO CHOOSE AND USE SMALL-CALIBER HANDGUNS, McLeod, Terence. Paladin Press, 2001. 1st edition. 80 pages. Softcover. $14.00

Small-caliber handguns are often maligned as too puny for serious self-defense, but millions of Americans own and carry these guns and have used them successfully to stop violent assaults. This is the first book ever devoted to eliminating the many misconceptions about the usefulness of these popular guns. "Pocket pistols" are small, easily concealed, inexpensive semiautomatic handguns in .22, .25, .32 and .380 calibers. Their small size and hammerless design enable them to be easily concealed and carried so they are immediately accessible in an emergency. Their purpose is not to knock an assailant off his feet with fire-breathing power (which no handgun is capable of doing) but simply to deter or stop his assault by putting firepower in your hands when you need it most. Concealable Pocket Pistols addresses every aspect of owning, carrying and shooting small-caliber handguns in a realistic manner. It cuts right to the chase and recommends a handful of the best pistols on the market today as well as the best ammunition for them. It then gets into the real-world issues of how to carry a concealed pocket pistol, how to shoot it under stress and how to deal with malfunctions quickly and efficiently. In an emergency, a small-caliber pistol in the pocket is better than the .357 Magnum left at home. Find out what millions of Americans already know about these practical self-defense tools.

The Custom Government Model Pistol, by Layne Simpson, Wolfe Publishing Co., Prescott, AZ, 1994. 639 pp., illus. Paper covers. $26.95.

The book about one of the world's greatest firearms and the things pistolsmiths do to make it even greater.

The CZ-75 Family: The Ultimate Combat Handgun, by J.M. Ramos, Paladin Press, Boulder, CO, 1990. 100 pp., illus. Soft covers. $25.00.

An in-depth discussion of the early-and-late model CZ-75s, as well as the many newest additions to the Czech pistol family.

Encyclopedia of Pistols & Revolvers, by A.E. Hartnik, Knickerbocker Press, New York, NY, 1997. 272 pp., illus. $19.95.

A comprehensive encyclopedia specially written for collectors and owners of pistols and revolvers.

ENGRAVED HANDGUNS OF .22 CALIBRE, by John S. Laidacker, Atglen, PA: Schiffer Publications, 2003. 1st edition. 192 pages, with over 400 color and b/w photos. $69.95

Experiments of a Handgunner, by Walter Roper, Wolfe Publishing Co., Prescott, AZ, 1989. 202 pp., illus. $37.00.

A limited edition reprint. A listing of experiments with functioning parts of handguns, with targets, stocks, rests, handloading, etc.

The Farnam Method of Defensive Handgunning, by John S. Farnam, Police Bookshelf, 1999. 191 pp., illus. Paper covers. $24.00

A book intended to not only educate the new shooter, but also to serve as a guide and textbook for his and his instructor's training courses.

Fast and Fancy Revolver Shooting, by Ed. McGivern, Anniversary Edition, Winchester Press, Piscataway, NJ, 1984. 484 pp., illus. $19.95.

A fascinating volume, packed with handgun lore and solid information by the acknowledged dean of revolver shooters.

German Handguns: The Complete Book Of The Pistols And Revolvers Of Germany, 1869 To The Present, by Ian Hogg. Greenhill Publishing, 2001. 320 pages, 270 illustrations. Hardcover. $49.95

Ian Hogg examines the full range of handguns produced in Germany from

THE HANDGUNS LIBRARY

such classics as the Luger M1908, Mauser HsC and Walther PPK, to more unusual types such as the Reichsrevolver M1879 and the Dreyse 9mm. He presents the key data (length, weight, muzzle velocity, and range) for each weapon discussed and also gives its date of introduction and service record, evaluates and discusses peculiarities, and examines in detail particular strengths and weaknesses.

Glock: The New Wave in Combat Handguns, by Peter Alan Kasler, Paladin Press, Boulder, CO, 1993. 304 pp., illus. $27.00.

Kasler debunks the myths that surround what is the most innovative handgun to be introduced in some time.

Glock's Handguns, by Duncan Long, Desert Publications, El Dorado, AR, 1996. 180 pp., illus. Paper covers. $19.95.

An outstanding volume on one of the world's newest and most successful firearms of the century.

THE GUN DIGEST BOOK OF THE 1911, by Patrick Sweeney. Krause Publications, Iola, WI, 2002. 336 pages, with 700 b&w photos. Softcover. $27.95

Compete guide of all models and variations of the Model 1911. The author also includes repair tips and information on buying a used 1911.

Hand Cannons: The World's Most Powerful Handguns, by Duncan Long, Paladin Press, Boulder, CO, 1995. 208 pp., illus. Paper covers. $22.00.

Long describes and evaluates each powerful gun according to their features.

The Handgun, by Geoffrey Boothroyd, Safari Press, Inc., Huntington Beach, CA, 1999. 566 pp., illustrated. $50.00.

A very detailed history of the handgun. Now revised and a completely new chapter written to take account of developments since the 1970 edition.

Handguns 2003, 14th Edition, edited by Ken Ramage, DBI Books a division of Krause Publications, Iola, WI, 2002. 352 pp., illustrated. Paper covers. $22.95.

Top writers in the handgun industry give you a complete report on new handgun developments, testfire reports on the newest introductions and previews on what's ahead.

Handgun Stopping Power "The Definitive Study", by Evan P. Marshall & Edwin J. Sanow, Paladin Press, Boulder, CO, 1997, soft cover, photos, 240 pp. $45.00

Dramatic first-hand accounts of the results of handgun rounds fired into criminals by cops, storeowners, cabbies and others are the heart and soul of this long-awaited book. This is the definitive methodology for predicting the stopping power of handgun loads, the first to take into account what really happens when a bullet meets a man.

Heckler & Koch's Handguns, by Duncan Long, Desert Publications, El Dorado, AR, 1996. 142 pp., illus. Paper covers. $19.95.

Traces the history and the evolution of H&K's pistols from the company's beginning at the end of WWII to the present.

Hidden in Plain Sight, by Trey Bloodworth & Mike Raley, Professional Press, Chapel Hill, NC, 1995. Paper covers. $19.95.

A practical guide to concealed handgun carry.

HIGH STANDARD: A COLLECTORS GUIDE TO THE HAMDEN & HARTFORD TARGET PISTOLS, Dance, Tom. Andrew Mowbray, Inc., Lincoln, RI: 1999. 192 pp., Heavily illustrated with black & white photographs and technical drawings. $24.00

From Citation to Supermatic, all of the production models and specials made from 1951 to 1984 are covered according to model number or series, making it easy to understand the evolution to this favorite of shooters and collectors.

High Standard Automatic Pistols 1932-1950, by Charles E. Petty, The Gunroom Press, Highland Park, NJ, 1989. 124 pp., illus. $14.95.

A definitive source of information for the collector of High Standard arms.

Hi-Standard Pistols and Revolvers, 1951-1984, by James Spacek, James Spacek, Chesire, CT, 1998. 128 pp., illustrated. Paper covers. $12.50.

Technical details, marketing features and instruction/parts manual of every model High Standard pistol and revolver made between 1951 and 1984. Most accurate serial number information available.

The Hi-Standard Pistol Guide, by Burr Leyson, Duckett's Sporting Books, Tempe AZ, 1995. 128 pp., illus. Paper covers. $26.00.

Complete information on selection, care and repair, ammunition, parts, and accessories.

How to Become a Master Handgunner: The Mechanics of X-Count Shooting, by Charles Stephens, Paladin Press, Boulder, CO, 1993. 64 pp., illus. Paper covers. $14.00.

Offers a simple formula for success to the handgunner who strives to master the technique of shooting accurately.

Illustrated Encyclopedia of Handguns, by A.B. Zhuk, Stackpole Books, Mechanicsburg, PA, 2002. 256 pp., illus. Softcover, $24.95

Identifies more than 2,000 military and commercial pistols and revolvers with details of more than 100 popular handgun cartridges.

The Inglis Diamond: The Canadian High Power Pistol, by Clive M. Law, Collector Grade Publications, Canada, 2001. 312 pp., illustrated. $49.95

This definitive work on Canada's first and indeed only mass produced handgun, in production for a very brief span of time and consequently made in relatively few numbers, the venerable Inglis-made Browning High Power covers the pistol's initial history, the story of Chinese and British adoption, use post-war by Holland, Australia, Greece, Belgium, New Zealand, Peru, Brasil and other countries. All new information on the famous light-weights and the Inglis Diamond variations. Completely researched through official archives in a dozen countries. Many of the bewildering variety of markings have never been satisfactorily explained until now. Also included are many photos of holsters and accessories.

Instinct Combat Shooting, by Chuck Klein, The Goose Creek, IN, 1989. 49 pp., illus. Paper covers. $12.00.

Defensive handgunning for police.

Know Your 45 Auto Pistols—Models 1911 & A1, by E.J. Hoffschmidt, Blacksmith Corp., Southport, CT, 1974. 58 pp., illus. Paper covers. $14.95.

A concise history of the gun with a wide variety of types and copies.

Know Your Ruger Single Actions: The Second Decade 1963-1973, by John C. Dougan. Blacksmith Corp., North Hampton, OH, 1994. 143 pp., illus. Paper covers. $19.95.

Know Your Ruger S/A Revolvers 1953-1963 (Revised Edition), by John C. Dougan. Blacksmith Corp., North Hampton, OH, 2002. 191 pp., illus. Paper covers. $19.95.

Know Your Walther P38 Pistols, by E.J. Hoffschmidt, Blacksmith Corp., Southport, CT, 1974. 77 pp., illus. Paper covers. $14.95.

Covers the Walther models Armee, M.P., H.P., P.38—history and variations.

Know Your Walther PP & PPK Pistols, by E.J. Hoffschmidt, Blacksmith Corp., Southport, CT, 1975. 87 pp., illus. Paper covers. $14.95.

A concise history of the guns with a guide to the variety and types.

La Connaissance du Luger, Tome 1, by Gerard Henrotin, H & L Publishing, Belguim, 1996. 144 pages, illustrated. $45.00.

(The Knowledge of Luger, Volume 1, translated.) B&W and Color photo's. French text.

LIVING WITH GLOCKS: THE COMPLETE GUIDE TO THE NEW STANDARD IN COMBAT HANDGUNS, by Robert H Boatman, Boulder, CO: Paladin Press, 2002. 1st edition. ISBN: 1581603401. 184 pages, illustrated. Hardcover. $29.95

In this book he explains why in no uncertain terms. In addition to demystifying the enigmatic Glock trigger, Boatman describes and critiques each Glock model in production. Separate chapters on the G36, the enhanced G20 and the full-auto G18 emphasize the job-specific talents of these standout models for those seeking insight on which Glock pistol might best meet their needs. And for those interested in optimizing their Glock's capabilities, this book addresses all the peripherals - holsters, ammo, accessories, silencers, modifications and conversions, training programs and more. Whether your focus is on concealed carry, home protection, hunting, competition, training or law enforcement.

The Luger Handbook, by Aarron Davis, Krause Publications, Iola, WI, 1997. 112 pp., illus. Paper covers. $9.95.

Now you can identify any of the legendary Luger variations using a simple decision tree. Each model and variation includes pricing information, proof marks and detailed attributes in a handy, user-friendly format. Plus, it's fully indexed. Instantly identify that Luger!

Lugers of Ralph Shattuck, by Ralph Shattuck, Peoria, AZ, 2000. 49 pages, illus. Hardcover. $29.95.

49 pages, illustrated with maps and full color photos of here to now never before shown photos of some of the rarest lugers ever. Written by one of the world's renowned collectors. A MUST have book for any Luger collector.

Lugers at Random (Revised Format Edition), by Charles Kenyon, Jr., Handgun Press, Glenview, IL, 2000. 420 pp., illus. $59.95.

A new printing of this classic, comprehensive reference for all Luger collectors.

The Luger Story, by John Walter, Stackpole Books, Mechanicsburg, PA, 2001. 256 pp., illus. Paper Covers. $19.95.

The standard history of the world's most famous handgun.

The Mauser Self-Loading Pistol, by Belford & Dunlap, Borden Publ. Co., Alhambra, CA. Over 200 pp., 300 illus., large format. $29.95.

The long-awaited book on the "Broom Handles," covering their inception in 1894 to the end of production. Complete and in detail: pocket pistols, Chinese and Spanish copies, etc.

MENTAL MECHANICS OF SHOOTING: HOW TO STAY CALM AT THE CENTER, by Vishnu Karmakar and Thomas Whitney. Littleton, CO: Center Vision, Inc., 2001. 144 pages. Softcover. $19.95

Not only will this book help you stay free of trigger jerk, it will help you in all areas of your shooting.

THE HANDGUNS LIBRARY

9mm Parabellum; The History & Development of the World's 9mm Pistols & Ammunition, by Klaus-Peter Konig and Martin Hugo, Schiffer Publishing Ltd., Atglen, PA, 1993. 304 pp., illus. $39.95.

Detailed history of 9mm weapons from Belguim, Italy, Germany, Israel, France, USA, Czechoslovakia, Hungary, Poland, Brazil, Finland and Spain.

The Official 9mm Markarov Pistol Manual, translated into English by Major James Gebhardt, U.S. Army (Ret.), Desert Publications, El Dorado, AR, 1996. 84 pp., illus. Paper covers. $12.95.

The information found in this book will be of enormous benefit and interest to the owner or a prospective owner of one of these pistols.

The Official Soviet 7.62mm Handgun Manual, by Translation by Maj. James F. Gebhardt Ret.), Paladin Press, Boulder, CO, 1997, soft cover, illus., 104 pp. $20.00

This Soviet military manual, now available in English for the first time, covers instructions for use and maintenance of two side arms, the Nagant 7.62mm revolver, used by the Russian tsarist armed forces and later the Soviet armed forces, and the Tokarev 7.62mm semi-auto pistol, which replaced the Nagant.

The P-08 Parabellum Luger Automatic Pistol, edited by J. David McFarland, Desert Publications, Cornville, AZ, 1982. 20 pp., illus. Paper covers. $13.95.

Covers every facet of the Luger, plus a listing of all known Luger models.

THE P08 LUGER PISTOL, by de Vries & Martens. Alexandria, VA: Ironside International, 2002. 152 pages, illustrated with 200 high quality Black & White Photos. Hardcover. $34.95

Covers all essential information on history and development, ammunition and accessories, codes and markings, and contains photos of nearly every model and accessory. Includes a unique selection of original German WWll propoganda photos, most never published before.

P-38 Automatic Pistol, by Gene Gangarosa, Jr., Stoeger Publishing Co., S. Hackensack, NJ, 1993. 272 pp., illus. Paper covers. $16.95

This book traces the origins and development of the P-38, including the momentous political forces of the World War II era that caused its near demise and, later, its rebirth.

The P-38 Pistol: The Walther Pistols, 1930-1945. Volume 1. by Warren Buxton, Ucross Books, Los Alamos, MN 1999. $68.50

A limited run reprint of this scarce and sought-after work on the P-38 Pistol. 328 pp. with 160 illustrations.

The P-38 Pistol: The Contract Pistols, 1940-1945. Volume 2. by Warren Buxton, Ucross Books, Los Alamos, MN 1999. 256 pp. with 237 illustrations. $68.50

The P-38 Pistol: Postwar Distributions, 1945-1990. Volume 3. by Warren Buxton, Ucross Books, Los Alamos, MN 1999. $68.50

Plus an addendum to Volumes 1 & 2. 272 pp. with 342 illustrations.

PARABELLUM - A Technical History of Swiss Lugers, by V. Bobba, Italy.1998. 224pp, profuse color photos, large format. $100.00.

The is the most beautifully illustrated and well-produced book on the Swiss Lugers yet produced. This splendidly produced book features magnificent images while giving an incredible amount of detail on the Swiss Luger. In-depth coverage of key issues include: the production process, pistol accessories, charts with serial numbers, production figures, variations, markings, patent drawings, etc. Covers the Swiss Luger story from 1894 when the first Bergmann-Schmeisser models were tested till the commercial model 1965. Shows every imaginable production variation in amazing detail and full color! A must for all Luger collectors. This work has been produced in an extremely attractive package using quality materials throughout and housed in a protective slipcase.

The Ruger "P" Family of Handguns, by Duncan Long, Desert Publications, El Dorado, AZ, 1993. 128 pp., illus. Paper covers. $14.95.

A full-fledged documentary on a remarkable series of Sturm Ruger handguns.

The Ruger .22 Automatic Pistol, Standard/Mark I/Mark II Series, by Duncan Long, Paladin Press, Boulder, CO, 1989. 168 pp., illus. Paper covers. $16.00.

The definitive book about the pistol that has served more than 1 million owners so well.

The Semiautomatic Pistols in Police Service and Self Defense, by Massad Ayoob, Police Bookshelf, Concord, NH, 1990. 25 pp., illus. Soft covers. $11.95.

First quantitative, documented look at actual police experience with 9mm and 45 police service automatics.

Shooting Colt Single Actions, by Mike Venturino, Livingston, MT, 1997. 205 pp., illus. Paper covers. $25.00

A definitive work on the famous Colt SAA and the ammunition it shoots.

Sig Handguns, by Duncan Long, Desert Publications, El Dorado, AZ, 1995. 150

pp., illus. Paper covers. $19.95.

The history of Sig/Sauer handguns, including Sig, Sig-Hammerli and Sig/ Sauer variants.

Sixgun Cartridges and Loads, by Elmer Keith, reprint edition by The Gun Room Press, Highland Park, NJ, 1984. 151 pp., illus. $24.95.

A manual covering the selection, use and loading of the most suitable and popular revolver cartridges.

Sixguns, by Elmer Keith, Wolfe Publishing Company, Prescott, AZ, 1992. 336 pp. Paper covers. $29.95. Hardcover $35.00

The history, selection, repair, care, loading, and use of this historic frontiersman's friend—the one-hand firearm.

Smith & Wesson's Automatics, by Larry Combs, Desert Publications, El Dorado, AZ, 1994. 143 pp., illus. Paper covers. $19.95.

A must for every S&W auto owner or prospective owner.

Spanish Handguns: The History of Spanish Pistols and Revolvers, by Gene Gangarosa, Jr., Stoeger Publishing Co., Accokeek, MD, 2001. 320 pp., illustrated. B & W photos. Paper covers. $21.95

STANDARD CATALOG OF SMITH & WESSON; 2ND EDITION, by Jim Supica and Richard Nahas.Krause Publications, Iola, WI: 2001. 2nd edition. 272 Pages, 350 b&w photos, with a 16 page color section. Pictorial Hardcover. $34.95

Clearly details 775 Smith & Wesson models, knives, holsters, ammunition and police items with complete pricing information, illustrated glossary and index.

STAR FIREARMS, by Leonardo M. Antaris, Davenport, IA: Firac Publications Co., 2002. 640 pages, with over 1,100 b/w photos, 47 pages in full color. Hardcover. $119.95

The definitive work on Star's many models with a historical context, with a review of their mechanical features, & details their development throughout production plus tables of proof marks & codes, serial numbers, annual summaries, procurements by Spanish Guardia Civil & Spanish Police, exports to Bulgaria, Germany, & Switzerland during WW2; text also covers Star's .22 rifles & submachine guns & includes a comprehensive list of Spanish trade names matched to manufacturer for arms made prior to the Spanish Civil War (1936-1939).

Street Stoppers: The Latest Handgun Stopping Power Street Results, by Evan P. Marshall & Edwin J. Sandow, Paladin Press, Boulder, CO, 1997. 392 pp., illus. Paper covers. $42.95.

Compilation of the results of real-life shooting incidents involving every major handgun caliber.

The Tactical 1911, by Dave Lauck, Paladin Press, Boulder, CO, 1999. 152 pp., illustrated. Paper covers. $22.00.

The cop's and SWAT operator's guide to employment and maintenance.

The Tactical Pistol, by Gabriel Suarez with a foreword by Jeff Cooper, Paladin Press, Boulder, CO, 1996. 216 pp., illus. Paper covers. $25.00.

Advanced gunfighting concepts and techniques.

The Thompson/Center Contender Pistol, by Charles Tephens, Paladin Press, Boulder, CO, 1997. 58 pp., illus. Paper covers. $14.00.

How to tune and time, load and shoot accurately with the Contender pistol.

The .380 Enfield No. 2 Revolver, by Mark Stamps and Ian Skennerton, I.D.S.A. Books, Piqua, OH, 1993. 124 pp., 80 illus. Paper covers. $19.95.

The Truth About Handguns, by Duane Thomas, Paladin Press, Boulder, CO, 1997. 136 pp., illus. Paper covers. $18.00.

Exploding the myths, hype, and misinformation about handguns.

Walther Pistols: Models 1 Through P99, Factory Variations and Copies, by Dieter H. Marschall, Ucross Books, Los Alamos, NM. 2000. 140 pages, with 140 b & w illustrations, index. Paper Covers. $19.95.

This is the English translation, revised and updated, of the highly successful and widely acclaimed German language edition. This book provides the collector with a reference guide and overview of the entire line of the Walther military, police, and self-defense pistols from the very first to the very latest. Models 1-9, PP, PPK, MP, AP, HP, P.38, P1, P4, P38K, P5, P88, P99 and the Manurhin models. Variations, where issued, serial ranges, calibers, marks, proofs, logos, and design aspects in an astonishing quantity and variety are crammed into this very well researched and highly regarded work.

U.S. Handguns of World War 2, The Secondary Pistols and Revolvers, by Charles W. Pate, Mowbray Publishers, Lincoln, RI, 1997. 368 pp., illus. $39.00.

This indispensable new book covers all of the American military handguns of W.W.2 except for the M1911A1.